D0406741

MASTERING CSS
with Dreamweaver CS4

Stephanie Sullivan
and Greg Rewis

New
Riders

VOICES THAT MATTER™

Mastering CSS with Dreamweaver CS4

Stephanie Sullivan and Greg Rewis

NEW RIDERS

1249 Eighth Street
Berkeley, CA 94710
(510) 524-2178
Fax: (510) 524-2221

Find us on the Web at www.newriders.com
To report errors, please send a note to errata@peachpit.com
New Riders is an imprint of Peachpit, a division of Pearson Education
Copyright © 2009 by Stephanie Sullivan and Greg Rewis

Editor: Wendy Sharp
Tech Editor: Dee Sadler
Production Editor: Becky Winter
Cover design: Aren Howell
Cover photograph: Brownie Harris
Interior design: Mimi Heft
Compositor: Danielle Foster
Indexer: JB Indexing

NOTICE OF RIGHTS

All rights reserved. No part of this book may be reproduced or transmitted in any form by any means, electronic, mechanical, photocopying, recording, or other-wise, without the prior written permission of the publisher. For information on getting permission for reprints and excerpts, contact permissions@peachpit.com.

NOTICE OF LIABILITY

The information in this book is distributed on an "As Is" basis, without warranty. While every precaution has been taken in the preparation of the book, neither the authors nor Peachpit shall have any liability to any person or entity with respect to any loss or damage caused or alleged to be caused directly or indi-rectly by the instructions contained in this book or by the computer software and hardware products described in it.

TRADEMARKS

Many of the designations used by manufacturers and sellers to distinguish their products are claimed as trademarks. Where those designations appear in this book, and Peachpit was aware of a trademark claim, the designations appear as requested by the owner of the trademark. All other product names and services identified throughout this book are used in editorial fashion only and for the benefit of such companies with no intention of infringement of the trademark. No such use, or the use of any trade name, is intended to convey endorsement or other affiliation with this book.

ISBN 13: 978-0-321-60503-0
ISBN 10: 0-321-60503-9

9 8 7 6 5 4 3 2 1

Printed and bound in the United States of America

This book is dedicated to our four boys—Cameron, Hunter, Devin, and Noah—we love and adore you. Anything's possible in this life. Follow your dreams.

"I just want to state what a wonderful book you guys wrote pertaining to CSS and Dreamweaver CS3. This is one of the best books around that breaks down the understanding of CSS." W.D.

"Thank you so much! As I am working through your book I think I have learned a new trick on every page. This is just fantastic!" A.G.

"I am new to CSS, and have read a few books. Yours is extremely well-written, and also, importantly, very well laid-out. With other books, it is harder to find one's place and follow along. Enjoyable reading." S.T.

"…I'm getting a much clearer understanding of CSS than I have by using any other resource." D.H.

"Of all the manuals that I have, yours has so far been the easiest to understand with its clear logical layout and language." B.G.

"I'm enjoying the book! The font used and font size makes it easy to read. The spacing, white space around content, and screen captures in color make this book one of my favorite resources. Of course, the information and instructions are excellent, as I knew they would be given yours and Greg's knowledge and experience. Thank you again for sharing your expertise with the web professional community." D.E.

"I bought your book recently and it's amazing! Just what I've been needing for a long time." G.I.

"… thanks for finally writing that advanced CSS book that I have been looking for." S.L.

"As advised I have completed chapter 2 and had the WOW moments. I was struggling with these problems for months without a solution and after completing chapter 2, I know what I was doing wrong. I am glad you came up with this book and I am glad I found it. It was money well spent. Thank you for writing the book." G.M.

"Great work on your efforts. This is my jump-in-with-both-feet-and-try-not-to-drown conversion from using GoLive for years. I can really appreciate the thoroughness with regards to compatibility issues and how to handle them before they become a problem." B.C.

"Thank you, your book is wonderful. I'm an ACE for Dreamweaver and started to learn CSS a few years ago with Eric Meyer's books and others, but I learn so much from yours by putting the two together… and I love working with your predefined templates, which I never used before… I'm also a Dreamweaver trainer for a company, and now I show them how to use the templates to help them, which I didn't do before!" N.T.

"I love your book and have recommended it to several people." R.P.

"I absolutely want to compliment you on your book. Never before (and I am studying CSS for quite a while) have I found things explained in such a clear and concise way. Many advanced CSS techniques suddenly become clear to me and even quite simple to achieve. Thank you very, very much for that. I think it's a pity that your book is written for Dreamweaver users only, because it would be very useful for every CSS developer." N.S.

Table of Contents

Acknowledgments

A variety of wonderful people offered help, input, and support toward the completion of both editions of this book. Most important are my boys, Cameron and Hunter, who support me during the "mom gone missing" times and cook easy, and most probably boring, stuff. Thanks so much, guys. I adore you both. You've grown into amazing men and my life wouldn't be the same without you. I wish you the best as you embark on your own life journeys.

There were many direct contributors as well. Thanks go to Dori Smith and Dee Sadler for jumping in and tech editing for us. You relieved my mind. Great job, you guys! To Joann Lavrich—I've sincerely appreciated your tireless beta testing of every chapter, at every step. You've been an angel. Hopefully, the errata will be minimal! To Sheri German and Vicki Stanton—kudos for helping us pull a couple of the chapters for the first book together. As we traveled and taught all over the world, your assistance was truly a lifesaver.

Linda Rathgeber, Scott LaPlant, and Robert Chafino all contributed to the designs we were graciously allowed to mutilate and simplify for our purposes here. You're all extremely talented and I'm sorry we couldn't allow your full creativity to shine. Thanks for pitching in and being such great sports! Much love also to Brownie Harris—world-class photographer and good friend. Your willingness to shoot this cover was definitely above and beyond. We're not in your usual John F. Kennedy Jr. or John Edwards league, but hey, you've now got another book cover credit anyway. Thanks go to Dionne Stokely for the photo retouching. None of us are perfect, are we? Darn.

To Wendy Sharp, our editor at New Riders—thanks for your eagle eye editing. You've made this a much more succinct book. Thanks also to Becky Winter, Mimi Heft, Danielle Foster, and Julie Bess, as well as the team who worked on the first edition, including Kate Reber, Owen Wolfson and Emily Glossbrenner. To David Fugate, our literary agent—you're a great negotiator and the most amazing, positive person. Thanks for all you continue to do.

Thanks also to the many people in the biz that led the way, mentored, advised, and steered me—too many to list here— you know who you are. To my friends Molly Holzschlag and

Eric Meyer—you continue to inspire me. To Ray West, who gave me both my first full-time writing opportunity at Community MX (www.communitymx.com) and my first speaking opportunity at TODCon (www.todcon.org), you are most awesome, sir! Thanks for your vision in our industry and your belief in my abilities to contribute to it. I'm forever in your debt. And going back to the very beginning—kudos to Stuart Nealy for convincing me not to learn C++ as planned. You knew the score, dude! Thanks for believing in me, getting me started in HTML and supporting me through some tough times.

Finally, to my co-author and life partner, Greg Rewis—I have immense admiration and respect. You rock. Thanks for taking this journey with me. May it last a very long time and expand to many more horizons. You are, indeed, the kettle. And to you, patient readers, thanks for waiting for, and buying our books. I hope it helps you learn, focus, and hone your skills in our ever-morphing industry. Remember, life is about learning. Always improve— always force yourself to stretch—always grow.

Ciao, Stephanie

This has truly been an incredible journey—one that started too many years ago and has seen several costume changes along the way. And yet, it seems like just yesterday that I began hacking my first web page together and viewing it in Mosaic (the idea of a site at that time was non-existent). Little did I know that I would owe so much to that fledgling technology. Since that time I have had the good fortune to make a career of working with cool software and traveling around the world to show it off. And of course, the side benefit is that I have gotten to know so many great people along the way. I obviously can't thank each of you by name—after all, there is a page limit to this book—but a few of you absolutely deserve special notice.

In addition to all of the folks Stephanie has already mentioned, I want to thank my guys, Devin and Noah. The two of you are the brightest spot in my life and the reason that I keep doing what I do. Thanks for "missing Dad" and being there with a hug after yet another long trip. Thanks as well to Gabriele. You are an amazing mother to our boys, as well as a talented painter. Thank you for letting us use your pictures in the book. And Frederic, I hope you like the new site—thanks for letting us build it.

On the professional side, I'd be remiss if I didn't thank Andreas, whose amazing entrepreneurship got this whole thing started. And to Beth, who "had to have that guy at Macromedia"—and no, I still don't wear an XXL. Thanks also to all of my colleagues at GoLive, then Macromedia, and now Adobe—but most importantly to the Dreamweaver team. To say you all are amazing is an understatement. Thanks for such a great product—it's hard to believe that CS3 could be topped, but you've done it again!

Finally, to Stephanie, what more can I say? Your passion and pursuit of excellence are truly inspirational. Thank you for finally letting me wear you down. Aota.

Cheers, Greg

Introduction

DEAR READER,

Welcome to Mastering CSS with Dreamweaver CS4!

Adobe Dreamweaver (DW) is the leading web authoring tool on the market; Cascading Style Sheets (CSS) is the recommended method for separating presentation from content to make site upkeep simpler and faster, as well as making a site friendlier to search engines. Yet it's a common misconception that it's tough to use Dreamweaver to build accessible, standards-compliant page layouts using CSS.

We're here to show you how easy it really is. Who are we? Greg is the Group Manager, Creative Solutions Evangelism at Adobe, and has been involved with Dreamweaver since version two. He demos and teaches it weekly, highlighting its CSS capabilities. Stephanie codes CSS for a living as a consultant and trains corporate web departments in CSS techniques, best practices, and web standards. She's the co-lead of the Adobe Task Force for WaSP (formerly the Dreamweaver Task Force) and wrote the CSS layouts in Dreamweaver CS3 (and included in Dreamweaver CS4) under contract from Adobe.

We wrote this book because we felt our combined knowledge about Dreamweaver and CSS could help you, our reader, grasp these tools in combination—the way we use them every day. And we wanted the opportunity to really discuss the CSS layouts contained in Dreamweaver CS3 and CS4, showing you how to use, extend, and really put them to work. We updated this book because of Dreamweaver's substantial, and welcomed, overhaul for Dreamweaver CS4.

Who Should Read This Book?

We wrote the book with a fairly specific reader in mind. We explain each concept on first encounter, so you don't need to have extensive knowledge of either Dreamweaver or CSS, but we do expect that you have at least a little familiarity with both. We're also assuming you have some rudimentary working knowledge of (X)HTML.

On the other hand, if you're a power user of either Dreamweaver or CSS, this book will hopefully expose you to that "other" side and open your mind to some new workflow possibilities. Stephanie even learned some new tips as she edited Greg's writing, and if pressed, Greg will admit he learned some new tricks with CSS. In the pages of this book, you'll hopefully have several "gee, I wish I'd known that on my last project" moments.

How Is the Book Structured?

Each chapter of the book is a stand-alone project. You don't have to do them in order, but they do build on each other, so starting at the beginning is probably best. Throughout the book, we'll try to show you different ways to use Dreamweaver and CSS, so you can figure out the best way for *you* to work.

We begin with a What's New in Dreamweaver CS4 chapter. This gives you an overview of the most significant changes Adobe has introduced in the latest version of Dreamweaver. Those changes are then integrated and discussed in more detail as you progress through the book's projects. Chapter 2 covers the basic principles of CSS, as well as giving an overview of Dreamweaver's CSS tools. Chapters 3, 4, 5, and 6 each begin with a different type of CSS layout and walk you through building the initial page structure for a website with it—just as we ourselves do during a typical work day—all while teaching Dreamweaver and CSS concepts. The beginning of each chapter gives a bit more explicit instructions, but as you progress, we assume you remember what was done earlier and we don't waste space with minutiae.

Errata from the first book has been corrected. Techniques and information have been updated based on current industry trends. Workflows, introduced in Dreamweaver CS4, and new tools are integrated along with updated screen shots. And in answer to many requests, we've created partial builds (contained in the files you'll download for each chapter) as you move through each project. The projects are in depth and can take some time to complete. Now you're able to check your work without moving way back in the text or undoing much of the work you've already completed, saving you time and frustration.

We hope, as you finish each chapter, you feel like you've had a personal coach by your side pulling you through it. And this book costs a lot less than your local fitness center charges you for a personal trainer!

Files and Reference Material

The files for this book are housed on Stephanie's website—w3conversions.com. They're contained in, you guessed it, the "book" directory (http://www.w3conversions.com/book/). Be sure to grab the files for the Dreamweaver CS4 version of this book since there are changes from the previous version. The website includes the reference links found in the book as well, so you can simply click instead of typing while reading the book (some of the link names are really long). Also, if any links change (if you encounter a 404, let us know), we'll be able to keep the site updated.

We suggest you start by going to the site and downloading all the necessary files. From this page on, we're going to assume that you have the files you need, rather than directing you to download files in each chapter. So let's get started!

About the Authors

Together Stephanie and Greg have over 25 years of experience in the web industry and are both recognized experts within the web community and their respective areas of expertise.

About Stephanie Sullivan

Founder and principal of web standards redesign company W3Conversions, Stephanie Sullivan is a CSS, accessibility, and (X)HTML expert, whose services are in demand by top firms across the United States. She regularly works with clients, large and small, to train their corporate web team, or to work behind-the-scenes transforming their in-house graphic designs into function-ing standard-based websites. Stephanie serves as co-lead of the influential Web Standards Project (WaSP) Adobe Task Force and is a partner at Community MX, a site offering over 2,900 tutorials to web developers seeking to increase their skills (at the time of this writing). She's an Adobe Community Expert, beta tester, and Dreamweaver advisor.

A tireless advocate of web community education, she is "List Mom" for the long-running WebWeavers discussion list for professional web designers, and a moderator of the search engine marketing discussion group SEM 2.0 run by Andrew Goodman. She answers questions almost daily in the forums at Community MX, where she also writes a widely read blog. She's a sought-after speaker and lends her voice to a variety of events each year, including Adobe MAX, An Event Apart, South by Southwest, HOW Design Conference, Voices That Matter, Web Design World, InterLab, and many, many more.

Stephanie headquarters her business in the desert of Phoenix, AZ, where she lives with her youngest teenaged son and two, part-time "semi-sons." Though an admitted workaholic, she escapes as often as possible from the little people inside her computer to play squash or get sandy playing beach volleyball. Her hobby, if only she had time? Studying brain function. Her guilty pleasure? 80s music. Nina Hagen anyone?

About Greg Rewis

Greg is a true "old-timer" in not only the web industry, but the computer industry in general. Having completed his studies at Louisiana State University in 1983, Greg sought out new adventures in Europe and ended up working for the US Army, attached to the National Security Agency. Little did he know that one of the systems he would be working on would later come to be known as the Internet.

Fate led him to an industry tradeshow in 1990 where he met "a couple of German dudes" demonstrating their new desktop publishing system, P.INK Press. A few conversations later and Greg was the Product Manager for P.INK, which eventually spun off into a new start-up, GoLive Systems, makers of GoLive Cyberstudio. When Adobe acquired GoLive, Greg left for the "greener pastures" of chief rival Macromedia. Greg wore a variety of hats at Macromedia—from sales engineer to Technical Product Manager for Dreamweaver to Evangelist.

With the acquisition of Macromedia by Adobe, Greg took on the role of Worldwide Web Evangelist. Through his role at Adobe, Greg has had the good fortune to travel around the world (more times than he cares to count) and talk with users of Adobe's products at seminars, conferences, and trade shows. Greg is now the Group Manager for Creative Solutions Evangelism at Adobe, leading a team of worldwide evangelists as they spread the word about Adobe's creative products and technologies.

You can follow Greg's adventures at http://blog.assortedgarbage.com.

CHAPTER 1

What's New in Dreamweaver CS4?

FROM THE MOMENT we saw the earliest of builds and heard what the Adobe engineering team had planned for Dreamweaver CS4, we knew this release would be amazing. Before we dive into CSS, let's take a quick tour of the new features of Dreamweaver CS4, with a focus on those that most affect our work in the rest of the book.

Work, Work, Work

Probably the most obvious of the new features is the new interface. In the CS3 revision, Flash got a new interface and with CS4 it's Dreamweaver's turn at the cosmetic counter—and if you're thinking that looks are only skin deep, you're wrong. These enhancements make the overall work environment much more flexible, and in turn make you more productive.

At the top of the Dreamweaver CS4 workspace you'll notice a new toolbar known as the Application Bar.

FIGURE 1.1 The Application Bar—a few icons, but loads of functionality.

FIGURE 1.2 Pick a workspace—
or make your own.

The Application Bar's four icons pack a lot of punch in terms of workspace enhancements. In previous versions of Dreamweaver, there were basically two workspaces: Designer and Developer. But the only real difference was the placement of the panels—either on the right side of the screen for the Designer, or the left side of the screen for the Developer. Now, however, Dreamweaver comes decked out with eight workspace variations.

Each of these predefined workspaces contains different combinations of panels and panel groups, as well as different placements and appearances for the panels. For example, the Designer workspace, which is the default workspace when you install Dreamweaver CS4, places the panels on the right side of the screen in their fully expanded state, with the Insert panel and Files panel open. This is similar to the Designer workspace in previous versions of Dreamweaver, but with two noticeable changes. First, the Insert panel is no longer a horizontal bar located at the top of the screen, under the menus, but is now a vertical panel grouped together with the other panels on screen. The second difference can only be seen when a document is open.

1. Create a blank HTML document.

You'll notice that the document opened in Split view with the code on top and the design on the bottom.

For years, this Split view with the code on top and design below (or code on bottom, design on top) has been the only way to view the two together. But by popular demand—and there were a lot of requests for this feature!—we now have another option, side-by-side.

N   *For old-school Dreamweaver users that prefer the Insert panel to be a horizontal, tabbed bar at the top of the screen, choosing the Classic workspace moves the panel back to its old position. However, this can also be done in any workspace by dragging the Insert tab up into the Application Bar.*

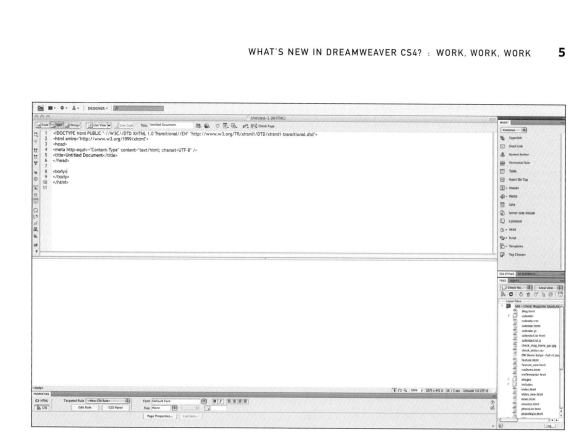

FIGURE 1.3 The default Designer workspace with an open document.

FIGURE 1.4 The Layout pop-up menu allows further customization of the workspace.

2. Click on the Layout icon on the Application Bar and choose Split Vertically.

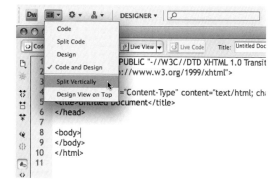

This places the code on the left and the design on the right by default, but the placement can also be reversed in the Layout pop-up menu.

3. Choose the Coder workspace from the Application Bar.

This workspace gives new meaning to minimal. There's one panel group, which is displaying the Files panel, along with the HTML document, which is now in Code view.

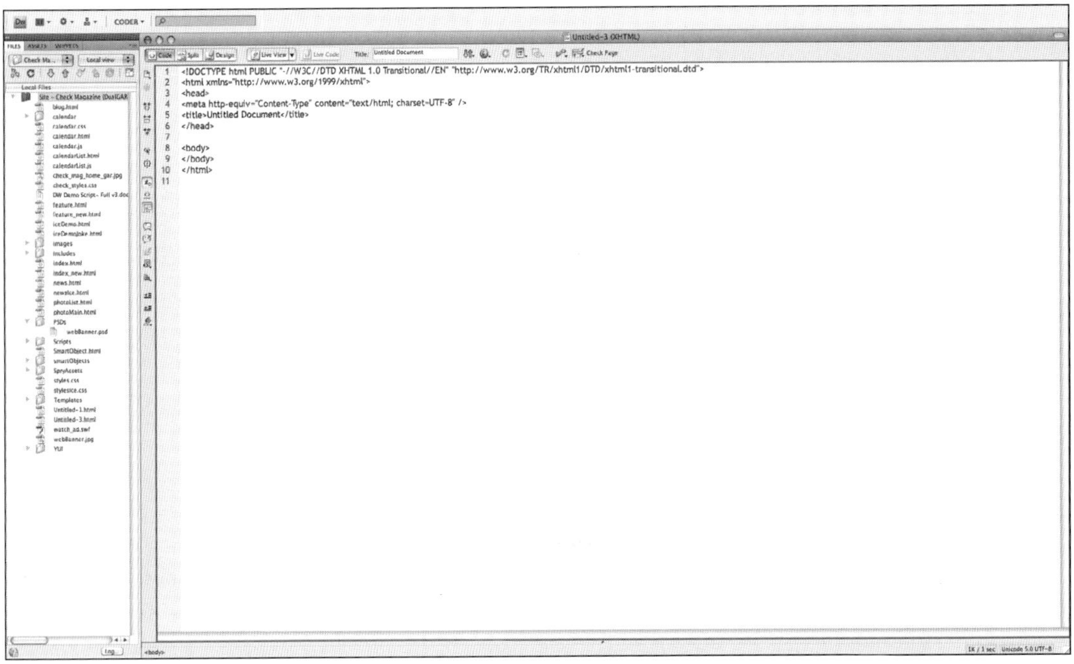

FIGURE 1.5 The Coder workspace is definitely all about the code!

If you are fond of this code-centric workspace, head back up to the Application Bar and choose Split Code from the Layout pop-up menu. This will place two copies of the code side-by-side (or stacked on top of each other, if you prefer), allowing you to scroll and work in different areas of the same document at one time! This can be extremely handy when working with CSS or JavaScript in the head of a document while needing to refer to elements of the HTML.

4. Choose the Designer Compact workspace from the Application Bar.

Suddenly all of the panels are back on the right-hand side of the screen, but they've turned into little rectangles! The ability to collapse panels down to an iconic state and save on precious screen real estate is one of the great benefits of the new interface.

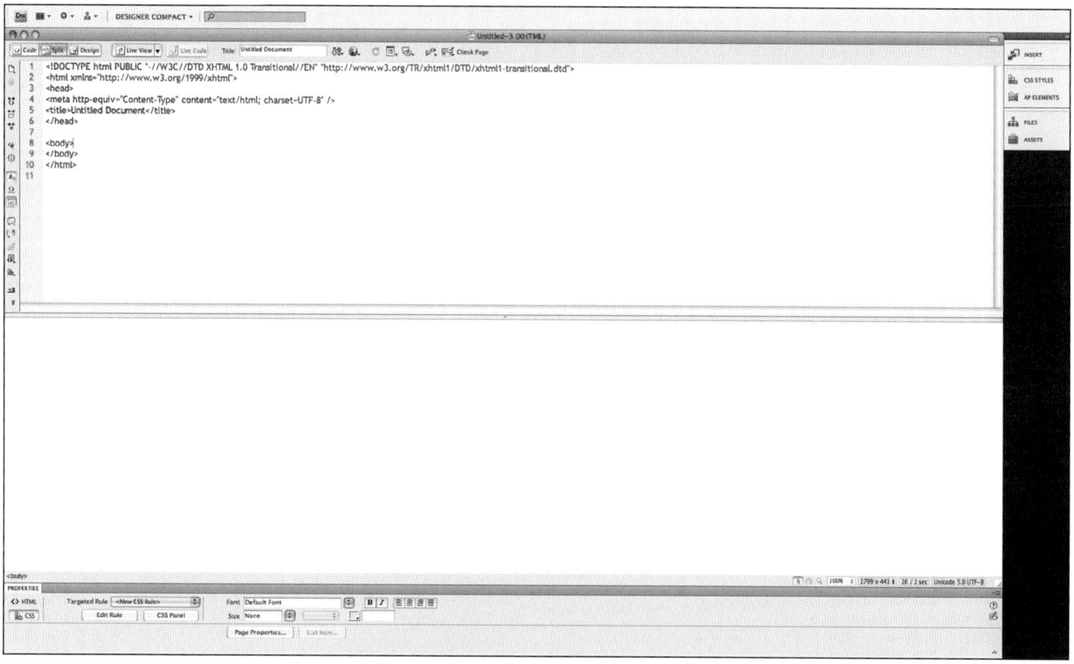

FIGURE 1.6 Hey, where did the panels go?

FIGURE 1.7 The Insert panel makes a reappearance.

5. Click on the Insert panel.

When panels are collapsed into their iconic mode, they pop out when clicked and then automatically hide themselves as soon as you click elsewhere. At first blush, this seems really cool—but quite honestly, we've found it a bit irritating, especially for panels (like the CSS panel) that we use a lot.

Now don't take that the wrong way—the iconic mode can be a great space-saver, but the showing/hiding thing gets old. Therefore, the Dreamweaver engineers gave us the ability to control this behavior.

6. With the Insert panel open, right-click on the Insert tab itself.

7. Select Auto-Collapse Iconic Panels.

   This option tells Dreamweaver to leave any panel open until you yourself close it.

FIGURE 1.8 Auto-Collapse Iconic Panels makes them play a game of peek-a-boo.

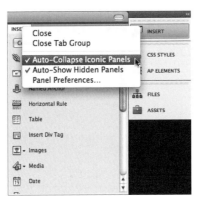

8. Click anywhere on the open HTML document and notice that the panel still remains open.

   When the Auto-Collapse option is not enabled, the panel can be closed by clicking on the panel's tab, or by clicking on the two triangles in the top-right corner of the panel or panel group.

9. Select the App Developer Plus workspace.

   In this workspace, notice that there are panel groups on both sides of the document. And the ones on the right-hand side are collapsed into iconic mode, while the ones on the left are expanded.

N *If you want even more screen real estate, the iconic mode for the panels can be made even smaller. Simply place your mouse close to the right or left edge of the panel's icon so that a small double-headed arrow appears. Click and drag toward the edge of the screen and the panel will pop closed, displaying only its icon. Dragging away from the screen edge expands the panel group back to the iconic mode with the name of the panel beside the icon. Continue dragging away from the screen edge to expand the panel group completely. Alternatively, you can toggle the panel group open and closed by clicking the two triangles.*

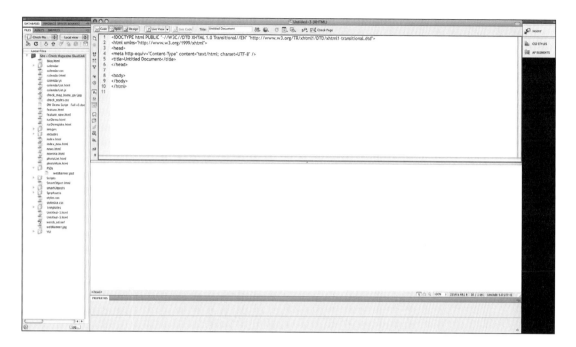

FIGURE 1.9 Panel groups can be placed on either side of the screen, seen here in the App Developer Plus workspace.

While you might be content with the default workspaces, you are also free to create your own. Each panel can be torn off of its default position and left to float on its own, or it can be grouped with another panel or panel group. In terms of flexibility, a panel or panel group can be docked in a variety of places now.

10. Click and drag the Files panel from its position over to the right-hand side of the screen until a light blue bar appears on the right edge of the screen.

11. Drop the panel into place.

    When dragging panels and panel groups, the blue bar indicates where the new position of the item would be. And you can literally go wild with the combinations.

12. Switch to a workspace that basically meets your needs, then experiment with dragging panels around to customize the workspace and deciding upon the way you want Split view to appear. Take your time, we'll wait.

13. From the Application Bar, click the Workspace pop-up menu and choose New Workspace. Give your new workspace a name and click OK.

Feel free to create multiple workspaces to meet the needs of your task at hand. Workspaces can be managed, that is, renamed or deleted, from the Workspace pop-up menu.

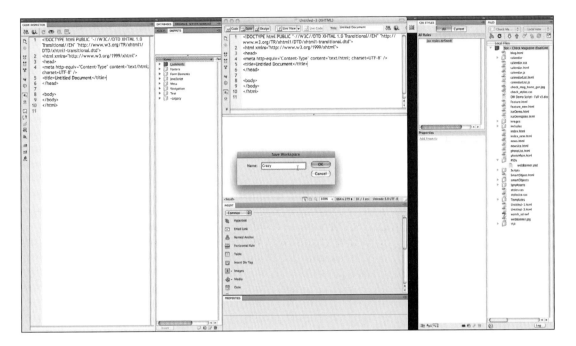

FIGURE 1.10 Okay, so this might be a little over the top!

Finally on the Application Bar are two other iconic pop-up menus, one for adding and managing extensions to Dreamweaver, and the other for creating and managing site definitions.

You'll also find a search field that connects directly to the new Dreamweaver community-based Help site, where you can find answers to questions and problems, links to tutorials, and much more.

Live View—More Than a Pretty Picture

As every web designer knows, half of the battle when using a WYSIWYG editor is figuring out why the browser(s) and editor vary in the rendering of the page. Although Dreamweaver's rendering in Design view has gotten better and better with each successive version, it's never been perfect. While there are a number of completely logical reasons for this, the reasons never matter when you're at deadline and having to coerce Dreamweaver into matching the browser's rendering.

To solve this, and ideally increase our productivity by limiting the trips we need to take to the browser, the Dreamweaver team created Live View, the sexiest new feature in Dreamweaver and the one that's most welcome from a CSS point of view. To create Live View, the team built a browser engine directly into Dreamweaver. The browser that they used is Webkit, arguably the most standards-compliant browser engine, and the engine used in Apple's Safari browser as well as Google's new Chrome browser.

FIGURE 1.11 Live View enabled in Split view.

Live View is a real browser's view of the page, so all of the functionality of the page, such as Ajax, JavaScript, or Flash, can be viewed and executed. Should you want to test a page without JavaScript or a plugin enabled, as we'll do in Chapter 6, the Live View drop-down menu can enable or disable JavaScript and plugins.

You can even use Live View while in Split view. Selecting elements on the page in Live View selects the corresponding HTML in the code. However, selecting elements from the code, though they're editable, does not highlight or select the corresponding element within Live View. Additionally, in order to see any changes made in the HTML or CSS, you must refresh the Live View mode (F5 is the shortcut).

FIGURE 1.12 A complete carbon copy—the page as seen in Dreamweaver CS4 in Live View and Safari 3.

It's Really All Related

As welcome a feature as Live View is, working with complex pages such as Ajax applications is still challenging, because of all of the external dependencies, including not only JavaScript files but CSS as well. Even the simplest web page today generally has a CSS file linked to it. Managing and understanding which supporting files are related to a given HTML page is the responsibility of the Related Files toolbar.

When this option is enabled in the General section of the Dreamweaver Preferences, a toolbar appears above each document's Document toolbar listing all of the files related to the HTML page. This includes not only CSS and JavaScript files but also server-side includes.

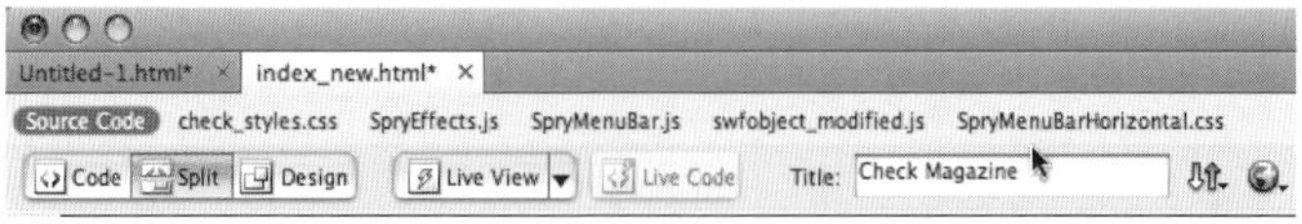

FIGURE 1.13 The Related Files toolbar lists all of the external documents necessary to render the page.

You can easily switch to any of the listed documents by clicking on their name in the Related Files toolbar. This is especially handy, as you'll see throughout the book, when working with your CSS files while watching the changes get applied in the Design view—or even Live View.

Code Comes Alive

As we've just mentioned, Ajax pages require not only HTML and CSS, but also JavaScript. And the JavaScript is responsible for changing the rendering of the page on-the-fly. This can be something as simple as applying a different CSS class or as complex as completely restructuring the HTML of the page. All of this, in turn, makes it very difficult to work on the layout of a page since it is likely to change once the JavaScript gets involved.

To solve this design challenge, the Dreamweaver engineers gave Dreamweaver CS4 two essential abilities. The first is called Live Code, which allows us to click the Live Code button and tell Dreamweaver to render, or interpret, the HTML code exactly as the browser sees and does it. You'll notice that the Live Code button, located to the right of the Live View button, is only enabled when Live View is enabled.

FIGURE 1.14 Live Code shows the code as it is rendered by the browser.

It's important to note that when Live Code is enabled, it is no longer editable. You can still click in the Design (Live Code) pane to select an element and it will be highlighted in the Live Code—you just can't edit it.

So what's the point if you can't edit? Well, that's simple—when working with pages that change as in the Ajax example, we often need to see what modification the browser has undertaken. At the point at which we wish to modify something that has been written by the JavaScript, such as the assignment of a different CSS class, Dreamweaver CS4 allows us to freeze the code. We can then not only see the code change, through the use of the new Code Navigator, we can see a cascade of all of the related documents and CSS rules and their declarations controlling the selected element. We'll be using the Code Navigator and Live Code extensively in Chapter 6.

FIGURE 1.15 The Code Navigator gives a quick look at everything related to a specific page element.

One final note: if you find yourself writing or editing JavaScript, Dreamweaver CS4 now provides enhanced code hinting for not only the Spry Framework for Ajax, but also for your own custom JavaScripts or other JavaScript frameworks. When a page is opened that contains links to JavaScript files, Dreamweaver will read those files and make a note of all of the functions contained within them. This allows Dreamweaver to provide intelligent code hinting and code completion, regardless of where the JavaScript has come from.

Give Me Data or Give Me Death

Speaking of Ajax, and more specifically of the Spry framework for Ajax, there are several new enhancements sure to put a smile on the face of anyone who is interested in standards—that'd be you, right?

Midway through the lifecycle of Dreamweaver CS3, the engineering team for Spry released version 1.6. This release brought a number of important advancements to the framework in the areas of progressive enhancement, including support for HTML data sets and unobtrusive JavaScript. Unfortunately, creating and using an HTML data set as well as externalizing JavaScript was a code-only, do-it-with-no-help endeavor in Dreamweaver CS3.

With Dreamweaver CS4, these features come to the forefront and really shine. A new data set wizard intelligently and easily steps you through the process of creating a data set—whether you're dealing with XML as a data source, or building a data set from an HTML page or snippet. The wizard examines and identifies elements, such as tables, divs, and so on, which can be used as data sources, then quickly builds master/detail relationships, data tables, or stacked elements that can be modified with CSS.

FIGURE 1.16 The new and improved Spry Data Set Wizard.

From a standards perspective, Spry was sometimes belittled because of its reliance upon non-standard attributes and embedded JavaScript. This practice flies in the face of true standards-based, progressive enhancement of pages. With Dreamweaver CS4 however, when we've completed the development process and are ready to deploy the page, a single command is all it takes to move the entire Spry-specific markup and JavaScript into an external JavaScript file.

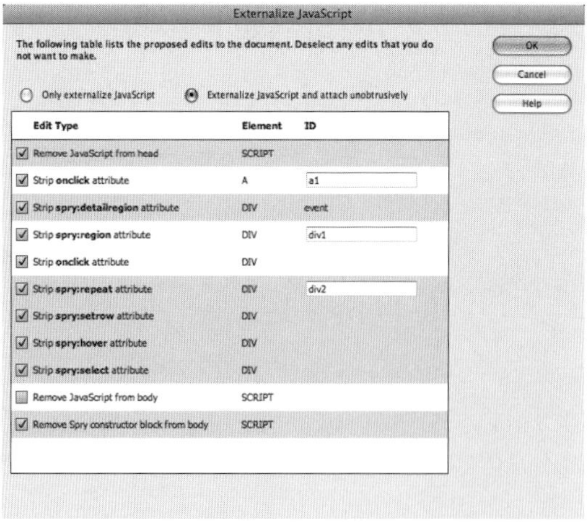

FIGURE 1.17 Choices, choices. The Externalize JavaScript command can move as much or as little as you want to an external file.

Spry aficionados will also appreciate the fact that three new form validation widgets and an interface element have been added to the Insert panel. These are the Validation Password widget, Validation Confirm widget, and Validation Radio Group widget along with the Tooltip widget.

The Validation Password widget allows for client-side validation of a password in a form, while the Validation Confirm widget checks to make sure that the password entered in the second password field matches that of the first field. And with the Validation Radio Group, you can even require that a radio button be selected before processing a form.

The Tooltip widget is exactly what it sounds like—it displays a tooltip when hovering over any designated element within the page—but instead of a single line or word like with alternative text or the CSS title attribute, the tooltip can contain literally any HTML markup including text, images, links, Flash, you name it.

FIGURE 1.18 The Spry Tooltip widget is a cool way to provide additional information or instructions to a viewer.

Ribbons and Bows

In addition to the list of major new features, there are a few useful changes to existing features. Not all of them will be important to you as you work your way through the projects in the book. But before moving on, let's go over a few of these more minor but still important changes.

The Property inspector has been around since the first version of Dreamweaver, and like a pair of old jeans, is probably one of the most comfortable tools for Dreamweaver users. But as Dreamweaver shifted to a more standards-compliant CSS-based method of building web sites, the Property inspector came under criticism, largely because it was designed to display text and table properties, not CSS. Dreamweaver MX 2004 added a few CSS features to the Property inspector, such as the ability to automatically create (and arbitrarily name) a style when you changed attributes in the panel. This, in turn, actually created a bit of chaos because people ended up with styles like Style1, Style2, Style3.... But in Dreamweaver CS4, the Property inspector has separated HTML from CSS, through two buttons on the left. Click the HTML button, and you get access to HTML specific aspects of a design, such as creating <p> elements, lists, and links. Click the CSS button for access to CSS specific tasks, such as creating or assigning a new CSS rule.

FIGURE 1.19 The Property inspector's two areas—offering more task-centric options.

Getting Flashy

In Dreamweaver CS3, changes to the way that Flash was placed into a page worked fairly well, but there were occasional situations in which a user did not receive content or alternative content. In CS4, a modified version of an open source JavaScript method known as SWFObject provides not only a standards-compliant method of embedding Flash content, but also an easy method for implementing alternative content. As a nice bonus, the required JavaScript is much smaller than the "old" way of doing things.

 *In Dreamweaver CS3 when you opened a page with any Flash content that was embedded with the older methods, you were prompted to update the page with the new method. This is no longer the case, meaning that you unfortunately will need to manually delete and re-embed your Flash content in each page of your site.*

This new method of embedding Flash also allows the designer to specify whether or not a given version of the Flash Player is required, and if they want to use Express Install—in other words to automatically upgrade and install the newest version of the Flash Player without actually leaving the page.

Getting Smart with Photoshop

Dreamweaver CS3 introduced the ability to copy and paste from a Photoshop layout into a Dreamweaver page, optimizing the image with the built-in Fireworks optimization engine, and remembering the link to the initial Photoshop file that the image in the HTML page came from. A small but significant step forward in Dreamweaver CS4 is the capability for Dreamweaver to be aware if the Photoshop document changes and notify you by placing a small icon with a half-red circle in the upper left of the image. If you select the image and click on the Update From Original icon on the Property inspector, Dreamweaver will re-import and optimize the image on the basis of the newly modified Photoshop document.

FIGURE 1.20 Houston, we've got a problem—the image is out of sync with the original Photoshop document.

With all good things comes a little bit of bad, however…this new functionality only works when you are working with a full PSD document. In other words, dragging a PSD file into a Dreamweaver page is the trigger that causes Dreamweaver to watch the PSD. If you simply copy and paste an area of a PSD into your web page, as we'll be doing in later chapters, Dreamweaver will remember which PSD the image came from, but it won't notify you when the document has changed. Obviously, this makes this feature most useful when dealing with individual items such as ad banners, badges, or any other frequently changing graphic.

When All Is Said and Done

FIGURE 1.21 Where's my magic cloaking device?

At the end of a project it's all about getting your files up to the real web server (although like we do, you probably upload things all through the workflow). One of the small but welcome additions that came along in Dreamweaver CS3 was the ability to upload/download via FTP in the background. No longer did you have to stare at your computer screen while tons of data was shuffled to and from the server. Dreamweaver CS4 enhances this capability with increased performance when transferring files, as well as the ability to connect to a broader range of servers.

In addition, individual files can now be excluded from a file transfer by cloaking them—it was previously only possible to cloak either an entire folder or all files of a given type. Now, we can simply select the file, right-click, and choose Cloak from the Cloaking submenu.

Finally, for many teams of designers and developers, it's also important to note that Dreamweaver CS4 now supports the content management system Subversion. This provides far superior asset and code management than Dreamweaver's built-in check-in/check-out can offer, including versioning and rollbacks.

And if all of this isn't enough, Dreamweaver's extensibility API has been updated to provide even greater enhancements both now and in the future—such as the ability to create AIR applications directly from within Dreamweaver (available now from the AIR section of the Adobe site), integration with other widgets such as those from Yahoo (YUI), jQuery, and much, much more. You'll even find a new

section of tools in Dreamweaver CS4 for InContext Editing—
a new technology that is still in early beta at this writing, but
should be out soon.

But for now, let's change the subject and get to the job of
Mastering CSS with Dreamweaver CS4!

CHAPTER 2

Laying the CSS Groundwork

OUR GOAL IN THIS BOOK is to give you lots of handy techniques that'll help you quickly create beautiful sites that conform to Web standards and are accessible to everyone, using the CSS layouts and tools of Dreamweaver CS4. But before we can really jump into projects, we want to be sure we're all on the same page (metaphorically) as far as understanding the terminology of CSS and the interface of Dreamweaver. This chapter, then, is a quick-and-dirty CSS primer, with some hands-on Dreamweaver exercises that'll get you up and running and familiar with Dreamweaver's CSS tools and the CSS layouts.

We'll start by introducing the basic concepts of CSS. We'll then create an equal height, two-column layout with header and footer that is similar to one of the CSS layouts in Dreamweaver—basically going through the very process that Stephanie used as she wrote the CSS layouts. By the end of this chapter, you should be able to look at the code of any of the CSS layouts included with Dreamweaver and understand most of what you see.

If you already have a strong understanding of basic CSS concepts, you may choose to move on to the next chapter. Or simply use this chapter as a review to find any cracks in the foundation of your CSS knowledge. On the other hand, if you're new to CSS and find the chapter overwhelming, relax—by the end of the book, you'll be able to return to this chapter and feel comfortable with all the concepts discussed.

Before we begin, let's save a new page based on the two-column fixed, left sidebar, header and footer layout in the CSS layout list in the New Document dialog box. We'll use this document as an example as we examine the concepts of web standards.

1. Launch Dreamweaver and select File > New. Select the Blank Page category. Select HTML under the Page Type category. Select 2 column fixed, left sidebar, header and footer from the layout category.

   In the far-right column we can see a graphical representation of the layout and a description of its specifications.

2. Leave DocType set to the XHTML 1.0 Transitional default. Leave Layout CSS on the Add to Head default. Click the Create button.

3. Save the document in the root folder of your site.

FIGURE 2.1 Choosing the 2 column fixed CSS layout.

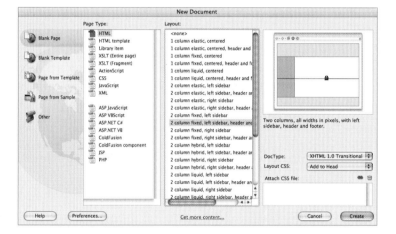

The Content/Design Equation

In order to understand solid standards-based design, you need to understand the two halves of the content/presentation equation: (X)HTML (for content) and CSS (for presentation).

In the early, early days of the web—yes, that means before YouTube and Facebook—HTML pages were simple. The few tags available were used to semantically define what the content was. For example, the h1 tag indicated that the enclosed text was a heading, and thus important. But during the wild days of the web in the late 90s, many designers applied values, such as weight, size, and color, directly to the text. They obviously wanted the text to take on a certain look, or presentation. But the fact that our *eyes* could see that the text was larger, bolder or a different color was useless to search engines and assistive technologies!

Today, our (X)HTML documents should include the page content, marked up in *semantic elements*—tags that actually describe the type of content contained within them. When our content has semantic meaning, the user agent (the browser in most cases) doesn't matter.

> ### What Are Web Standards?
>
> In a nutshell, what we're calling web standards in this book are really just best practices for building web sites. Building sites in this manner means following three principles:
>
> **Separate content and its presentation.** If you create the essential structure of the document in the (X)HTML page, you can code the information once, and output to many different devices.
>
> **Use Cascading Style Sheets for the design.** If you've been around the web long enough, you'll remember the wretched days of using browser-sniffing JavaScript to determine how to display content based on which browser and platform someone was using. Or the endless search for a printer-friendly version of a page (which we unfortunately run into even today). Or creating text-only versions to minimally satisfy accessibility requirements. When you use Cascading Style Sheets to design your pages, these resource-consuming, economy-draining activities are a thing of the past. The simple text document known as a CSS file gives the (X)HTML document its look with a few well-crafted rules.
>
> **Design for universal accessibility.** Not everyone on the web can access, or see, our pages in exactly the same way. The goal is to give everyone the same content, in a reasonably acceptable presentational style, without crashing the system. Standards-compliant browsers will render the pages one way. Buggy browsers, such as Internet Explorer 6 and earlier, will need adjustments to render correctly. Assistive technologies (AT) will have access to all our content without the presentational markup getting in the way. And older browsers will still present the essential content, although with fewer presentational enhancements.

The (X)HTML Document

Several concepts are essential to understanding proper, well-formed (X)HTML documents: the doctype, character encoding, document flow, semantics, and inline versus block elements.

The Doctype

At the beginning of each web standards compliant document, the **Document Type Definition** (also called DTD or doctype), declares the document standard to which the file conforms. The nice thing about document standards is that there are so many of them—especially on the web! To this end, there are a number of different doctypes, each with its own set of rules for the standards with which it aspires to comply.

Take a moment to look at the various doctypes listed in the drop-down list of the New Document dialog box.

Dreamweaver uses the XHTML 1.0 Transitional doctype as its default. Unless the site has more specific requirements, this is a good doctype to use because of its backward compatibility with older web pages and its forward compatibility with the future of the web (we hope). XHTML 1.0 Transitional allows *deprecated elements*, which are mostly presentational elements and attributes such as `font`, `align`, and `bgcolor`. The XHTML 1.0 Strict or HTML 4.01 Strict doctypes do not allow those elements to be used.

Let's take a look at the page we just created. Move back to the page you created and look for the following code at the top. (Switch into Code or Code and Design view if necessary.)

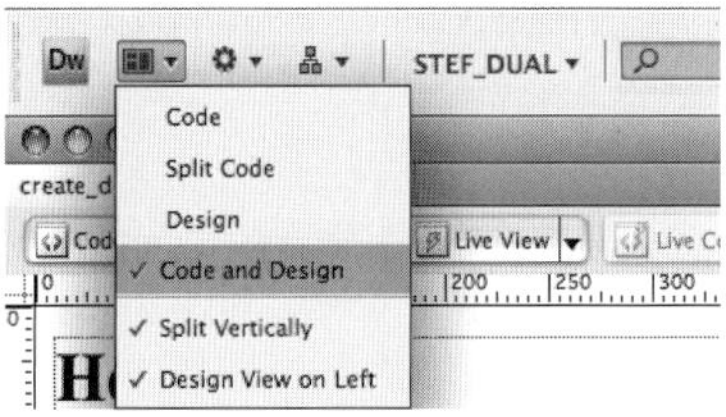

FIGURE 2.2 The Application Bar showing the Layout widget.

N   *The Application Bar, which is accessed using Window > Application Bar, contains a variety of useful workflow widgets. The Layout widget allows you to control the way you view your document—Design, Code, Code and Design, Split Vertically, etc. Working in Code and Design view is a great way to keep an eye on your code (and even learn if you're a beginner), as well as allowing you to jump back and forth between the two views effortlessly.*

```
<!DOCTYPE html PUBLIC "-//W3C//DTD XHTML 1.0 Transitional//EN"
"http://www.w3.org/TR/xhtml1/DTD/xhtml1-transitional.dtd">
<html xmlns="http://www.w3.org/1999/xhtml">
```

What this code is telling us is that the page uses XHTML 1.0 Transitional and will be compared against its rules as provided in the URL that follows. If you **validate** the page—check that it's free of errors—at the World Wide Web (W3C) consortium validator, the W3C would use that particular doctype as the basis of its tests.

Unfortunately, many web designers have neglected to include the doctype in their pages—and, in fact, even our beloved Dreamweaver included an incomplete doctype for several earlier versions. When this happens, pages will render in **quirks mode** instead of **standards mode**. In other words, they will render according to the methods of older, more forgiving browsers. This means our carefully constructed CSS might not display as we expect.

Character Encoding

Go back to the two-column CSS layout and look at the code beneath the doctype. The code should look like the following:

```
<meta http-equiv="Content-Type" content="text/html;
charset=UTF-8" />
```

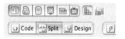 *To learn more about doctypes and the various rendering modes, read the article Rendering Mode and Doctype Switching http://www.communitymx.com/ content/article.cfm?cid=85fee by Holly Bergevin of Community MX. The article includes a list of doctypes, as well as a list of resource links for learning everything you ever wanted—or didn't want—to know about doctypes.*

This is the **character encoding** for the page, which is the system whereby each character we type is turned into computer bits. Until fairly recently, developers used character sets that expressed a limited number of languages, such as `charset=ISO-8859-1` for Western European languages. When the developer wanted to add a special character, such as a copyright symbol or an accent mark, they used a **character entity**. An example of this would be the character entity `&eacute;` that we use to represent the French accent acute.

More and more developers are using a universal character encoding called Unicode. In essence, Unicode allows us to use characters from almost any writing system in the world. The Dreamweaver CS4 default for both CSS and XHTML documents is a flavor of Unicode called UTF-8, which has backward compatibility with ASCII. Because of the increasing internationalization of the web, as well as the ability of browsers to support Unicode, UTF-8 is a solid choice for character encoding.

The Natural Flow of the Document

Another important concept to understand is the natural **document flow**. The flow of the document is what we see if we remove all CSS control from a page. We'll view this in real time, using the page we've been looking at already.

1. Right-click on the top of the document to verify that the Style Rendering toolbar is displayed.

2. Click the Toggle Displaying of CSS Styles icon (the second from the right) to turn CSS styles completely off.

3. View the page in Design view.

FIGURE 2.3 The Style Rendering toolbar at the top of the document window.

In the absence of any positioning techniques, page elements will flow one after the other in the order that they appear in the source code of the document.

Document Semantics

While our styles are toggled off, let's consider another important part of marking up our document. When moving content from a copywriter to the web, we must choose which elements to use to contain various portions of the content—this is called *semantics*. Think of your document in outline form—what text should be section headings, and how much weight do those headings hold? Once that's determined, that text should be marked up with h1, h2, h3, and so on. It should be hierarchical and logical. The text between the headings should be in paragraph elements.

Semantics is simply about being logical. At this stage, we don't think of the function of the content or what it will look like. We only think about what it logically *is* and mark it up consistently. Lists of information should be marked up as ordered, unordered, or definition lists. Blockquotes should only be used to contain quotations (and *not* to cause an indented area of the page—yes, you know who you are!).

What does it really matter, you say? For people using assistive technology (AT) such as screen readers, it can be helpful to access the page as a list of headings, then choose the portion of the page they want to read. Perhaps you're not concerned about accessibility; after all, that's such a small portion of the population. We bet you're concerned about search engines, though. Search engine spiders view your page very much like AT. In fact, search engines put greater weight on key words and phrases that are in heading elements. So though you can style text to *look* like a heading, it won't carry as much weight with the spiders as text that has been marked up to *be* a heading. And let's not forget user agents that may not display your style sheets at all. (Certain mobile devices come to mind.) Having your page marked up in a logical fashion makes it easier for those users to scan and digest the content. There are also CSS benefits to good semantic mark-up and we'll talk more about those later in the chapter.

Inline Versus Block Elements

When we place text, images, and other content in an (X)HTML page, each semantic element flows one after the other in the natural order in which we insert it in the source code of the document. But another variable within the flow affects how elements behave: their status as a block or inline element.

Block elements are 100% as wide as their parent container and stack vertically on top of each other. It's as if there is an inherent line break between each element. Look, for example, at the **h1** text labeled Main Content at the top of the document. It occupies its own block of space. The next element, the dummy text that sits in a paragraph, flows underneath it. Block elements do not, by default, sit next to each other.

Inline elements, on the other hand, flow horizontally and only require the amount of space they use (instead of the set width of block elements). Starting at the left, text characters, links, and images (all examples of inline elements) flow one after the other until all available horizontal space runs out. The next inline element then moves down to start a new line, just like the wrapping effect in your word processor. The browser calculates how many elements are going to fit on a line and then makes an invisible box that is tall enough for the highest elements in the line.

FIGURE 2.4 Inline and block elements within the natural flow of the document.

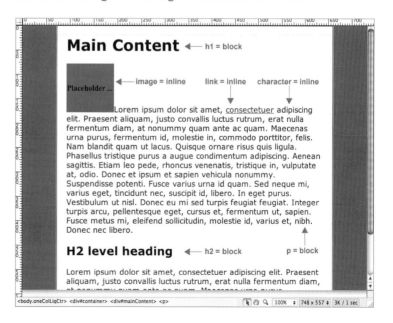

FIGURE 2.5 Dreamweaver gives you a host of visual aids to choose from.

N *If you haven't toggled your CSS styles back on, it's best to do that now.*

FIGURE 2.6 A div ends when the content within it ends.

Building with Divs

The **div** is a generic empty box that lets you divide a page into discrete areas. For example, a developer might divide a page into header, sidebar, main content, and footer sections, using divs with descriptive names such as header or footer. Look at the CSS layouts and see if you can locate this code:

`<div id="mainContent">` or `<div id="header">`

The div gives us yet another element that we can use to divide and style unique areas of the page. It has an intrinsic behavior, however, that confuses new CSS coders: although the div is a block element, it ends when the content within it stops flowing vertically. If you look at the light gray background color on the `sidebar1` div in your document, you can see how its outlines end when the content within ends. Dreamweaver's default method of outlining page elements makes the end of the div very clear.

This behavior presents challenges when we try to extend background color on a column so that it goes to the bottom of the layout. We will explore the faux column technique, a common method to give the illusion of two equal height columns, in later chapters of this book.

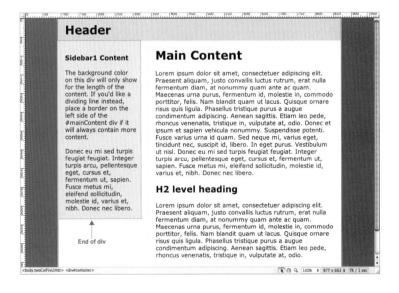

The CSS Document

The (X)HTML page is not just pure content but has semantic markup that describes the content's meaning. This markup provides the "hooks" to use CSS (Cascading Style Sheets) to style, and sometimes shift, the content.

CSS Syntax

Style sheets are made up of CSS rules that contribute to the design and placement of elements. Each CSS rule is made up of a selector and a declaration block. The declaration block, in turn, is made up of one or more declarations, each of which is a property with a value. Let's break this down by referring to **Figure 2.7**:

FIGURE 2.7 The anatomy of CSS syntax

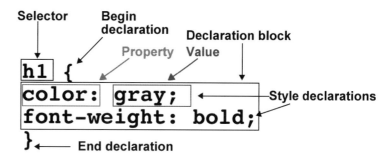

The **h1** element is the **selector** (an element in this case) that we want to style. Next comes the **declaration block**, which is the series of property and value pairs such as `color:gray;` and `font-weight: bold;`. As you can see in the example above, the declaration block begins and ends with a curly bracket. Each individual property and value pair within is a **declaration**. For the first declaration, the **property** is color and the **value** is gray. Each declaration ends with a semi-colon.

CSS Selector Types

When working with CSS in Dreamweaver, the New CSS Rule dialog box gives you four CSS selector options—Tag, Class, ID and Compound.

TAG SELECTORS (ALSO CALLED ELEMENT OR TYPE SELECTORS)

The most basic option is a selector that redefines the look of every instance of a specific tag or element. Returning to the **h1** example, if you want the color of all your **h1** text to be gray instead of black, you could write a rule for the **h1** element. Redefining an element is a global operation that affects every element of the same type on the page. Using element selectors to first redefine all common values will help you to write more efficient CSS.

As you can see in the following image, once you select "Tag (redefines an HTML element)", a drop-down list appears that lists all HTML elements in alphabetical order.

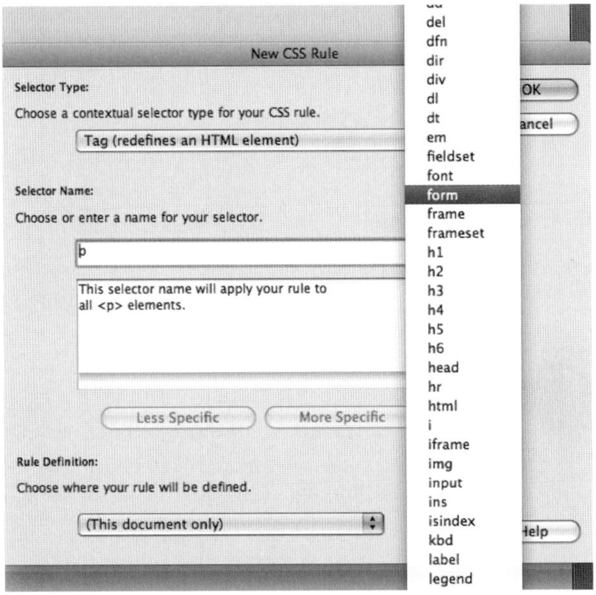

N *Many people, as well as Dreamweaver, use the terms tag and element interchangeably. However, the text inside the h1 is actually the element. The <h1> and </h1> surrounding it are the tags. Thus, tag selectors and element selectors are referring to the same thing. Since they're more commonly known as element selectors, we'll be using that terminology more often in the book.*

FIGURE 2.8 The Tag selector and its drop-down list

CLASS SELECTORS

The class selector is applied to anything on the page that includes its attribute in the (X)HTML code. Classes are used on an as-needed basis, and should be applied sparingly. If you've ever worked with styles in a word processor or page layout application, classes work in the same way. For example, you might add a class to a paragraph element:

```
<p class="warning">
```

In the style sheet, the class might include these properties and values:

```
.warning {
  font-weight: bold;
  color: #FF0000;
}
```

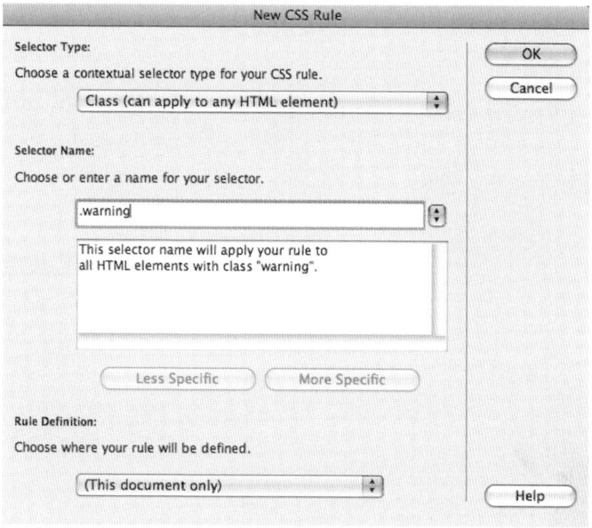

FIGURE 2.9 The Class selector

Selectors for class names begin with a period and then use a descriptive name, referring to the purpose of the class, not its appearance (although many a new CSS designer has been guilty of creating a .boldRed class!). We can use a class as many times as we like within a page to give elements consistent styling. For instance, we might want all of the important text within a paragraph to have the same visual properties and thus define a class called warning to set the appearance of the crucial text within the paragraph.

ID SELECTORS

The ID selector is applied to the single element on the page that includes its attribute in the (X)HTML code. ID selectors are commonly used to identify a specific area of the page, such as the mainContent div in our example:

```
<div id="mainContent">.
```

In the CSS, you might create a rule that moves the `mainContent` div 225 pixels from the left side of the page.

```
#mainContent {
  margin-left: 225px;
}
```

FIGURE 2.10 The ID selector

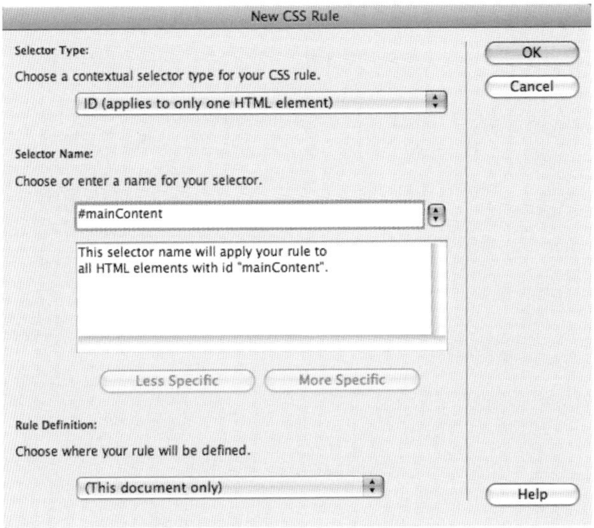

Note that in the style sheet, selectors for IDs begin with a hash mark or octothorpe (#). Each ID name must be unique, and unlike classes can only be used one time on each page.

COMPOUND SELECTORS

The Compound selector type, as it is known in Dreamweaver, is used most often for **pseudo selectors** and **descendant selectors** (though Dreamweaver allows you to type absolutely anything into this box, including child, sibling, attribute, compound lists, and any other selector). Let's look at what each term means.

Pseudo Selectors The most common example is pseudo-class selectors for anchors (links). These are the `a:link`, `a:visited`, `a:hover`, and `a:active` styles that we see listed in the drop-down list next to the Selector Name input when Compound selector is chosen. They represent various link states: `a:link` is the initial state of the link; `a:visited` is the state of the link after the user has already visited it; `a:hover` is the interactive state of the link when the visitor passes the mouse over it; and `a:active` is the state of the

N *When you want to apply the same properties and values to a number of selectors, you can group them, by writing them together and separating them with a comma and a space. This is called a grouped selector. Don't place a comma after the last selector in the list. Because Internet Explorer does not use the a:focus rule for keyboard navigators, but instead uses the a:active rule, we always group :hover, :active, and :focus together so that all types of users will see the same hover-type state when activating a link. We place :focus last to be sure IE keyboard navigators see the :hover style we intend.*

link when the user clicks the link but has not released the mouse button. There is also the **a:focus** state, which can be styled like the **a:hover** state (and grouped together), and is activated by those who are using a keyboard rather than a mouse to navigate through links (and indicates that a link can accept keyboard events). While this pseudo class does not appear within Dreamweaver's drop-down list, it can simply be typed into the field as **a:focus**.

We can use CSS to style these link states to display their differences visually. The one thing that must be remembered with these specific pseudo-class selectors is that they must follow a specific order in the style sheet:

- **a:link**

- **a:visited**

- **a:hover**

- **a:active**

- **a:focus** (when included)

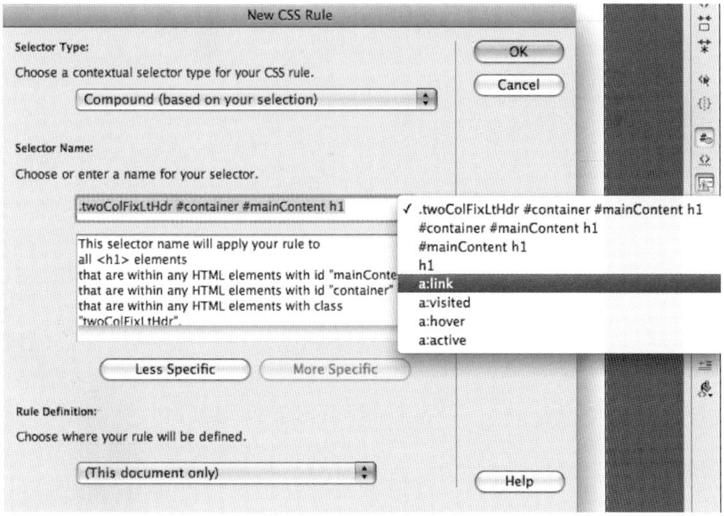

FIGURE 2.11 The Compound selector—pseudo-class selectors

Descendant Selectors Understanding the document tree—the structure of the (X)HTML document and the relationships between the elements—is the first step in writing highly efficient and compact CSS. The document tree is similar to a family tree with ancestors, siblings, and children. Learning to target an element using its descendants is a powerful tool.

Let's use the example of a document containing the body element with a container that holds `mainContent` and `sidebar1` divs. In `sidebar1`, we have some nested unordered lists creating the navigation. In `mainContent`, we have h1, h2, and paragraph elements. Visually, as a family tree is rendered, it might look like this:

FIGURE 2.12 All elements are descendants of the body.

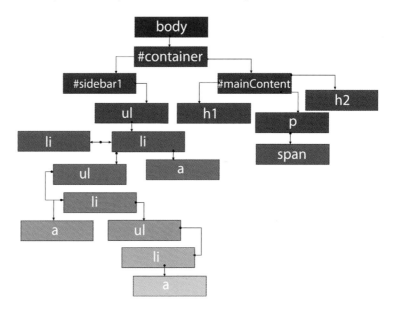

Earlier we mentioned that redefining the look of a specific element or tag is a global operation. If **h1** is defined as gray, every **h1** on the page will be gray. But what if we need to create different looks for the same element in different areas of the page? For example, we may want **h1** to be red in the sidebar (**#sidebar1**), but green in the main content (**#mainContent**). We then set individual looks for the h1 tag by writing the style in a specific context. A rule addressing **#mainContent h1** will target the **h1** tag only when it is in the main content area of the page. And a rule for **#sidebar1 h1** will target the **h1** tag only when it is in the sidebar area of the page. (Note the use of a space between the ID and the element name.)

FIGURE 2.13 The Compound selector—descendant selector

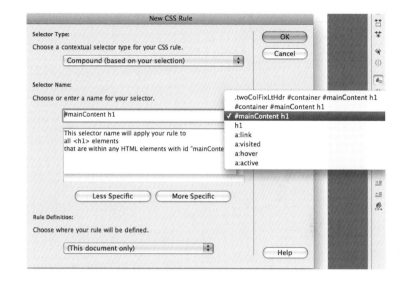

To read a complex descendant selector, always start at the end of the selector and work backward. For instance, `.twoColFixLtHdr #sidebar1 li a` *selects any anchor (link) element contained in a list item that is contained within an element with the ID of sidebar1 that is contained within an element with the class* `twoColFixLtHdr`*. If you need help figuring it out, the selectoracle at http://gallery.theopalgroup.com/ selectoracle/ can help.*

The CSS layouts in Dreamweaver CS4 only use descendant selectors; however, the CSS specifications allow for other advanced selectors. These selectors, such as the adjacent sibling and the child selector, aren't consistently supported yet, but are available in IE7 (among other browsers). You can familiarize yourself with more selector types at the W3C: http://www.w3.org/ TR/REC-CSS2/selector.html.

By choosing New CSS Rule from either the CSS pane of the CSS Property inspector or the CSS Styles panel and choosing Compound as our selector type, Dreamweaver auto-fills the full path to the element we're targeting, creating a very complex descendant selector. Most of the time, you don't need to be *that* specific (but you do have the option). Comparing Figure 2.11 and 2.13, you can see that Dreamweaver will show you more and less specific selector names. Our cursor was in the **h1** element in the **mainContent** div. You can create a more or less specific rule using the buttons below the description box, or using the drop-down on the right of the Selector Name.

There are many varieties of CSS layouts available to us in Dreamweaver, and we may want to use more than one within a site. For example, we might want to use both a two-column and three-column layout within the same site. In order to give different values to the **mainContent** div in the two-column page versus the **mainContent** div in the three-column page, each CSS layout has a class assigned to the body element.

In the following code, you can see the class attribute that the CSS layouts add to the body of the two-column fixed-width page and the three-column fixed-width page:

```
<body class="twoColFixLtHdr">
<body class="thrColFixHdr">
```

This code shows how we add a class prefix to the `mainContent` for each layout creating a descendant selector:

```
.twoColFixLtHdr #mainContent
.thrColFixHdr #mainContent
```

Now each rule that has a class prefix will maintain unique styles for different page types within one style sheet. We'll take a closer look at combining the style sheets for several CSS layouts later in this book.

Now that you understand basic CSS syntax and selector types, let's look at the kinds of style sheets in which we might use them.

The Cascade

There are many ways in which rules can be applied to our document. Though it may seem a bit mundane, it's important to understand the C in CSS, which is, of course, the cascade—the order in which rules are applied—and how it affects the page.

Doesn't this seem rather counterintuitive? We give the user the ability to create their own styles, but as authors, we can override their preferences. Sad, but them's the rules, pardner!

Style sheets operate in a hierarchy in which certain sheets take precedence over others. In the absence of any other style sheet, the browser style sheet determines how the page looks. But users can create user style sheets and set them as the defaults in their browser preferences, and those styles will take precedence over equivalent browser styles. Finally, author style sheets that we designers and developers create for our pages have the final authority over the look of the page.

THE BROWSER STYLE SHEET

There are a variety of ways to zero many defaults at once. We won't try to set any universal rules, but will simply zero values out as needed in the exercises, in order to keep the steps clear.

Browsers apply default style sheets that set the presentation of all HTML elements. Formats such as the large size on level one headings, the gaps between paragraphs, the indents on lists, and other basic style information give the page a minimal design.

To see specific browser's style sheets, visit http://meiert. com/en/blog/20070922/ user-agent-style-sheets/ to see some examples that Jens Meiert has posted.

Though the different browsers use similar values in their default style sheets, they are, unfortunately, not exactly the same. As we start to create our own custom rules, we don't have a level playing field—the changes we make can affect users differently depending on which browser they're using. In order to create a style sheet that looks the same to every user, we should start by "zeroing out" margins, padding, and borders on many (X)HTML elements in order to override the default browser values. With everything set to "0", we can then go on to set our own values expecting that the effect will now be the same in each browser.

THE USER STYLE SHEET

The next style sheet in the hierarchy comes from a user who adds a style sheet that overrides some browser styles. This style sheet may designate a larger font size, for example, to make it easier for a person to read the text. Most browsers allow users to set a custom user style sheet in the browser preferences. These preferences override the browser style sheet, but not the author style sheet.

THE AUTHOR STYLE SHEET

The top dog in the hierarchy is the style sheet created by us, the web page authors. But there are three different ways in which our rules can be organized and applied: as external, embedded, and inline styles. The closer to the element we get, the more precedence a style takes. Inline styles take precedence over embedded style sheets, and embedded style sheets take precedence over external style sheets.

External style sheets are exactly what their name implies: they are separate, or external, documents that include all, or a portion of, our CSS rules. The file name ends with the .css extension, and a link to this external CSS document goes in the head of the (X)HTML document.

If we were to create a new document based on a CSS layout in Dreamweaver CS4 and select the Create New File option in the drop-down list next to Layout CSS, you would see code like this in the head of the (X)HTML page:

```
<link href="twoColFixLtHdr.css" rel="stylesheet"
type="text/css" />
```

There are several different ways to create a link to a file in Dreamweaver. If you're selecting a CSS layout, you can choose Create New File or Link to Existing File. You can also link to a CSS file from within an existing (X)HTML document by clicking the Attach Style Sheet icon at the bottom of the CSS Styles panel (it looks like a link in a chain). Or you can link the style sheet from Text > CSS Styles > Attach Style Sheet. And of course lastly, you

---

N   *Though the W3C recommends using the* !important *operator to force a value in the user style sheet to take precedence, not all browser manufacturers have implemented the operator at this time. In the browsers where it works, however, the* !important *operator tells the browser that this declaration, no matter where it comes in the cascade, should be honored. It is written as* font-size: 45px !important;

N   *Some designers use the* @ import *notation rather than linking style sheets. This is another way to reference the style sheet in the head. One of the advantages of importing is that older browsers do not understand it and will ignore the style sheets. This is often preferable to the wacky way they might otherwise render (or attempt to render) the styles. Using this method, an older browser will get a plain but readable page that simply renders the normal flow of the document.*

can do it the most boring way—you can manually type it in the source code!

Embedded styles are placed within the head of the document. If we view our page in Code view, we can see the opening and closing style tags, some HTML comments to hide the CSS rules from older browsers that don't understand them, and nested with that, the actual CSS rules.

A single rule is shown for simplicity.

```
<style type="text/css">
<!--
.fltlft {
    float: left;
    margin-right: 8px;
}
-->
</style>
```

Embedded styles only apply to the single page in which they reside. Many developers embed styles while experimenting with the layout, and after they are satisfied with the result, they export the styles to an external style sheet. (Dreamweaver CS4 provides an easy way to export styles to an external style sheet that we'll use later.) When creating a new document using a CSS layout, it's easy to embed the rules in the head of the document. Simply set the Layout CSS drop-down list to Add to Head (which is the default). When creating a new rule, choose "This document only" in the New CSS Rule dialog to embed the rule in the head.

N *When using Dreamweaver's CSS Styles panel, you can view the source of a rule in the All view. If the CSS is embedded in the head, it will be shown indented under <style> and if it's in a CSS document, it will be shown indented below YourPageName.css. Inline styles are not shown in the All view, but are shown in the Rules pane as <inline style>, which you can see if you hover over the selector while in the Current view.*

Inline is a style that we apply directly to an individual element within the markup of the page. To style an h1 element, for example, we could add the style attribute along with the appropriate values:

```
<h1 style="font-size: 160%; color: red;">Inline Style</h1>
```

While arguments can surely be made for the use of inline styles, we rarely use them, as there's no easy way to update them.

CONFLICT RESOLUTION

When there is only one rule for a given element, we know which properties the browser will apply. But what if there are conflicting rules for the same element? What if we have two **h1** rules, for example, in one style sheet? In situations where rules have the same degree of importance, the rule that comes last has the final say: whichever **h1** style comes last in the style sheet wins.

But what if those two **h1** rules exist in different style sheets? In that case the browser follows the hierarchy of the kinds of style sheets. If you were napping, author style sheets take precedence over user style sheets, and user style sheets take precedence over the default browser style sheet. Now try to stay awake!

If the two **h1** rules are in different author style sheets, the browser loads the author style sheets in the order in which they appear in the source code. So, whichever **h1** rule is loaded last (according to which sheet it is in) will win.

If one of the **h1** rules is in an external sheet while the other is in the head, the embedded style takes precedence over the external style, and any inline styles take precedence over the embedded style. The style closest to the element wins.

Again, the order of precedence is as follows:

- *Browser*

- *User*

- *Author*

- *External*

- *Embedded*

- *Inline*

In other words, unlike the real world, it's good to come in last!

And Now for Something Really Confusing…Specificity!

Even though we just said that the last rule wins, sometimes rules have greater *weight*, regardless of where they appear. This means that even though they may not be last, they still win!

FIGURE 2.14 Dreamweaver shows you the specificity of the selector when you hover over the selector name in the Rules pane of the CSS Styles panel.

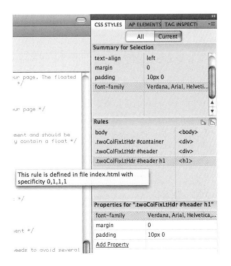

Let's consider two rules that define the color of text in a paragraph:

```
#mainContent p { color: blue; }
p.warning { color: red; }
```

N *In our example, p.warning is not the same as the descendant selector p .warning. The space matters! The p .warning rule selects any element with the class of warning that is within, or a descendant of, a p element. The p.warning rule would select any p element with a class of warning placed on it.*

The `#mainContent p` rule states that the text is blue, and the `p.warning` rule states that the text is red. Which one wins? How is their weight, or importance, calculated? The W3C considered this scenario too, and came up with a conflict resolution technique called specificity.

We calculate specificity by counting, within each selector, the number of:

- inline styles (=a)
- ids (=b)
- classes (=c)
- element names (and pseudo-elements) (=d)

The digital scheme is displayed as four hyphenated numbers (a-b-c-d), although it can also be written in comma-delimited style as well (a, b, c, d). In essence, read the value as a number: rules with higher numbers in the higher place value places win (it's not really base 10, however). Let's look at an example.

`#container #mainContent ul` has two IDs and one element name. Using the above formula, a=0 b=2, c=0, d=1 so we get the specificity of 0-2-0-1.

N *Zoe Gillenwater of Community MX wrote an article that goes into detail on the subjects of inheritance, cascade, and specificity. You can find it at http://www.communitymx.com/abstract.cfm?cid=2795D. The article includes a complete listing of the properties that elements inherit, and those they do not.*

In our paragraph color example, the specificity of `#mainContent p` is 0-1-0-1, while `p.warning` is 0-0-1-1. As a result, the text would stay blue, even if we applied the class of `warning` to a paragraph within it. In order to "beat" the specificity of `#mainContent p` and make the text in a paragraph red, we would have to make a more specific rule such as: `#mainContent p.warning`. This would give us a specificity of 0-1-1-1.

And don't think it helps to have larger numbers in the c or d slots. A selector with a specificity of 0-1-4-1 does not beat one with 1-0-0-0. And you thought high school algebra was complicated!

Inheritance

Inheritance is the process by which the value of a CSS property on one element passes down to a child element.

A general rule of thumb is that child elements inherit text-related properties but not box-related properties. But before that makes sense, we should probably discuss the box model.

Understanding the Box Model

The box model is an essential CSS concept—with some associated problems. Remember when we discussed inline and block elements? Each block element generates a box—invisible by default—that can be given padding within to push the content away from the edges of the box, borders on its edges, and margins to hold it away from other elements. The values for these properties can be applied as global values for the box or as individual values for each side. Inside the padding is the actual content area where we place our page elements.

By default, the width of the box will be 100% of the width of its parent container. (The parent container could be a div or even the body element.) The box will expand enough vertically to enclose the content within it, but no further. Of course, we can also assign a width and even a height to the element. Seems straightforward, right?

Unfortunately, Internet Explorer 5 and 5.5 render the page using a broken box model and many of us initially learned to code our pages using this incorrect math. Internet Explorer 6 (and even 7) will emulate the broken box model rendering when there is no doctype or an incorrect doctype. This is known as **quirks mode**.

The box model problem also applies to heights. But since the box by default expands vertically as long as there is additional content, this does not usually create problems like those that occur with explicit widths. Heights should rarely be used since in most cases it's better to allow the page to flow.

The W3C specs state that to determine the overall width of a box, we should add the padding and border values to the width we specified for the content within our box. But in quirks mode, that crazy Internet Explorer squeezes the padding and border into the width given to the content, arriving at a much different overall size. Margins do not have an effect on the calculations—they are always an additional value and simply hold the box away from other elements.

Other browsers, including Firefox, Netscape, Opera, Safari, and IE7 (with a correct doctype), are standards-compliant, and follow the guidelines of the W3C. However, documents with no doctype also trigger quirks mode, which varies from browser to browser.

Let's look at an example: If we set the width of a box to 250 pixels and then add 20 pixels of padding and 5 pixel borders to each side, a standards-compliant browser will read the total space that the element occupies as 300 pixels. Internet Explorer, in quirks mode, will stuff the padding and borders into the box content width—so the element would only take up 250 pixels of space on the page! Let's give the Internet Explorer team some credit—the broken box may model make logical sense, but it's not what the spec says, and it's not what we work with in standards mode.

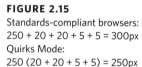

FIGURE 2.15

Standards-compliant browsers:
250 + 20 + 20 + 5 + 5 = 300px
Quirks Mode:
250 (20 + 20 + 5 + 5) = 250px

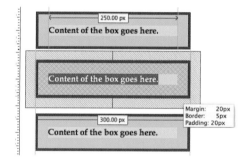

Figure 2.15 illustrates how tools within Dreamweaver can help with visualization. Go to the Visual Aids menu of the Document toolbar and be sure CSS Layout Box Model is enabled. If you click the edge of a div on your page, you'll see something similar to what is seen on the middle box in the illustration. Dreamweaver displays a hatch pattern, showing you where the padding, margin, and border are, as well as a tooltip giving their dimensions. You'll also notice the green guides—on the top box, they're at the edges of the content (shown by the lightest blue color) and on the bottom box, they're on the outside of entire box (outside the dark blue border). These guides can be accessed by clicking and holding the ruler on the outside edge of Dreamweaver and dragging across your document. The guides are "magnetic" and will stick to the edge of the element. Once there, simply place your cursor between the two guides and click Ctrl. The width between the two guides magically appears—no clicking necessary!

RULER TIP

With layouts that need to be pixel-precise, especially when using fixed widths, we may run into undesired results in browsers rendering in quirks mode. We need to have a way to render the box in both older and standards-compliant browsers to the same width. This brings us to the unsavory topic of methods to deal with the challenges of the browser minefield.

Browser Anomalies

As you know, older versions of Internet Explorer pose more CSS challenges than standards-compliant browsers such as Safari, Firefox, Netscape, and Opera. Let's take a look at how the box model problem is corrected for early versions of IE in the two-column CSS layout.

INTERNET EXPLORER CONDITIONAL COMMENTS

Because Internet Explorer has so many *unique* ways of rendering CSS properties, we're fortunate that the Microsoft engineers had pity on us. As a workaround for all its quirks and headaches, they created something called the **Conditional Comment**. It allows us to set up conditions under which we can feed unique rules to targeted Internet Explorer versions. You can target all versions of IE, or just specific versions such as 5, 5.5, 6, or 7. You can even target less than a version or greater than or equal to a certain version using a specific syntax.

What follows is the basic syntax for Internet Explorer Conditional Comments (IECC) that are added to the head of the document. First, we set up the conditional statement that sniffs out a targeted version of Internet Explorer (highlighted in the example). Then we code a certain set of styles or a link to a style sheet containing those styles.

The following IECC selects all versions of Internet Explorer:

```
<!--[if IE]>
<style type="text/css">
Rules for all versions of Internet Explorer go here.
</style>
<![endif]-->
```

John Gallant and Holly Bergevin of Community MX wrote an in-depth article about the box model and its problems and solutions. You can read the article at http://www.communitymx.com/abstract.cfm?cid=E0989953B6F20B41.

In the example we have one style block within an IECC and one linked CSS file within an IECC. Either can be used. The CSS layouts use a style block due to certain development limitations, but we like to move those styles into a separate style sheet that can be applied to every page for ease of updating. Who wants to update each page later if something changes? Not us! Dreamweaver does not yet have the capability of automating this process so you'll need to move these styles by hand.

The following Conditional Comment targets Internet Explorer 6 and below:

```
<!--[if lte IE6]>
<link rel="stylesheet" type="text/css"
href="ie6andLessDocHere.css" />
<![endif]-->
```

When targeting anything other than a single, specific version of IE, the basic targeting syntax opportunities are as follows:

- gt: greater than the version number specified

- gte: greater than or equal to the version number specified

- lt: less than the version number specified

- lte: less than or equal to the version number specified

N *You can go to Microsoft's site to view the proper syntax for IECCs. Or you can download Paul Davis' IECC extension for $10 from Community MX. It will add the proper syntax to the head of the page for you using Dreamweaver. http://www.communitymx.com/ abstract.cfm?cid=C433F*

Let's view our document in Code view. We are going to look at the IECC containing the box model fix for the sidebar1 div. In the style sheet, the sidebar1 rule's content has a width value of 200 pixels. The left padding is 20 pixels, and the right padding is 10 pixels. In standards-compliant browsers, the total will be 230 pixels. Browsers rendering in quirks mode will include the padding in the total, and compute the final overall width as 200 pixels. We need an IECC that targets Internet Explorer 5 and gives it a value of 230px so that when it includes the 30 pixels of padding, the overall box will be 230 pixels like the standard box model.

Locate the following code in the head of the document:

Place CSS box model fixes for IE 5* in this conditional comment.

```
<!-[ if IE 5]>
<style type="text/css">
.twoColFixLtHdr #sidebar1 { width: 230px; }
</style>
<![endif]-->
```

The hasLayout Property

In addition to its funny math in calculating the box model, Internet Explorer has a mysterious property called hasLayout. No such property exists as part of the CSS specifications, and no other browser uses it. It's the cause of many, many bugs.

The CSS Styles Panel

The CSS Styles panel has two modes: you switch between them by selecting either the All or Current buttons at the top of the panel.

In All mode, the panel has two panes. The All Rules pane shows all the rules that affect the document, no matter how they are applied. Whether the rules are embedded, linked, or imported, they appear in this pane. When you select a rule in the All Rules pane, its properties and values appear in the Properties pane.

In Current mode, the top pane shows a summary of all the properties and values that are affecting the element that's currently selected. This allows us to see the effect of the cascade on our element. When an element isn't doing exactly what we think it should and we need to troubleshoot, this comes in handy! Perhaps the text is red when we think it should be black: we can look in the Summary for Selection, find the color property, hover over it, and see what rule is overriding the red color.

The middle pane of the Current mode has two sections—About and Rules. These are followed, just as in All mode, by a Properties pane showing all property/value pairs set on the currently selected element.

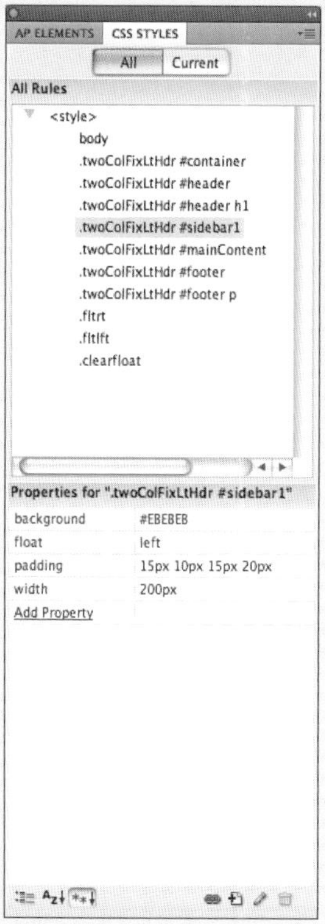

FIGURE 2.16 Below the All Rules pane, the Properties pane shows the properties and values from the rule currently selected.

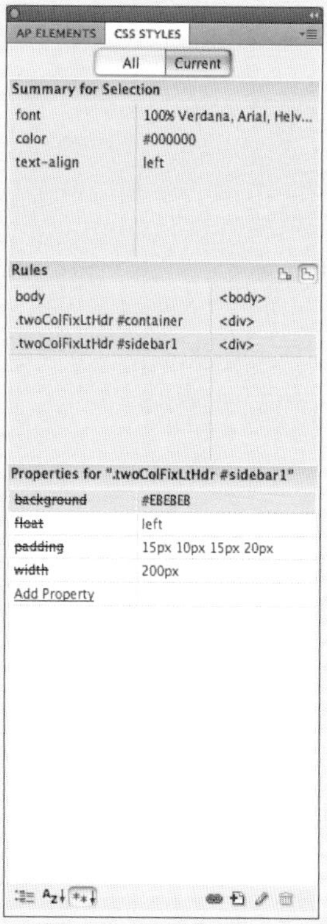

FIGURE 2.17 The Rules pane of the CSS Properties panel is a great tool for moving up the cascade and examining a selector's specificity.

If you select a property/value pair (declaration) in the Summary for Selection area, the About pane shows what rule contains the declaration as well as the CSS document in which it resides, and the Properties pane changes to show the specific rule.

Switching the middle pane to Rules view shows the cascade, from the body to our currently selected element. This is a handy way to move up and down the cascade viewing the various declarations in the property pane. Hovering over a rule shows us where the rule is contained as well as its specificity. This is another great troubleshooting tool since we can see when one rule is overriding another and if the latter needs to be made more specific to affect our element.

In the Properties pane, we can select an element and then use the Rules pane to move up the cascade to see what is affecting the element—or not affecting it. If the rule isn't inherited, Dreamweaver draws a line through it. When we hover over the rule, Dreamweaver creates a pop-up that explains why its property is not being applied.

With so many ways to utilize the CSS Styles panel, we find ourselves practically living there sometimes, usually in Current mode with the Rules pane selected.

So what is it? In general, think of hasLayout as a way in which Internet Explorer creates boundaries between, and relationships among, all page box areas. It's not a tangible property so much as an effect on surrounding objects and a way of calculating dimensions that economizes browser resources.

Some elements, such as the body, have hasLayout set to true by default. Some properties trigger hasLayout when we use them in style sheets. Height, width, and float directions all add hasLayout. Sometimes hasLayout needs to be triggered deliberately to fix an Internet Explorer bug.

Let's look at our page again and locate the following code:

Place CSS fixes for all versions of IE in this conditional comment

This proprietary zoom property gives IE the hasLayout it needs to avoid several bugs

```
<!--[if IE]>
<style type="text/css">
   .twoColFixLtHdr #sidebar1 { padding-top: 30px; }
   .twoColFixLtHdr #mainContent { zoom: 1; }
</style>
<![endif]-->
```

N   *If you want to read a comprehensive reference on* hasLayout, *you can find the definitive guide at http://www.satzansatz. de/cssd/onhavinglayout.html— we'll warn you, though, you'll need a lot of coffee—it's heavy reading!*

The #mainContent rule is adding a declaration to trigger hasLayout in Internet Explorer so that it draws the relationships among the divs more accurately. We are using the proprietary IE zoom property, a common way to fix bugs relating to a lack of hasLayout in the document. Don't ask us why (it's beyond the scope of this book)— it just works—and by using an IECC it validates and affects no other browser.

Manipulating the Natural Flow

Positioning Techniques

CSS positioning properties allow us to manipulate the natural flow of the document and arrange boxes on the page into a pleasing and user-friendly design. This is the final concept you need to understand before we can dig in to actually creating a CSS layout.

The different positioning types (static, absolute, relative, and fixed), as well as the use of floats for positioning, cover most layout situations. After we explore how each positioning type works, we will do some exercises to put some of them into action.

STATIC POSITIONING

Static positioning is the page default; the elements flow one after the other, filling the browser window with block and inline elements in their source order. Static positioning basically means that the element has no position—just the regular page flow.

Though it is the default, it's sometimes useful to explicitly set a layout to static positioning when we need to reset elements that have another kind of positioning applied to them. For example, printers can have trouble with pages with any kind of positioning; only one page may emerge from the printer or elements may be cut off. We can create a print style sheet that resets positioned elements to static so that they print properly.

FIGURE 2.18 Within a container, three boxes, left at their default static positioning.

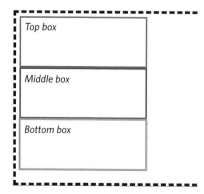

RELATIVE POSITIONING

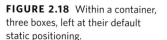 *You can also use negative values for these properties.*

Relative positioning lets you give an element position in relationship to its static place in the flow of the document. If you set an element to relative positioning but don't set values for the top, right, bottom, or left property, the element remains in exactly the same place in the flow of the document as if it were using static positioning. But once you set these properties, the element will shift away from its natural spot in the page by the defined amount. The space it filled in the flow, however, remains. Thus, if you give the element a 50px top and 50px left declaration, it will shift 50px in each direction, but there will be 50px of white space above and to the left of it. Nothing will fill that area.

FIGURE 2.19 A relatively positioned middle box with the white space shown.

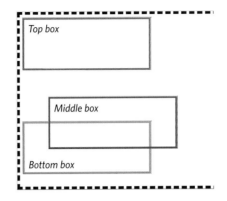

ABSOLUTE POSITIONING

Absolute positioning (AP) can be used to place objects on the page at precise X (horizontal) and Y (vertical) coordinates. The values of the AP elements derive their starting point from the last positioned parent element. This may not be the immediate parent: If the AP element's parent uses static positioning, it's not considered positioned, so the AP element looks farther up the document tree for a positioned ancestor. It may work its way all the way up the document tree to the body element (which is considered positioned) and set the X and Y coordinates from that point.

FIGURE 2.20 Since the outer container still has its default static positioning, the box gets its 50px x/y coordinates from the last positioned parent—the body element.

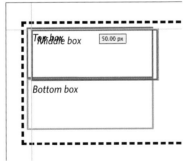

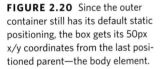

If you want your absolutely positioned element contained within a specific parent element, be sure to set the value of the parent element's position to relative. As stated earlier, relative positioning with no assigned values doesn't affect the element except to give it a position that its children can use to figure their own position values from.

Once the parent element has positioning, we can set values for top or bottom, and right or left for our absolutely positioned element. (We don't use both right and left, or both top and bottom, because these coordinates would fight each other, and that's such an ugly sight!)

Remember that (X)HTML provides a natural flow for the elements that begins at the top left of the browser window. Although we shift the elements around with CSS, the flow defines the ways in which they relate to one another—that is, except for AP elements. AP elements aren't very friendly. They're loners. Although they derive their position from a parent, they're outside the natural flow on the page; other elements can't relate to them and don't know where the AP elements begin or end. This can result in content overlapping and other unsightly messes unless the use of AP elements is carefully planned. You will see this in action in the exercises that follow.

FIGURE 2.21 Absolute positioning, from the parent element (guides at 50px from screen edge).

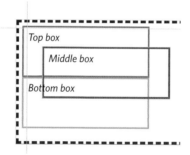

FIXED POSITIONING

Like absolute positioning, elements with fixed positioning are set at a specific X and Y coordinate on the page. However, the position is always set in relation to the visible area of the browser window, known as the **viewport** (not the parent element like AP elements). When the visitor scrolls the page, the fixed content remains in an exact location on their screen.

Fixed positioning can be creatively used for background images, or navigation areas. Even when you scroll to read more content, the navigation area remains in the same place. Unfortunately, the first version of Internet Explorer that supports fixed positioning is Internet Explorer 7 (and the sooner that's adopted, the sooner we're all in better shape). Advanced CSS designers use scripts to force earlier versions of Internet Explorer to simulate the effect of fixed positioning; however, in our experience some of them result in a stuttering scroll or flashing page refresh. If you're targeting early versions of IE, a lot of thought (and testing) should be used before deciding upon a fixed positioning solution.

We've just seen one way elements can be manipulated—using positioning. In this exercise, we are going to change the natural behavior of an image so that text wraps around it using the float property.

> **N**   *Dreamweaver shows fixed positioning as static within Design view (meaning it remains in the natural flow). Switching to Live View renders a fixed position perfectly.*

Floating Images

1. Open starter.html from the sample files for this chapter. This page contains semantically marked text elements very much like that used in the CSS layouts.

2. In Design view, place the cursor in front of the first paragraph of dummy text, beginning with Lorem Ipsum, below the Main Content heading.

   We are going to add a dummy, or placeholder, image to the page.

3. From the Insert menu, select Image Objects > Image Placeholder (or insert it from the Common tab of the Insert bar—7th icon). Use the following values in the dialog:

   - Name: **Placeholder**
   - Width and Height: **200**
   - Color: **#CCCCCC**
   - Alt text: **Placeholder**

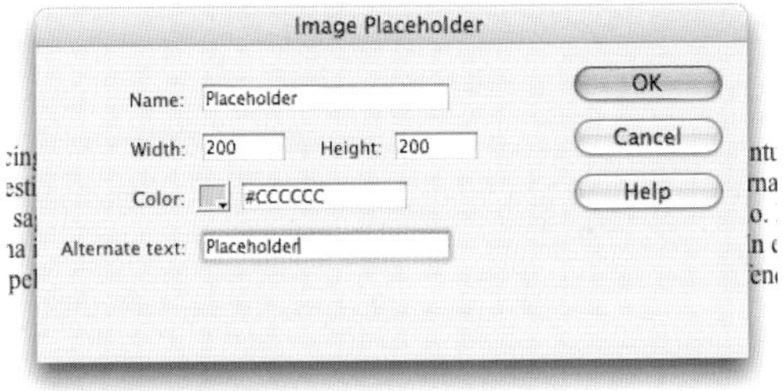

FIGURE 2.22 The Image Placeholder Image dialog box

By default, images are inline elements. Thus, the placeholder image will appear at the baseline of the first line of text.

> **N**   *When the image placeholder is selected, you'll notice on the image Property inspector a Fireworks icon below the alt attribute. Clicking this will open a canvas of your defined size in Fireworks to create the image the placeholder is reserving space for.*

4. Click the plus button at the bottom of the CSS Styles panel to bring up the New CSS Rule dialog box. Select Class from the Selector Type drop-down list. In the Selector Name field, type **.fltlft**. For Rule Definition, select the radio button for "This document only".

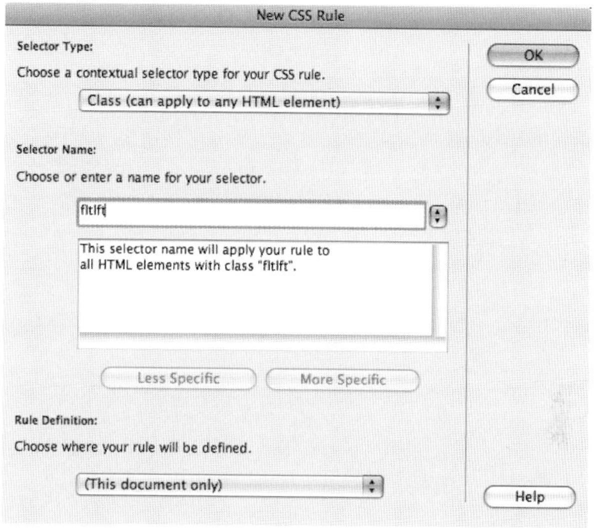

FIGURE 2.23 Rule definition for
the left floating image class

FIGURE 2.23 Rule definition for
the left floating image class

*Remember that class iden-
tifiers begin with a period. If you
select the Class Selector Type in
the New CSS Rule dialog, however,
Dreamweaver will automatically
add the period for you.*

As we mentioned earlier, many designers develop their pages
by first embedding the styles in the head of the document, and
then later, after the layout is complete, they export the styles to
an external style sheet. Add to Head is the default method in the
Layout CSS drop-down list for the CSS layouts.

5. When the CSS Rule definition for the `.fltlft` dialog box
   appears, select the Box category. Select left from the Float select
   list. Deselect the "Same for all" checkbox under Margin. In the
   Right field, type 8. Leave the unit of measurement at pixels.

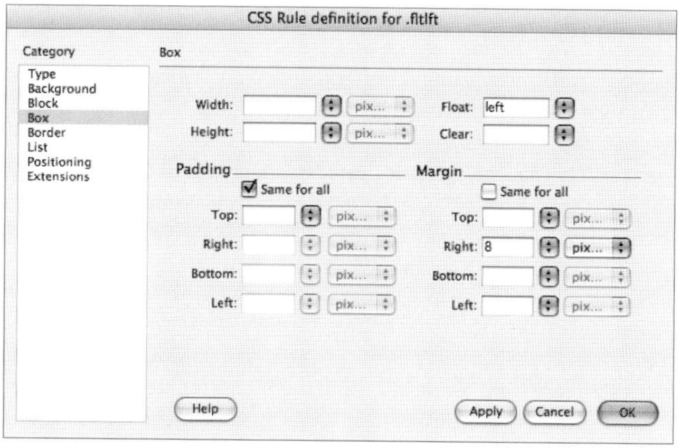

FIGURE 2.24 Float properties

6. Click OK.

7. Click the image on the page to select it. Select the **.fltlft** class from the Class select list in the image Property inspector.

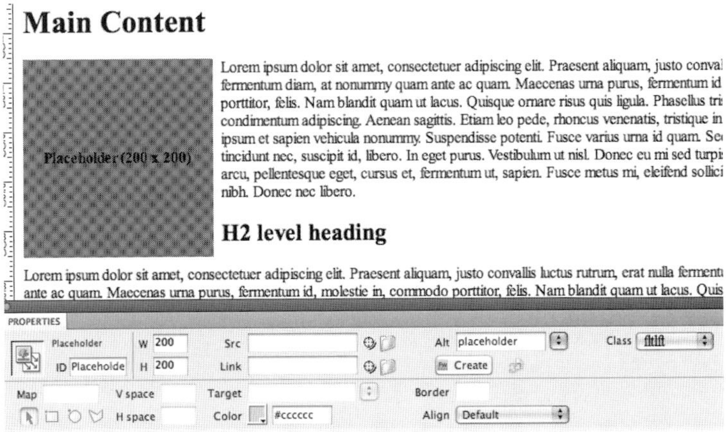

FIGURE 2.25 After applying the
fltlft class to the image, the text
wraps around it.

FIGURE 2.25 After applying the fltlft class to the image, the text wraps around it.

The text now wraps around the image. However, the next heading and its paragraphs wrap around the image as well. Sometimes this effect is what we're after, but other times we want to make the next heading and its text appear below the image. This is a job for the CSS **clear** property.

Applying a Clearing Element

1. Select the **h2** text "H2 level heading." Click the Split button in the document toolbar to enter into a split screen with both code and design views showing.

You'll see that the **h2** text is also selected in code view.

2. In Code view, place your cursor right before the **<h2>** or click the h2 on the tag selector at the bottom of the document window and arrow once to the left. The tag selector causes Dreamweaver to not only select the content of an element but also the tags themselves.

3. In Code view, type a **br** element to create a line break and give it a class of **clearfloat**. Since we are using the XHTML Transitional 1.0 Doctype, add the space and forward slash before closing the element.

```
<br class="clearfloat" />
```

To select the heading, you can either click and drag, or click within it three times. One click puts your cursor into the heading, the second click selects the word your cursor is in, and the third click selects all the text within the h2 element.

FIGURE 2.26 Adding a class to the br element.

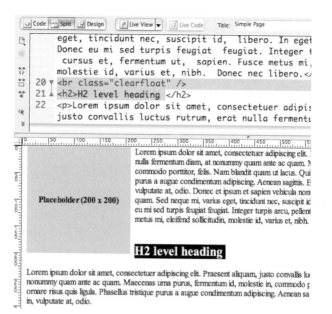

The tag selector is on the bottom area of the document window. It contains the hierarchy of our page all the way to the element we've selected. For example: <body><div#container><div #mainContent><h1>. When we say to click an element in the tag selector, be sure not to confuse that with the selector type that Dreamweaver identifies as a tag selector (the one we prefer to call an element selector). When the tag selector is referenced, click the tag specified on the bottom of your document. Yes, it's quite confusing.

This exercise will demonstrate how a clearing element works using a pared-down page. In this case, adding a clear: both property to the h2 would also cause it to move down below the floated image.

The break will provide a "hook" to add some properties via CSS that will clear the float while making sure it doesn't add any dimension to the page. Remember that browsers add their own default styles to elements, and thus add space that we may not want. In this case, the break is only there for the purpose of stopping the float effect so that the text that starts with the h2 doesn't wrap around it. There are various elements (such as a div) and other methods we could have used to clear the image, but this way is stable with older browsers and gives us a reusable element (with a class) that we can later apply to clear a floated column. (This method does add non-structural markup to the page to clear the float, and as such, some disagree with the method, but we do not yet live in a perfect web standards world!)

4. Click the plus button in the CSS panel to create a new rule called **clearfloat**.

   Dreamweaver autofills the name if the cursor is left either in, or right after, the **
** element we just created.

5. When the New CSS Rule dialog box appears, make sure Class is selected for the Selector Type and the Selector Name is auto-filled as **clearfloat**. For the Rule Definition option, make sure that the radio button for "This document only" is selected.

6. In the New CSS Rule dialog for the `.clearfloat` class, select the Type category. Choose Font-size 1px and set the Line-height value to 0. Select the Box category. Assign a value of 0 to Height. In the Clear select list, select both. For the Margin, leave same for all checked and type 0.

FIGURE 2.27 Removing sources of dimension that the browser style sheet might add.

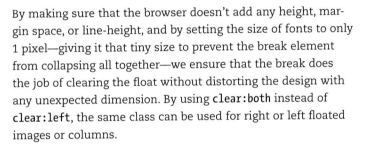

By making sure that the browser doesn't add any height, margin space, or line-height, and by setting the size of fonts to only 1 pixel—giving it that tiny size to prevent the break element from collapsing all together—we ensure that the break does the job of clearing the float without distorting the design with any unexpected dimension. By using `clear:both` instead of `clear:left`, the same class can be used for right or left floated images or columns.

7. Click OK.

The **h2** text and subsequent paragraphs now appear beneath the image.

FIGURE 2.28 The result of applying the clearing element.

Inserting a Div Tag

Continue using the page from the previous exercise (and delete the image holder and break element from the HTML, leaving the clearing class we created in the head), or open *create_div.html* from the Chapter 1 files. In this exercise, we will divide the page into different sections such as header, footer, and sidebar. The **div** element will be the building block to which we will give descriptive names that have semantic meaning.

1. Select the **h1** text Header. Click the <h1> in the tag selector at the bottom of the Document window to make sure that Dreamweaver includes both the opening and closing tags for the text.

FIGURE 2.29 Using the tag selector to select the complete h1 element in Classic mode. Note that your Insert bar may be grouped with the panels.

2. From the Insert toolbar, with the Common category selected, click the Insert Div Tag button.

FIGURE 2.30 Clicking the Insert Div Tag icon.

The Insert Div Tag dialog box appears.

N *If you aren't using the Classic workspace or haven't moved the Insert panel back to the top of your custom workspace, you'll see it in the form of a panel on the side of your document.*

3. For Insert, leave the menu at Wrap around selection.

You want the opening Div tag to go before your selection, and the closing Div tag to go at the end of your selection so that it encloses all the text within.

4. Leave the Class field empty, and in the ID field, type **header**. Click OK.

FIGURE 2.31 Filling out the Insert Div Tag dialog box.

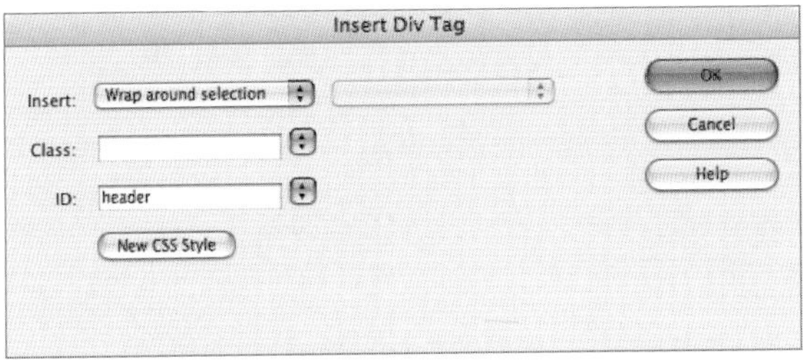

N *If you do not see the dashed line, you may have turned off the CSS Layout Outlines under Visual Aids (the Eye icon) in the Document toolbar.*

Dreamweaver adds a dashed line around the area around the div or division of the page. The line is just a visual effect to help you see where each div on the page lies. You will not see this line in a browser.

5. Select all the text from the Main Content **h1** title to the closing **p** tag of the paragraph after the **h2** level heading.

FIGURE 2.32 Ensuring that Dreamweaver includes opening and closing tags.

```
27 ▼ <h1>Main Content </h1>
28   <p>Lorem ipsum dolor sit amet, consectetuer adipiscing elit. Praesent
     aliquam, justo convallis luctus rutrum, erat nulla fermentum diam,
     at nonummy quam  ante ac quam. Maecenas urna purus, fermentum id,
     molestie in, commodo  porttitor, felis. Nam blandit quam ut lacus.
     Quisque ornare risus quis  ligula. Phasellus tristique purus a augue
     condimentum adipiscing. Aenean  sagittis. Etiam leo pede, rhoncus
     venenatis, tristique in, vulputate at,  odio. Donec et ipsum et
     sapien vehicula nonummy. Suspendisse potenti. Fusce  varius urna id
     quam. Sed neque mi, varius eget, tincidunt nec, suscipit id,  libero.
     In eget purus. Vestibulum ut nisl. Donec eu mi sed turpis feugiat
     feugiat. Integer turpis arcu, pellentesque eget, cursus et, fermentum
     ut,  sapien. Fusce metus mi, eleifend sollicitudin, molestie id,
     varius et, nibh.  Donec nec libero.</p>
29   <h2>H2 level heading </h2>
30   <p>Lorem ipsum dolor sit amet, consectetuer adipiscing elit. Praesent
     aliquam, justo convallis luctus rutrum, erat nulla fermentum diam,
     at nonummy quam  ante ac quam. Maecenas urna purus, fermentum id,
     molestie in, commodo  porttitor, felis. Nam blandit quam ut lacus.
     Quisque ornare risus quis  ligula. Phasellus tristique purus a augue
     condimentum adipiscing. Aenean  sagittis. Etiam leo pede, rhoncus
     venenatis, tristique in, vulputate at, odio.</p>
31   <h3>Sidebar1 Content</h3>
```

N *Dreamweaver has a tendency to exclude the opening and/or closing tags of your selection, so it is a good idea to click the Split or Code view button and make sure the opening* h1 *and closing* p *are also selected. If you're not in Split view, click the Split button in the Document toolbar so that you see both code and design.*

N *You can also wrap your selection in a div element using Insert > Layout Objects > Div Tag or by right-clicking your selection and choosing Wrap Tag. Then type directly into the box as you would in Code view.*

6. From the Insert toolbar, again click the Insert Div Tag button. Leave the menu set to "Wrap around selection" as before. In the ID field, type **mainContent**. Click OK.

7. Select the Sidebar1 Content heading and the two paragraphs that follow it.

Again, use code view to make sure that everything from the opening of the first **h3** to the closing tag of the second paragraph is included in the selection.

8. Click the Insert Div Tag button on the Insert toolbar and keep the same settings. In the ID field, type **sidebar1** and click OK.

9. Put your cursor within the text that reads Footer and select the **<p>** tag that appears in the tag selector at the bottom of the document window.

N *Be aware of your naming conventions when creating your own CSS selectors. Using* #rightside *or* #leftcolumn *is not best practices since a column can easily change positions when using CSS. Likewise, using a class name like* .redtext *or* .bluelink *could cause some confusion if color decisions change later in the project. Using* #sidebar1 *and* #sidebar2 *or .alert and .navlink is a much more semantic way to name your selectors. Think of the use of the selector instead of its visual look whenever possible.*

10. Insert a Div Tag from the Insert toolbar as before. This time, name the ID **footer** and click OK.

Your finished page will have four sections, each with dashed lines around them to provide a visual representation of where each div begins and ends.

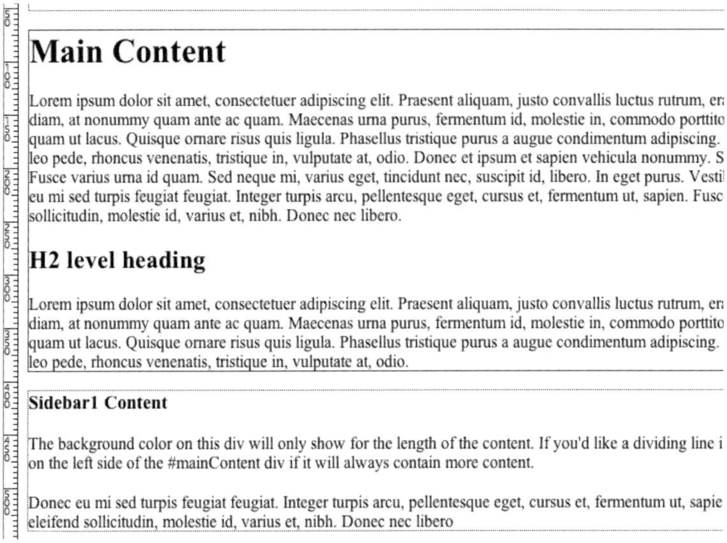

FIGURE 2.33 The page divided into divisions.

FIGURE 2.33 The page divided into divisions.

Columns with Absolute Positioning

Now that you have the page divided into sections, you can manipulate these by using different kinds of positioning techniques. Make sure your CSS Styles panel is open. If you do not see it on screen, go to Window > CSS Styles.

1. Continuing with the same file, place your cursor into the **side-bar1** div and choose **<div#sidebar1>** from the tag selector. Click the new rule icon at the bottom of the CSS Styles panel.

    The New CSS Rule dialog box will appear.

2. Select the ID (applies to only one HTML element) from the Selector Type select list.

3. If you properly selected the sidebar div, Dreamweaver auto-fills the Selector Name field based on the name given (**sidebar1**). If the proper selector name isn't pre-filled, it's easy enough to type the proper name in directly.

4. For Rule Definition, choose (This document only). Click OK. The CSS Rule definition for **#sidebar1** dialog box will open.

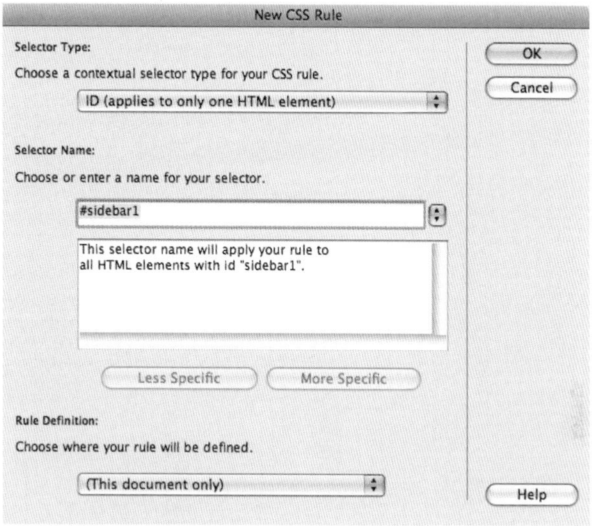

FIGURE 2.34 The #sidebar1
New CSS Rule dialog.

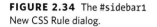

5. Select the Background category. In the Background-color input, type **#ebebeb**. Select the Positioning category. For Position, choose absolute; for Width, type 200 and choose pixels (the default) as the unit of measurement. In the Placement section, for Top, type 80 and for Left, type 10. Choose pixels for the unit of measurement for both fields.

   The values for top and left are in relationship to the body, since that is the last positioned parent container of the **#sidebar1** div.

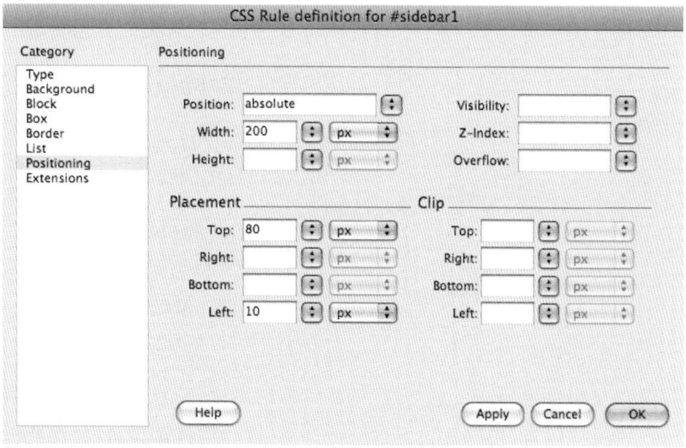

FIGURE 2.35 Positioning values
for #sidebar1.

6. Click OK.

You will probably be surprised at the result that appears in Design view in the Dreamweaver document window. The `sidebar1` div now partially covers the content area. As we mentioned earlier, an element with absolute positioning is taken out of the natural flow of the document. The other content no longer "sees" it and as such can't react to it. We will fix this in the next part of the exercise.

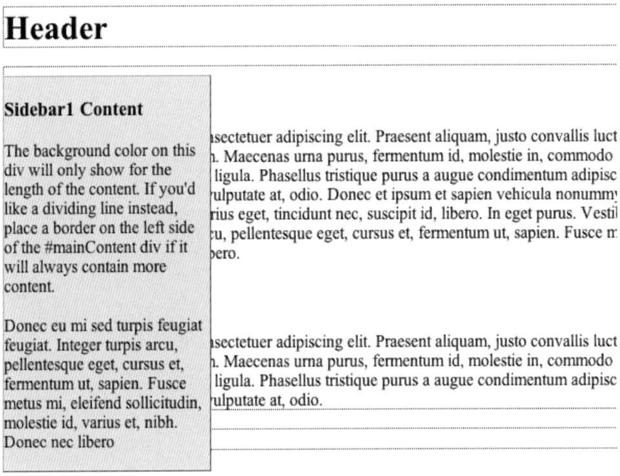

FIGURE 2.36 The `sidebar1` div is taken out of the document flow.

Header

Sidebar1 Content

The background color on this div will only show for the length of the content. If you'd like a dividing line instead, place a border on the left side of the #mainContent div if it will always contain more content.

Donec eu mi sed turpis feugiat feugiat. Integer turpis arcu, pellentesque eget, cursus et, fermentum ut, sapien. Fusce metus mi, eleifend sollicitudin, molestie id, varius et, nibh. Donec nec libero

...sectetuer adipiscing elit. Praesent aliquam, justo convallis luct... ...n. Maecenas urna purus, fermentum id, molestie in, commodo ...ligula. Phasellus tristique purus a augue condimentum adipisc ...ulputate at, odio. Donec et ipsum et sapien vehicula nonumm... ...rius eget, tincidunt nec, suscipit id, libero. In eget purus. Vesti... ...u, pellentesque eget, cursus et, fermentum ut, sapien. Fusce m... ...ero.

...sectetuer adipiscing elit. Praesent aliquam, justo convallis luct... ...n. Maecenas urna purus, fermentum id, molestie in, commodo ...ligula. Phasellus tristique purus a augue condimentum adipisc ...ulputate at, odio.

7. As in step 1, click the New CSS rule button. Use the same ID Selector Type as before but give this rule the name `#mainContent` in the Selector name field. Click OK.

8. In the CSS Rule definition, select the Box category. Under Margin, deselect the "Same for all" checkbox so that it is empty.

   We want to apply a unique margin to the Left field only.

9. Type 225 for the value, and make sure pixels, the default unit of measurement, is selected. Click OK.

   The result should look much better to you. Remember that margin is the area outside the box. We've now carved out a 225-pixel margin for the sidebar area to slip into.

This is a pretty good method for creating the look of side-by-side columns. There is, however, one potential problem. As long as the main content column is longer than the sidebar column, the footer will appear below both columns and all will be well. If the sidebar column is longer—as it might be if there were navigation links above the sidebar text—then the footer will slide under the sidebar1 div. Just as the `mainContent` div did not see the absolutely positioned `sidebar1` div, the `footer` div will be equally unaware of its existence. Try removing a big chunk of text from the `mainContent` div to see this in action.

The next method for creating side-by-side columns gives you the flexibility of either column being longest.

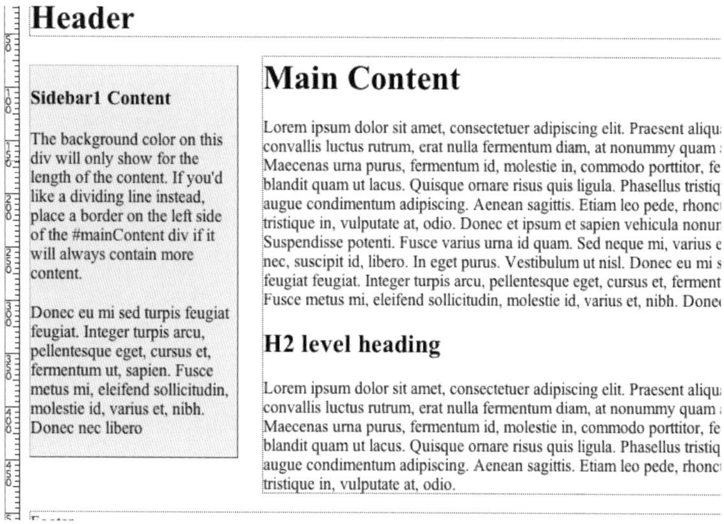

FIGURE 2.37 Carving a left margin for the `mainContent` div.

Header

Sidebar1 Content

The background color on this div will only show for the length of the content. If you'd like a dividing line instead, place a border on the left side of the #mainContent div if it will always contain more content.

Donec eu mi sed turpis feugiat feugiat. Integer turpis arcu, pellentesque eget, cursus et, fermentum ut, sapien. Fusce metus mi, eleifend sollicitudin, molestie id, varius et, nibh. Donec nec libero

Main Content

Lorem ipsum dolor sit amet, consectetuer adipiscing elit. Praesent aliqua convallis luctus rutrum, erat nulla fermentum diam, at nonummy quam : Maecenas urna purus, fermentum id, molestie in, commodo porttitor, fe blandit quam ut lacus. Quisque ornare risus quis ligula. Phasellus tristiq augue condimentum adipiscing. Aenean sagittis. Etiam leo pede, rhonci tristique in, vulputate at, odio. Donec et ipsum et sapien vehicula nonur Suspendisse potenti. Fusce varius urna id quam. Sed neque mi, varius e nec, suscipit id, libero. In eget purus. Vestibulum ut nisl. Donec eu mi s feugiat feugiat. Integer turpis arcu, pellentesque eget, cursus et, ferment Fusce metus mi, eleifend sollicitudin, molestie id, varius et, nibh. Done

H2 level heading

Lorem ipsum dolor sit amet, consectetuer adipiscing elit. Praesent aliqua convallis luctus rutrum, erat nulla fermentum diam, at nonummy quam : Maecenas urna purus, fermentum id, molestie in, commodo porttitor, fe blandit quam ut lacus. Quisque ornare risus quis ligula. Phasellus tristiq augue condimentum adipiscing. Aenean sagittis. Etiam leo pede, rhonci tristique in, vulputate at, odio.

Floating Columns

Continue with the page we've been using or use float.html from the Chapter 1 files. If you continue with our page, copy and paste some extra Lorem Ipsum text into the `mainContent` area to see the effect we're going to demonstrate more clearly.

1. In the All pane of the CSS Styles panel, select the `#sidebar1`. (You may need to click the arrow next to the `style` element to expand the list of rules.)

2. Click the trashcan icon at the bottom of the panel to remove it (or right-click and choose Delete).

3. Select and delete the `#mainContent` rule as well. Your page will revert to the normal flow with non-positioned divs. Be sure to change your CSS Styles panel back to the Current pane.

FIGURE 2.38 Selecting the #sidebar1 rule and clicking the trashcan to delete it.

When we want to float a div next to a non-floated element, we must place it in the source code before the element we want it to align with. Let's cut the `sidebar1` div and paste it before the `mainContent` div.

4. Put your cursor into the `sidebar1` div. Click `<div#sidebar1>` in the tag selector at the bottom of the document window to make sure the entire div is selected. Choose Edit > Cut.

5. Put your cursor into the `mainContent` div. Click `<div#mainContent>` in the tag selector and press the left arrow key on your keyboard to place your cursor in front of the `main-Content` div. Choose Edit > Paste.

Now that your `sidebar1` div is in front of the `mainContent` div, we'll create a rule for it.

FIGURE 2.39 Moving the sidebar1 div before the mainContent div.

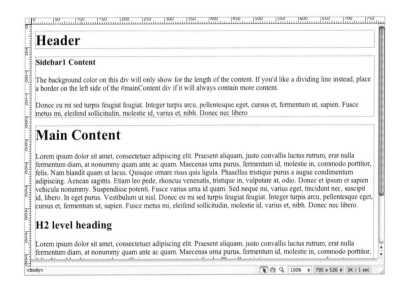

6. Click the New CSS Rule called `#sidebar1`. In the dialog, select the Background category, and give the Background-color a value of #ebebeb as we did earlier. Select the Box category and set the width to 200px.

Remember, floats should have an explicit width; otherwise, the div will continue to fill 100% of its parent container.

7. Next to Float, select Left. Click OK.

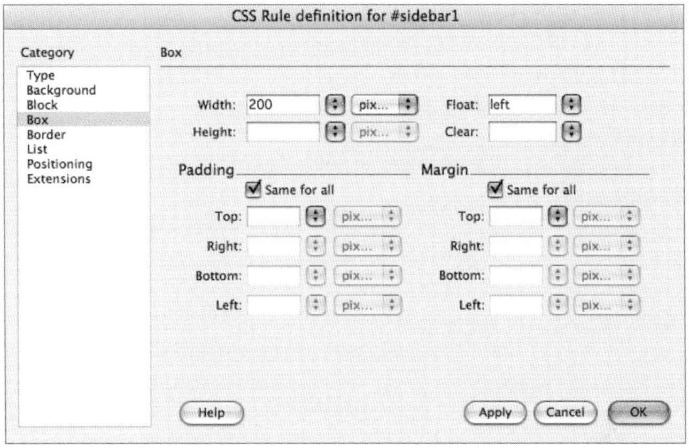

FIGURE 2.40 Adding the float property to the `sidebar1` div.

Now the `sidebar1` div is floated to the left of the `mainContent` div. However, you'll notice that once the content in `sidebar1` reaches its end, the `mainContent` div wraps around it (this is where the extra text you added to the `mainContent` div pays off). The default behavior for floats is that the elements that follow wrap around them. The `mainContent` div makes space for the `sidebar1` div, but there is not really a true two-column look all the way down the page. We'll fix this by again carving out a left margin space on the `mainContent` div.

FIGURE 2.41 The float wrapping effect on columns.

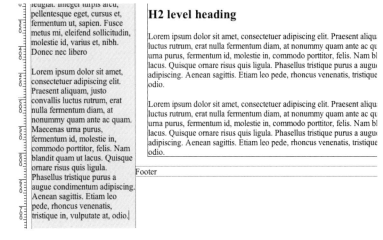

8. Create a `#mainContent` rule as you did in the last section. Select the Box category on the left. Deselect "Same for all" under Margin. Give Left a value of 225 pixels.

The look of two columns is now back.

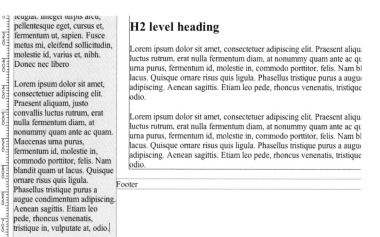

Using a margin to create the look of columns is the method used for the CSS layouts in Dreamweaver. The mainContent *div could be given a width and floated next to the side column creating the same effect. We'll get into more detail about this in the next chapter.*

As we look at the results, they look fairly similar to what we achieved using absolute positioning in the previous exercise. By floating our divs, however, we can allow either column to be longest without overlapping the footer div.

Clearing a Floated Column

Continue with the file from the previous exercise. Just as we discussed doing in the absolutely positioned exercise, let's make the two columns unequal lengths with the sidebar1 being the longest.

Copy the content of the side column and paste it in after the last paragraph, doubling the length of the sidebar1 div.

FIGURE 2.42 The footer creeps up under the mainContent div.

Hmm, that's strange. The extra text in the left column is still overlapping the footer div, though not the footer text. Think back to the image floating exercise. The floated image was taller than the paragraphs next to it, and the h2 crept up to the space next to the image. Text stays next to a float until the float ends and then wraps below—unless the float is cleared.

Since the float is taken out of the flow of the document, elements following the float or containing the float don't know exactly where it ends. But unlike the non-communicative absolutely positioned element, the shy float has a friend, the clearing element. When properly cleared, the other elements know where the float ends because of its relationship to the clearing element. The clearing element tells them where the end of the float is.

We haven't added a clearing element yet, so the `footer` div begins in the flow, right after the last element of which it's aware, the `mainContent` div. In fact, you can see that the footer has moved up under the floated sidebar div. However, a floated div will never overlap the content of a div/box; thus, the text stays out to the right of `sidebar1`. Let's solve this problem.

1. Put your cursor anywhere in the `mainContent` div, and select `<div#mainContent>` in the tag selector at the bottom of the document window to select the entire content area.

If you're not in Code and Design view, use the Layout widget on the Application Bar to change your view.

2. Press your right arrow key once.

3. In Code view, place a break element between the closing tag for the `mainContent` div and before the opening tag of the `footer` div and give it the class `clearfloat`.

```
</div>
<br class="clearfloat" />
<div id="footer">
   <p>Footer</p>
</div>
```

You already created the `clearfloat` class in the image floating exercise, so not only will Dreamweaver allow you to select it in the code hints as you type, but as soon as you return to Design view, the effect should be apparent. The footer now clears the `sidebar1` column!

In developing the CSS layouts for Adobe, one goal was to remain consistent across layouts and another was to keep the layouts solid and simple as starter points that users could develop more fully. In this example, we could apply a clear property to the footer div, but with further development by the user, the results could be unexpected. We chose a clearing method that's very solid and reliable in older browsers.

Before you continue to the next exercise, delete the extra text that you pasted into the `sidebar1` column.

Centering a Layout

1. Click anywhere in the page and then click `<body>` in the tag selector at the bottom of the document window.

   This will select everything on the page.

2. Insert a Div Tag from the Insert bar. Allow it to wrap around the selection, give it an ID of `container`, and click New CSS Rule.

   The dialog shown will be auto-filled with `#container`.

3. For Rule Definition, choose this document. Click OK.

4. Select the Background category and for the Background-color, select white (#FFF).

5. Select the Box category. Set the Width to 780 pixels.

   This width allows users with a screen resolution of 800 by 600 to view the page without encountering horizontal scrollbars. Using 20px less than a full 800px width allows for the room taken up by the browser chrome, e.g., the scrollbar area, window borders, and so forth.

   The same theory applies if you are supporting a minimum of 1024 by 768. Remember to leave room for browser chrome when choosing your width.

6. Deselect "Same for all" under Margin. Select **auto** from the select lists next to Right and Left.

7. Click OK on both dialogs.

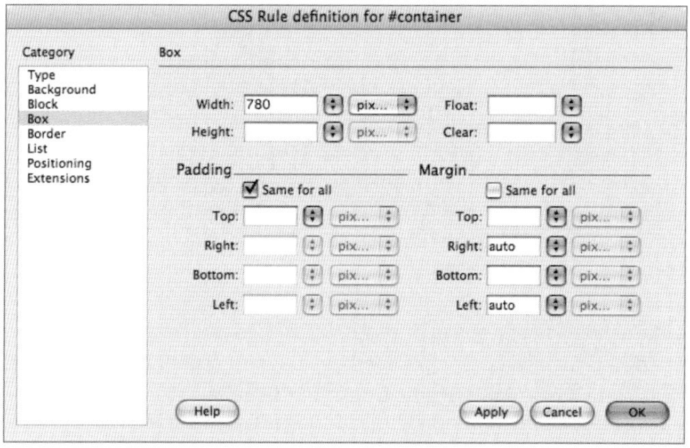

N   *The width you choose to support should be based on your site's statistics if you have access to them. At the writing of this book, 800 x 600 resolutions were on average, down to about 25% of all users.*

FIGURE 2.43 Setting auto margins on the container to center it.

In a perfect world, that would be it. A width, accompanied by the **auto** value for the right and left margins, will center a div in modern browsers.

When we look at the page in Internet Explorer 4, 5, or 5.5 (6 and above when in quirks mode), we see a very different result: the auto margins are ignored. We'll have to use one simple line of wizardry to support these browsers.

Fortunately (we guess), these browsers get something else wrong: they center block elements as well as inline elements when you use **text-align: center;**. Therefore, if we add this declaration to the body rule of the page, these browsers will center everything on the page.

1. Select the body element on the tag selector. Create a new rule for the body.

2. Select the Background category and type **#666** in the Background-color field.

3. Select the Block category. From the Text-align select list, select center. Click OK.

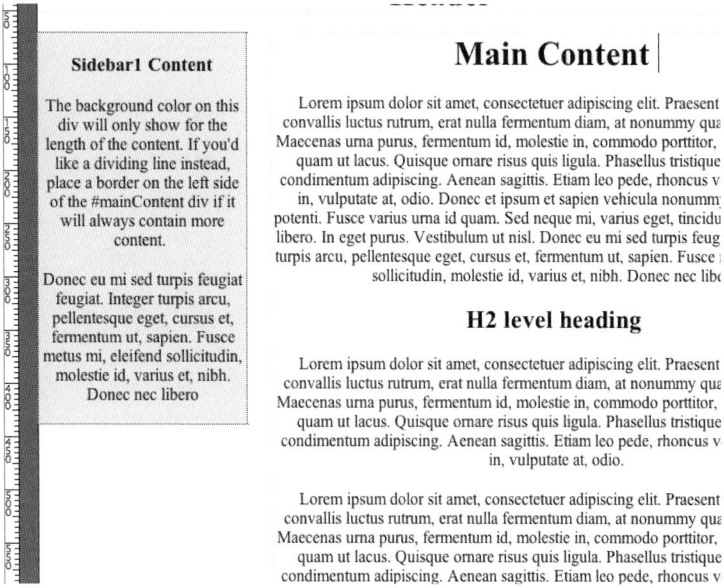

FIGURE 2.44 Setting text align to center on the body.

N *If you have an IECC for version 5 of Internet Explorer in your page, you can place the text-align: center declaration on the body rule within it. When hidden in an IECC, there's no need to reset the value of the text-align property back to left for other browsers.*

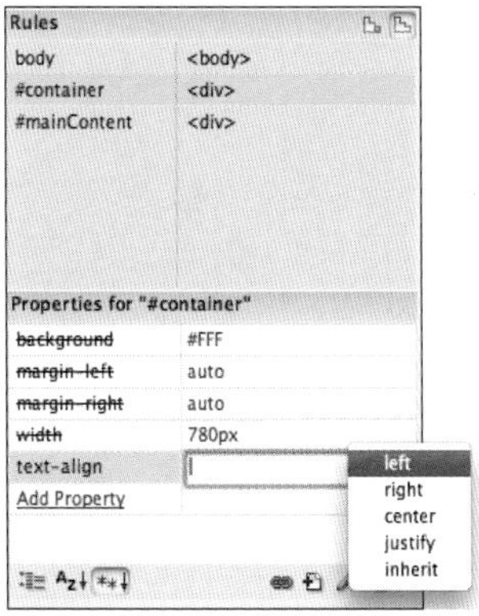

Sidebar1 Content

The background color on this div will only show for the length of the content. If you'd like a dividing line instead, place a border on the left side of the #mainContent div if it will always contain more content.

Donec eu mi sed turpis feugiat feugiat. Integer turpis arcu, pellentesque eget, cursus et, fermentum ut, sapien. Fusce metus mi, eleifend sollicitudin, molestie id, varius et, nibh. Donec nec libero

Main Content

Lorem ipsum dolor sit amet, consectetuer adipiscing elit. Praesent convallis luctus rutrum, erat nulla fermentum diam, at nonummy quam Maecenas urna purus, fermentum id, molestie in, commodo porttitor, quam ut lacus. Quisque ornare risus quis ligula. Phasellus tristique condimentum adipiscing. Aenean sagittis. Etiam leo pede, rhoncus v in, vulputate at, odio. Donec et ipsum et sapien vehicula nonumm potenti. Fusce aliquam urna id quam. Sed neque mi, varius eget, tincidu libero. In eget purus. Vestibulum ut nisl. Donec eu mi sed turpis feug turpis arcu, pellentesque eget, cursus et, fermentum ut, sapien. Fusce sollicitudin, molestie id, varius et, nibh. Donec nec libe

H2 level heading

Lorem ipsum dolor sit amet, consectetuer adipiscing elit. Praesent convallis luctus rutrum, erat nulla fermentum diam, at nonummy quam Maecenas urna purus, fermentum id, molestie in, commodo porttitor, quam ut lacus. Quisque ornare risus quis ligula. Phasellus tristique condimentum adipiscing. Aenean sagittis. Etiam leo pede, rhoncus v in, vulputate at, odio.

Lorem ipsum dolor sit amet, consectetuer adipiscing elit. Praesent convallis luctus rutrum, erat nulla fermentum diam, at nonummy quam Maecenas urna purus, fermentum id, molestie in, commodo porttitor, quam ut lacus. Quisque ornare risus quis ligula. Phasellus tristique condimentum adipiscing. Aenean sagittis. Etiam leo pede, rhoncus v

Rules		
body	\<body\>	
#container	\<div\>	
#mainContent	\<div\>	

Properties for "#container"		
background	#FFF	
margin-left	auto	
margin-right	auto	
width	780px	
text-align		left
Add Property		right
		center
		justify
		inherit

FIGURE 2.45 Adding a property/value pair directly into the Properties pane of the CSS Styles panel.

Of course, due to inheritance, everything is now centered, including all of the text. That's not exactly what we had in mind. We'll need to reopen the container rule (or simply type in Code view) to reset the text back to its default left alignment. The container will stay centered via the text-align property in the body rule, and all the divs nested in the container will align left via the text-align property for the container.

1. With the `#container` rule selected, on the Properties pane of the CSS Styles panel, click Add Property.

2. Set the text-align property to left by either typing the values into the inputs or choosing them from the select lists.

N *If we were supporting version 5* of Internet Explorer, this would be the point where we'd create an IECC with the adjusted values for IE's faulty box model.*

We now have a basic reconstruction of a CSS layout. To complete the layout, we would need to add the missing text formatting, margins, and padding that are in the two-column fixed CSS layout that comes with Dreamweaver CS3 and Dreamweaver CS4. But instead we'll dive into a real layout in the next chapter.

CSS Management

Though it's not really pertinent to this unfinished layout, we'll still take a moment here to discuss CSS organization. There are many methods used to keep CSS documents organized. What is *the best* in our opinion is what works best for you. Nonetheless, some method of organizing your document must be used.

Some people divide their CSS into multiple documents, placing color information into one, font and text information into another, and placement in yet another. Others prefer to keep all their CSS in one style sheet and divide rules into logical groupings with comments in between. This is the method we prefer. We place the body selector first, followed by any element selectors with their global values. We then move on to the page sections (divs) with the container first, followed by the header, various columns, and finally the footer. Within those sections, we place the descendant selectors that control that sections elements. We complete the document with any classes that will be reused—and that's usually the smallest number of rules.

When you create a selector using the CSS Styles panel or the CSS area of the Property inspector, Dreamweaver places the rule at the bottom of the document. It doesn't have to stay there. Dreamweaver has excellent CSS management capabilities from within the CSS Styles panel.

1. Go to the All pane of the CSS Styles panel.

   We'd like to create the order we just discussed.

2. Select the body rule at the bottom and drag it all the way to the top of your list of rules.

3. Shift-select the two classes (`.fltlft` and `.clearfloat`) and drag them to the bottom of the list.

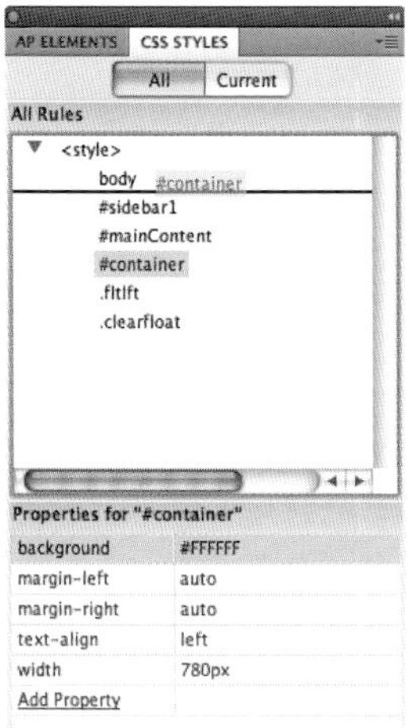

FIGURE 2.46 The black line between rules indicates where the rule will be when released.

4. Drag the `#container` rule to be directly below the body selector.

The order of our CSS rules now follows the order of our (X)HTML.

Many people like to write the CSS in the head of their document during development. But on completion of the project, those rules should *always* be placed into an external style sheet. Dreamweaver's CSS management capabilities make it simple to move your rules to an external style sheet (or even between style sheets).

5. Shift-select all the rules for our page.

6. Right-click and choose Move CSS Rules.

A dialog will appear giving you the ability to move the rules to an existing style sheet or to create a new style sheet.

7. Choose "A new style sheet" and click OK.

The Save Style Sheet File As dialog appears.

8. Type a name into the Save As: input and choose the directory yosu'd like to place your style sheet into. Click OK.

Dreamweaver moves all the rules into a new external style sheet and links to that style sheet in the head of your document.

FIGURE 2.47 Dreamweaver indicates CSS rules in the head using `<style>` and linked style sheets by showing their name with the rules within shown indented below it

9. Right-click the empty `<style>` block shown above the newly linked style sheet. Choose Delete.

Dreamweaver removes the empty style block from the head of the document.

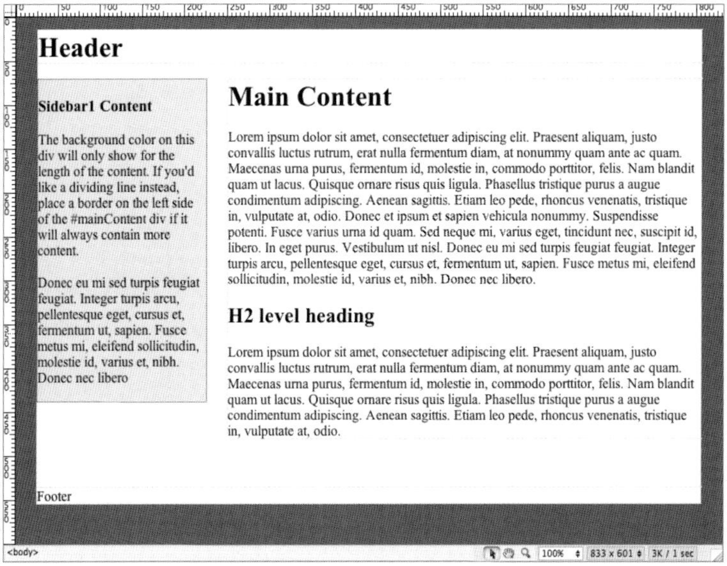

FIGURE 2.48 The final result, centered in all browser versions—even early and quirks mode browsers.

To read more about the escaping margin effect that comes as a result of margin collapse, read The Practice of CSS Column Design: Boxes in Columns by John Gallant and Holly Bergevin at http://www.communitymx.com/abstract.cfm?cid=CB7B3.

You should now have a basic understanding of the core CSS principles that allow you to create functional CSS layouts, based on one of Dreamweaver's more common web layouts: two-column, fixed-width with header and footer. With this knowledge of essential CSS concepts behind us, let's delve into different types of layouts as well as more complex techniques we can apply to real web sites.

Margin Collapse

The CSS layouts contain almost no styling for text elements. However, in the header and footer divs, you'll find that the top and bottom values have been "zeroed out." We establish the breathing room around the elements with padding instead. The reason for this is called **margin collapse**. The top and bottom margins for such elements often do not stay contained inside their parent div. Instead, they spill outside it, holding the div away from the div above or below and causing a confusing gap if you don't understand what's going on.

This is not a bug but is actually the proper behavior, though in some cases it's undesirable. For example, if we have two paragraphs stacked one after the other, we wouldn't want the 10 pixels of margin space on the bottom and the 10 pixels of space on the top of the second paragraph to be added together, morphing the space into a height of 20 pixels. The W3C provides for this contingency by collapsing the 20 pixels into one 10-pixel value (if the margins that are touching have unequal values, the largest will be used). This collapsing effect influences how margins interact within divs. Of course, the effect works differently in Internet Explorer. Go figure!

In addition to removing margins by applying a 0 value, adding even one pixel of padding or a border at the top and/or bottom of the containing element fixes the problem too. In the CSS layouts, an IECC was used to give IE more padding on the sidebars. Since IECCs do not appear in the CSS Styles panel, this can be nearly invisible to people who do not work in Code or Code and Design view. This IECC requires us to change the padding value within IECC when we change the layout values from their defaults, possibly causing confusion.

A better solution might have been to remove the top margin from the first element in the sidebars (as was done in the header and footer). People wanting to add a margin back to their elements might have been confused by the margin collapse behavior, but it would have shown up in the CSS Styles panel. Apologies for any confusion or hair-pulling that may have ensued if you didn't find that immediately.

Our recommendation is to remove that rule from the IECC and either remove the top margin using a descendant selector, or create a class that removes the top margin from any element you place it on.

```
.noTop {
  margin-top: 0;
}
```

CHAPTER 3

Using the Fixed, Centered CSS Layouts

PROBABLY THE MOST COMMON layouts on the web, especially with blog-type sites that have become so popular, are fixed-width layouts. These layouts have an overall pixel width, side columns with specific pixel widths, and are usually displayed in the center of the browser window, though that's not required.

One reason this layout style is used so often is that when you have static sizes for most elements, interactions are more predictable. That makes the layout easier to design and code, because there are fewer unknowns.

For this chapter, we'll use a fictitious client, a horticulture site. We'll look at how to center your layout, create full-length columns, use and position background images, style and size fonts, and rearrange the pages and float the main content div to change your source order. We'll see some good uses for absolute positioning and discuss the print media type. We've got a lot to cover, so let's dive in!

Beginning to Build

FIGURE 3.1 A screen shot of the final outcome shows what we'll be creating in this chapter.

Before proceeding, define a site within Dreamweaver CS4 and create a folder to contain your files. If you're unfamiliar with defining a site, go to Help > Dreamweaver Help > Working with Dreamweaver sites > Setting up a Dreamweaver site to learn more. If you're using our sliced images, place them into a directory called images within your site definition.

Let's begin by creating a new page using File > New. Choose Blank Page on the left of the dialog. Select Page Type: HTML. For Layout:, choose the 2 column fixed, right sidebar, header and footer layout. For DocType: choose XHTML 1.0 Transitional and set Layout CSS: to Create New File. Click Create.

FIGURE 3.2 Create a new page using the fixed-width CSS layout.

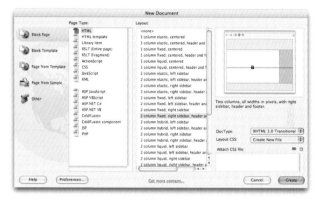

When prompted, save the CSS document with the default name (or any name) into the root of your site definition. Save the HTML document as index.html. Dreamweaver has just created a solid, structure-only document so we can start creating our web site. Notice that all the divs are shades of gray. This lets us see where everything is, but isn't meant to stay: we'll be removing the gray as we change the various rules.

FIGURE 3.3 Dreamweaver CS4 gives us a totally gray palette to start.

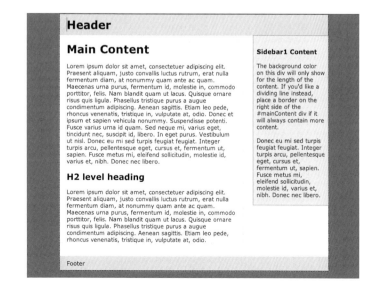

Preparing the HTML Document

 *If you have the screen real estate available, we've found keeping our design/code split view in its new vertical split state to be one of our favorite changes in Dreamweaver CS4. And if you're on dual monitors, you can choose the Dual Screen Workspace Layout. You can view the HTML source in the Code Inspector while looking at other related files (like your CSS) in the vertical split code view. Awesome!*

In Code view, we see the class `twoColFixRtHdr` on the body and preceding nearly every selector in our style sheet. Every CSS layout in Dreamweaver has a class on the body, with a similar pattern. It can be deciphered as follows:

- `twoCol`—two column

- `Fix`—fixed-width

- `Rt`—right column

- `Hdr`—header and footer

Following this pattern, a three-column, elastic layout with header and footer would have the class `thrColElsHdr`. A three-column, elastic layout without header and footer would be missing the `Hdr` at the end of the rule, leaving it as `thrColEls`.

These classes were created to keep the CSS code succinct while still letting us combine layout types (see Chapter 6). But when all pages of the site use the same layout, it becomes difficult to view all the information for descendant selectors in the Current view of the CSS Styles panel because the names are so long. Since the class isn't necessary unless you're combining layout types, we'll remove them at the outset using Find and Replace. For example, we'll turn `.twoColFixRtHdr #header h1` to just `#header h1`, which takes up considerably less room.

FIGURE 3.4 Dreamweaver's new layout tool gives us access to a new vertical split view.

FIGURE 3.5 Each document's related files are shown at the top of the document window.

1. At the top of the document window, click on your CSS file in the related files space. If you're in Split view, you'll see the CSS right next to your design view. In your CSS document, select the text `.twoColFixRtHdr` (as well as the space that follows it) on any of the descendant selectors.

2. Select Edit > Find and Replace (Cmd+F).

   Dreamweaver automatically adds our selected class to the Find portion of the dialog.

3. Leave the Replace area blank (and be sure Current Document is selected).

4. Click Replace All and save.

   All of the initial classes on your descendant selectors will be removed.

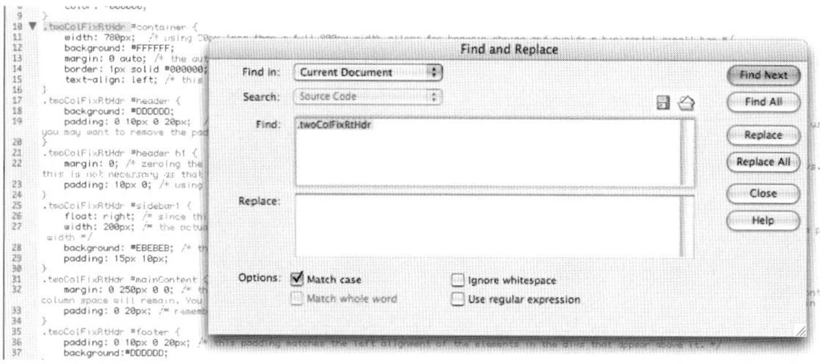

FIGURE 3.6 Use the Find and Replace dialog to strip the class names out of your pages.

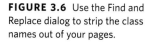

5. Click on Source Code in your related files toolbar and do the same in your HTML document since the Internet Explorer Conditional Comments (IECC) are contained there.

6. Finally, as shown in Figure 3.7, remove the class from the body element by right-clicking the body tag on the tag selector at the bottom of your document.

FIGURE 3.7 Use the tag selector to remove the class from the body element.

7. Choose Set Class > None.

Preparing the Comp

The point of this chapter is the techniques we teach and integrate into the CSS layout, not the look of the comp. To the graphic designers among you—make your layout more beautiful!

N   Take a moment to look at the code in the CSS document. Within it are many, many comments that explain all the rules and declarations and describe what might be otherwise unexpected interactions between elements. Each type of CSS layout has comments specifically applicable to that layout.

You don't have to use a graphics program to create page layouts using the CSS layouts. You could simply build the pages in Dreamweaver using a graphics program to create background glows and drop shadows, the rounded corners, and so on. We find, however, that either wire-framing and/or building the design in a graphics program is a much quicker and more efficient way to visualize our final outcome—before we get into the code at all. For this particular chapter, we created the overall look in Fireworks, although we didn't add the Latin text and headings.

 *You'll find this comp (the term we use for our source file) in the source directory of your download for this chapter (along with all the exported slices).*

The first step, before we begin to slice the comp, is to envision how it will be divided as HTML. Think in terms of vertical and horizontal lines. Though our page may not be all horizontal or vertical—it may be very curvy—we still have to break it up into square and rectangular areas to code. Don't ever feel limited by straight lines, however. There are creative ways to include portions of graphics into the tops and bottoms of sibling or child page divisions. We'll look at those as we progress through the chapter.

FIGURE 3.8 At the end of the day, most Web pages are simply headers, footers, and columns.

 *You'll find that your slice's exported size, created from Fireworks, is substantially smaller than Photoshop. If you own Fireworks, we recommend that you do your web optimization there, even if you design in Photoshop. Fireworks now understands almost all of a Photoshop file except for extremely complicated effects.*

For this chapter, we used Fireworks because we appreciate its vector and export capabilities for the web. (We'll use Photoshop in Chapter 4.) The slices we created are named within the comp. If you're following along in a classroom setting, or would like to practice slicing the comp as well, simply save the file under another name and delete the slices in the Web layer. If you don't have access to Fireworks, you can re-slice and Save for Web & Devices in Photoshop.

Styling the Body Element

Let's begin our work with the body selector. As you get more comfortable in the code space, you may find yourself doing more writing and editing of code within Code view itself as we do. In this chapter, however, our instructions will use the CSS Styles panel and CSS dialog. Feel free to work within your comfort zone and type directly in Code view using Dreamweaver's code hinting and code completion if that's what you prefer.

1. With the body tag selected on the Tag selector at the bottom of the document, click the edit (pencil) icon at the bottom of the CSS panel.

   Dreamweaver will open the CSS Rules definition dialog.

   N *There are a couple of different ways to find the color. You can choose the color in your graphics program, and copy and paste it into Dreamweaver. Or, with both Dreamweaver and your comp in the same space, you can click and hold the Color Picker in the CSS Styles panel edit dialog (next to Background color), and release the eyedropper over the background color in the graphics program: Dreamweaver will automatically fill the sampled background color into the Background color input.*

2. In the Background category > Background color, remove the default #666666 and replace it with the background color of the overall page in our comp, #7F98C3.

3. In the Type category, add a 1.5 value for line-height. In the drop-down list next to it, choose multiple as the unit of measure.

   This will set the line height as a multiple of the size of the font of the element. It will appear in your CSS code with no unit of measurement and is generally recognized as the most consistent way to set line-height.

4. Click the drop-down list next to the Font input. Choose Edit Font List at the bottom.

   The Edit Font List dialog will appear. The fonts on our system will appear in the Available fonts list on the right. Instead of using one of the standard font lists Dreamweaver provides, we're going to create a new list. When we've completed it, the order will be Helvetica Neue, Helvetica, Arial, sans-serif.

5. Choose Helvetica Neue if it's shown in the list and click the left arrow key.

   It will be moved to the Chosen fonts list on the left. If it doesn't exist on your system, no worries. You can still use it in your font list. Simply type the name into the input below the Available fonts list and then click the left arrow button to move it to the Chosen fonts list.

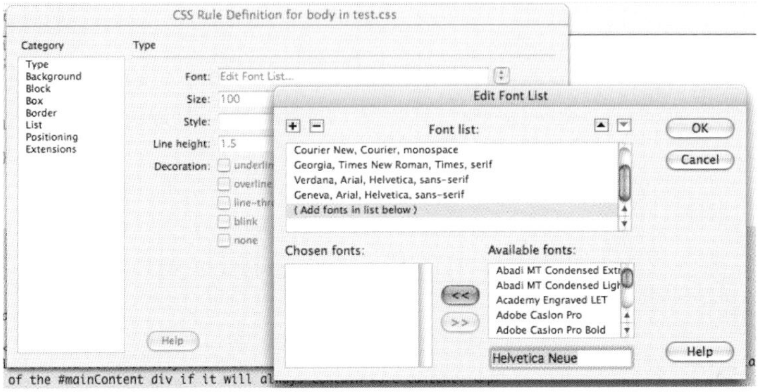

FIGURE 3.9 Creating a new font
list using a font that doesn't exist
on the system.

6. Create the complete list by continuing with Helvetica, Arial,
and the generic sans-serif. Click OK.

7. Choose the font list we just created from the drop-down list.
Click OK in the CSS Rules definition dialog.

Styling with Font Cascades

We can create any font cascade we'd like. But here are a few things to keep in mind:

The order the fonts appear in matters. The browser attempts to render the text beginning with the first
font on the list. But that only works if that font exists on the user's system! If it doesn't, the browser
moves through each font in order, finally ending with the generic font family (serif or sans-serif most
commonly). For this reason, put your most desired font first in the list, followed by the next-most desired
font and so on.

Sometimes we'd like to use a font for the Mac that doesn't exist for Windows, which means we need
to also include a more common font for Windows users. If you do this, be sure that the Mac-only font
comes first if the Windows font also exists for the Mac; otherwise the less-desirable font will be rendered on both platforms.

When creating new font cascades, test the default size of the fonts you choose. Make sure to create a
font cascade that uses fonts in similar sizes in order to ensure that your user will see what you expect!

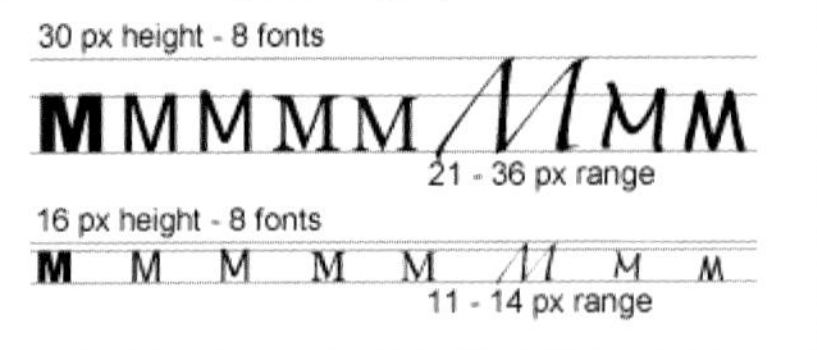

FIGURE 3.10 Font sizes, even
at the "same size" vary from
family to family.

Using Shorthand Properties in CSS

N *For the sake of space in the book, when we post code blocks, we don't include the comments. We do include them in our code, however, so the files will sometimes look slightly different.*

Your body rule should now look like this (though the order may differ):

```css
body {
    font: 100%/1.5 "Helvetica Neue", Helvetica, Arial, sans-serif;
    background: #7F98C3;
    margin: 0;
    padding: 0;
    text-align: center;
    color: #000000;
}
```

If you look at the font property, you may notice that your CSS may not look like ours. If you have individual font values on each line instead of all in one line, it is due to the way the CSS preferences are set in Dreamweaver: we keep our preferences set to write shorthand.

So what in the world is shorthand anyway? Simply put, shorthand lets you specify several values with a single property. It can be quite a space saver in CSS documents and once you get used to it, it makes it much easier to read your pages.

Order is generally quite important when using shorthand, because one property name may have several values following it.

Let's look quickly at a couple of shorthand examples, beginning with the `font` property. There are six possible values for `font`: `font-style`, `font-variant`, `font-weight`, `font-size`, `line-height`, and `font-family`. If one of these values is not declared, the default for the value is used.

In the case of our style sheet, you can see that we declared the `font-size`, `line-height`, and `font-family`. This means the other three properties are left at their default values. Our shorthand declaration equals this block of code:

```css
font-style: normal;
font-variant: normal;
font-weight: normal;
font-size: 100%;
line-height: 1.5;
font-family: "Helvetica Neue", Helvetica, Arial, sans-serif;
```

The shorthand for applying background values is similar to font shorthand. The property is called **background** and it has five possible values: `background-color`, `background-image`, `background-repeat`, `background-attachment`, and `background-position`. Thus, `background: #7F98C3 url(images/body_back.jpg) repeat-y left top;` is equal to:

```
background-color: #7F98C3;
background-image: url(images/body_back.jpg);
background-repeat: repeat-y;
background-attachment: scroll;
background-position: left top;
```

Border is a similar property. It allows us to set the width, style, and color of the borders of a box. It does not allow us to make one of the sides different than the other, however. To do that, we need to declare that value separately. So for instance, if we want to set the width of the left side border of our box to be 2px and the rest to be 1px, we could write it like this:

```
border: 1px solid #000;
border-left-width: 2px;
```

The first line sets the entire box to have a 1px black border with a solid style. The second line overrides the width of the left border. Remember the cascade—to override the 1px border, the 2px border must come after it.

Font, background, and border are the most common mixed value shorthand properties.

Two other shorthand properties that we'll use throughout the book are margin and padding. The shorthand for these properties allows us to set all four sides of the box at once. Both properties are written in the same way: the specific order is top, right, bottom, left. People use different tricks to remember the order: you can think of the rule as trouble, from the acronym TRBL, or more simply, as clockwise (start at the top and moving around the box). After years of experience, we still find ourselves using our tricks of choice as we write our code.

In the border example, you see the color defined as #000. This is equivalent to #000000. Some colors can be converted to shorthand and others can't. RGB color is written with a hash mark, immediately followed by either three or six characters—#RRGGBB or #RGB. That means a value like *#006699 is equivalent to #069 and #FF9933 is the same as #F93. However, a value like #C3C3C3 cannot be shortened.*

For example, `margin: 0 20px 10px 15px;` is equal to:

```
margin-top: 0;
margin-right: 20px;
margin-bottom: 10px;
margin-left: 15px;
```

When the values of all four sides are the same, only one value needs to be used since it applies to all four sides: `margin: 0;`

Notice there is no unit of measurement after the 0. This is because, no matter what unit you place after zero—pixels, percent, em units—the value is still the same, zero.

If you're using equivalent top and bottom values as well as equal side values, you can use only two values: `margin: 10px 15px;`

This indicates that the top and bottom values are 10px and the right and left are 15px.

Finally, if your top and bottom sides have different values from each other, but the sides are the same, you can use three values in your shorthand: `margin: 0 20px 15px;`

This tells the browser to render 0 on the top margin, 20px on the right margin, 15px on the bottom, and the lack of a fourth value indicates that the left side is equivalent to the right side. So it's 20px as well.

As you can see, shorthand is cool and it's absolutely the way we want to write our code. It's much too handy to not use, so throughout the rest of the book, we'll be using shorthand. Let's make sure you can do the same!

Dreamweaver CSS Preferences

The key to having Dreamweaver automatically write the shorthand for us, saving tons of time, is in the preferences. Dreamweaver actually gives you a lot of power within its preferences, but many people never venture in. Let's bravely enter!

1. Go to Edit > Preferences. (On the Mac, go to Dreamweaver > Preferences).

2. From the Category list, choose CSS Styles.

3. Make the following choices:

When creating CSS rules: Use shorthand for: (Check all properties)

When editing CSS rules: Use shorthand: According to settings above

When double-clicking in CSS panel: Edit using CSS dialog

While we're in the preferences window, let's look at one more thing.

4. From the Category list, choose Code Format. There's a little-noticed setting there—Advanced Formatting. Click the button that says CSS.

FIGURE 3.11 CSS Code formatting preferences—awesome!

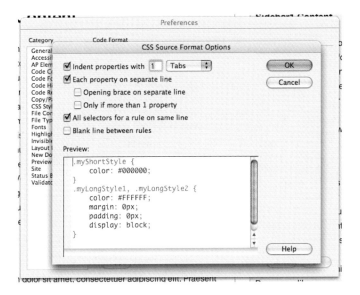

Dreamweaver opens the CSS Source Format Options dialog. This dialog allows us to set the way Dreamweaver, by default, writes our CSS. We're not going to change anything here now, but if you have a specific style you prefer to write your CSS in, it's likely you can set the indentation, or the way Dreamweaver spaces your lines and other formatting preferences, to suit your personal style.

The CSS formatting preferences can be handy in other situations as well. If you inherit a style sheet from someone else, formatted in an unusual way, you can choose Commands >

Apply Source Formatting to the page and it will be reformatted according to your preferences. In addition, some people like to remove most of the white space before uploading their CSS by putting all declarations for a rule on one line. Though we find it difficult to work this way as we develop a site, it's quite simple to change your preferences to place the entire rule on one line, apply the new source formatting, and then upload the style sheet. Once that's complete, change the preferences back to your usual way to work. Voilà! An instant removal of white space without all that tedious hand deletion we used to have to do.

5. Click OK to close and save your Preferences.

Using Background Images

Back to our layout!

This fixed-width comp is designed to be centered in the browser's viewport. Centering is a common technique since on today's larger monitors left-aligning the design can leave a lot of space to the right. Centering an element, like the container div, is accomplished by using a width and the auto value for the left and right margin. Our design has an overall glow highlighting each side of the page, which wraps around the bottom, giving it the illusion of a three-dimensional object.

The design also contains a right column that needs to go all the way down to the footer, no matter how much content it contains. You may remember that in Chapter 2 we mentioned that the background color of a div ends when the content ends. There is no reliable way (outside of using JavaScript) to force columns to be equal in size and thus the color on one column will end shy of the other column. We'll create the illusion of equal height columns using a technique called faux columns.

Faux, in French, means false. During the faux painting craze of the 90s, many homes were painted using techniques that created the illusion of wood, stone, marble, or even a window, plant, or animal in a room where there was none. That's the same idea behind the faux column technique—we'll be creating the illusion of a column going to the footer of our page. It's almost as if we're painting with graphics.

Creating the "Faux" Right Column

Take a look at the current gray sidebar1 column for a good example of how a column ends when the content in it ends. (In fact, if you read the text within, it warns you of this fact.)

FIGURE 3.12 The gray column on the right ends when the content ends.

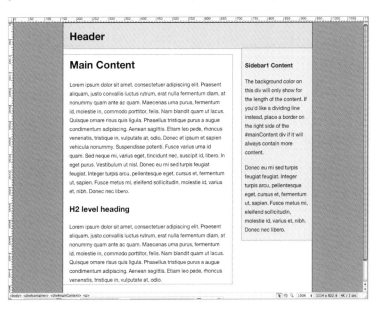

N   *Sadly, there wasn't space in this book to teach how to slice in Fireworks and Photoshop. If you're unfamiliar with either program, their help files can be very helpful. Have a look there or do a search at Adobe's Developer Connection or Community MX—other great sources of information.*

Adding a background image or color on the `sidebar1` div doesn't fix the problem, because the background still ends where the content does, so instead we'll place the background image on the element containing `sidebar1`. In the case of the CSS layouts, that element is the container div that holds the entire layout.

You may use the `column.gif` slice created for you in your images directory. Or, in your graphics program of choice, create a slice from the white edge at the right of the comp to the left edge of the column. Make the slice about 10-15px high. Export it as a gif.

FIGURE 3.13 The columns slice, shown on the gray Fireworks canvas.

1.   Click anywhere in your page and on the tag selector at the bottom, choose `<div#container>`. In the CSS Styles panel, click the Edit Style icon (pencil).

2. From the CSS Rule Definition dialog, choose the Background Category and set the following values:

Background image: (use the Browse button to create the correct path to the image) `column.gif` (in your images directory)

Repeat: repeat-y (this is the vertical axis)

Click Apply and look at your page.

The `repeat-y` property will allow the graphic to repeat from the top of the container div to the bottom. And yes, this includes behind both the header and the footer, so we'll make sure we have a background color or image in those divs to cover this faux technique.

Notice, though we have a column, it's on the left side of our page. The default value for a background image is to be applied to the element at the top left, so that's where our column has settled. Since our column is on the right side of the content div, we'll have to set the horizontal position of our `column.gif` to begin on the right side of the element.

3. Add to your Background properties the following:

Horizontal position (X): right

Vertical position (Y): top

Click OK.

Now we can see, that though covered by the background on the `sidebar1` div, our column has moved to the right side of our layout. Our container code should now look like the following:

```
#container {
    width: 780px;
    background: #FFFFFF url(images/column.gif) repeat-y
right top;
    margin: 0 auto;
    border: 1px solid #000000;
    text-align: left;
}
```

4. Click into the `sidebar1` div, right-click the background property in the Properties pane of the CSS Styles panel and choose delete. This will get rid of Dreamweaver's default gray column.

N *The y axis is a vertical repeat and the x axis is a horizontal repeat. Setting your image with these values allows you to have a narrow slice that repeats over and over, saving bandwidth.*

N *Be aware that with the new Related Files toolbar, making a change to your CSS using the CSS styles panel will "dirty" your page as if it were open (shown by the asterisk next to the name). If you're going to preview that page in a browser, Dreamweaver will prompt you to save it. If you use Live View within Dreamweaver, you can view the changes without saving. Know that if you're working in Split view like we are, with the related CSS file in the code pane, you may need to place your cursor into the CSS page so that it has focus (and not your page's Design view) to actually save the CSS file.*

FIGURE 3.14 The nifty, new Live View button!

N   *If you'd like to check your work along the way, the files for this chapter contain a folder called builds. The file that ends the last section and begins this one is index_1.html.*

Let's have a look at the page in Dreamweaver's new Live View. Our blue-gray column runs all the way to the footer even though it's obvious the div stops well before it. If you want to peek under the header or footer, remove the background color and you'll see how obvious it is that this is a faux or false column.

Creating the Outer Glow

Our comp didn't just have a column running the full length, did it? The technique we just used, with the small graphic containing only the side column, works nicely to create equal columns, but we've also got the outer glow or drop shadow appearance around the overall page. We can use the same technique with a different image to create this effect.

Create a slice (or use the one provided in your images directory) from the outer edge of the left glow to the outer edge of the right glow. Ours is 10px tall and 700px wide (this includes the blue glow area outside the white page portion which is an equal 9px on either side). Leave the right column we just applied in this image visible when you export this slice. We'll be replacing that right column graphic now. Export the slice as **body_back.jpg** into the images directory.

FIGURE 3.15 Overall page slice, including the column, shown on the gray Fireworks canvas.

N   *No matter how wide you create your page graphic, be sure you have equal amounts of glow on both sides. Otherwise, you're going to have to tweak values to make it appear centered.*

1. Select the container div. Click the edit icon and in the Background category, remove the Background color and browse to the **body_back.jpg** image. Click Apply.

   We've removed the background color since it's no longer needed. The image contains the white page color as well as the column and outer page glow.

2. Remove the X and Y placement values for the background image.

   Since the graphic and the div will be the same width, there's no need to specify where the graphic should begin. It will begin at the top, left by default.

   We can see that the image from our comp is not the same width as the CSS layout. The image we're using is 700px wide. Our container needs to match that width. Remember the 9px blue glow on either side of the image? That isn't *really* part of the white page area. We need to account for that.

3. In the Box Category, uncheck the "Same for all" box and set 9px of padding for both the left and right.

   Remember that padding is added to the overall width of the box in the standard box model. We'll have to subtract 18px from our desired width.

4. Set the width to 682px.

   700px - 9px - 9px = 682px. Border is also added to the box model, but since we don't need the border in this design, we'll remove it.

5. In the Border Category, remove the border from all sides of the container and click OK. Your code should now resemble:

```
#container {
    background: url(images/body_back.jpg) repeat-y;
    margin: 0 auto;
    text-align: left;
    width: 682px;
    padding-right: 9px;
    padding-left: 9px;
}
```

Check your page in Live View. Wow! It's really beginning to take shape, isn't it?

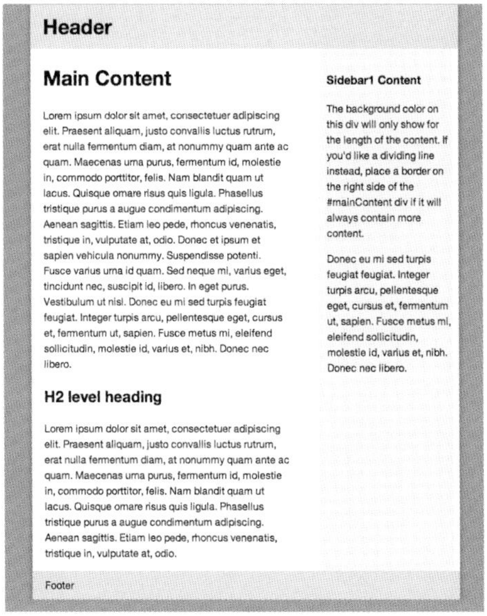

N   All the CSS layouts come with a border to allow you to visualize the edges of the layout more easily. Many times you'll want to remove it.

FIGURE 3.16 Our partially completed page—we've got the column and the glow!

N *You can test this full page effect by leaving the column.gif on the #container and exporting the white page with blue glow as a slice (without the gray column). Place it on the body selector as a background image set to repeat-y with a position of center top.*

If our design didn't have the glow around the bottom of the page, we could actually put an image on the body element containing just the page side glow, leaving the single column on the container. In that case, the page side glow effect would run the full length of the browser viewport, regardless of the content within. With some designs, this may be desirable.

One issue to remember if you choose to put a background image of any kind on the body element is that Internet Explorer 7 has zoom capability. This can be lovely for people with low vision: they can scale the entire page up, images and all, not just the text. But Microsoft got one little thing wrong. Background images on the body element don't scale up with the rest of the page. Thus, text could end up on a background color you didn't anticipate, making it illegible. This can be especially problematic with the faux column technique when the image is placed on the body element.

Luckily, there's a simple fix. If we place a background color or image on the HTML element, IE7 will zoom the background on the body element. Why? Who knows, it's IE. But it works and it's valid. If you'd like to keep your CSS organized, you could place the fix into a style sheet that's fed only to IE7 using an Internet Explorer Conditional Comment (IECC) (see Chapter 2.) Otherwise, place the fix in your regular CSS, but leave a comment next to it so that you or any developer that comes after you know why it's there.

```
html { background: #FFF; } */ this color forces IE7 to zoom
the body background image /*
```

Creating the Header

Most of the time, we work on our pages in a specific order. First come backgrounds and faux columns. Then, we move from the top down, from the header to the footer. We'll turn our attention to the header area now.

N *This example may be fairly pedestrian, but let your creative brain think about the possibilities opened up by the techniques we're going to demonstrate.*

The comp our designer handed us has a couple interesting design elements. The flower in the header overhangs the left side of the page and the small flower at the bottom right slightly overhangs the right side.

It's obvious from the comp that the client still wants to cater to the 800x600 resolution crowd. In order to keep the main area of the page centered in the browser window and not have the over-hanging design elements go outside the viewport, the overall page (measured from the outside of each flower) is 770px.

Be sure to allow approximately 15px for browser chrome—the outer area of the browser—when choosing the width to create your comp. An 800px resolution target would have a maximum width of 785px. A 1024px target shouldn't exceed 1009px. In fact, many people choose a 980px resolution. If your client has statistics on who uses their site, use them to help decide on a target width. Resolution statistics can vary widely based on the audience of the web site.

The images directory contains an image called `lg_flower.jpg`. If you're slicing, leave the background in and slice from the top of the page to each edge of the flower. Make sure to include the drop shadow under the flower. (Our image measures 218px x 250px.)

FIGURE 3.17 The large flower overhanging the edge of the page glow.

Absolute Positioning—Not Always Evil

With CSS, there can be a variety of ways to create the same effect. In this case we're going to use a positioning technique. Remember in Chapter 2, we discussed the problems with absolute positioning since the element is taken out of the flow of the page and nothing on the page reacts to it? In many cases, we want to avoid absolute positioning an element that contains text and is given a height. In this case, however, the image is a static height and width and contains no text that could cause the size to vary. This is a safe element on which to use absolute positioning.

Sometimes the fact that the absolutely positioned element is taken out of the flow of the page can be advantageous. We can place our image anywhere in the HTML of the container and set the positioning so it will appear at the top, where we want it. In light of that, since this is a decorative page element we can move the code for it down to the bottom of our page. This keeps non-essential code out of the top area of our page, moving our text up, which is always a good thing for search engine spiders searching for tasty words.

There is some argument over whether a non-essential decorative element should be described to the non-sighted using the alt attribute. We would argue that most people (including those with sight) are coming to the web site for information, not to hear descriptions of the design. In this case, we chose to use an empty alt attribute. No matter your decision, the alt attribute should either be filled in with a brief description or given the alt="" *(called empty) alt attribute to keep Assistive Technology (AT) from reading aloud the name of the image.*

1. With your page in Split view (our favorite way to work), place your cursor in the footer. Click `<div#footer>` on the tag selector and press the right arrow key on your keyboard.

   This will place your cursor between the end of the `#footer` and the end of the `#container`.

2. In the Common category of the Insert pane, click the image icon (sixth from the left). Navigate to `lg_flower.jpg` and select it. In the Image Tag Accessibility Attributes dialog, choose `<empty>` from the drop-down next to Alternate Text. Click OK.

   In the Design view portion of your document, you'll see that the image is simply sitting down at the bottom of the page. We need to create a rule to position it up in our header area.

3. Select the flower image. On the bottom of the CSS Styles panel, click the New CSS Rule icon (document with +).

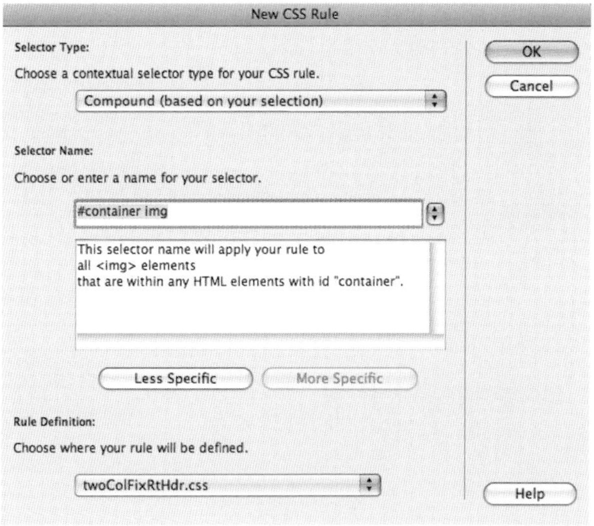

FIGURE 3.18 The Selector name is pre-filled in the New CSS Rule dialog.

Dreamweaver opens the New CSS Rule dialog with the Selector name pre-filled (`#container img`). Since it opens with the path to the image as the descendant selector name, we need to change it a bit.

4. Leave Selector Type: set to Compound. Change the Selector Name to `#container .overhang` and leave Rule Definition set to your external CSS page. Click OK.

5. In the Category list, select the Positioning category. Choose the following values:

 Position: Absolute

 Placement Top: 0

 Placement Left: -65px

 Click OK.

N *An absolutely positioned element will continue up the document tree until it finds a positioned ancestor and will calculate its x and y coordinates from that point. If it doesn't find an element to position from along the way, it will position itself from the body element.*

6. Right-click the image. In the Property inspector, choose **overhang** from the class drop-down list.

 Notice in the Design view the image has moved up to the top, but it's certainly not right where we want it. In fact, it's negatively margined off the left edge of the page!

 Remember that an absolutely positioned element positions itself off its last *positioned* ancestor. Since the container has been left with its default static positioning, it's not considered positioned at all. It takes at least relative positioning for an element to be considered positioned. So the image is calculating its negative left position off the body element, its last positioned ancestor.

7. Select the **#container** rule and in the Properties pane of the CSS Styles panel, click Add Property. Type position (or choose it from the drop-down list) on the left column and choose relative from the drop-down list on the right column (value).

The flower is now in its proper position, but as you can see, the other page elements aren't aware it's there. We'll deal with that as we go.

Adding the Logo

Slice the logo from the comp or use the **logo.jpg** image in the images directory.

FIGURE 3.19 The logo surrounded by the gray of the Fireworks canvas.

1. Place your cursor into the header. Right-click the `<h1>` element on the tag selector and choose Remove tag.

   Dreamweaver will remove the **h1** that surrounds the word header, leaving the word highlighted. (You won't be able to see the word, only the highlighting since the flower image is sitting on top of it.)

2. Press Delete/Backspace to remove the highlighted word and in the Common category of the Insert pane, insert the `logo.jpg` image. Type Horticulture as Art into the alt attribute. Click OK.

   You'll notice that the `logo.jpg` is inserted into the header, but it's sliding beneath the flower due to the absolute positioning. The header doesn't have as much space as in the comp and is still the default gray.

3. Select `<div#header>` in the tag selector. In the Properties pane of the CSS Styles panel, change the value of the background property from the default #DDDDDD to the shorthand #FFF.

4. Change the padding values to be 40px on the top, 0 on the right , 20px on the bottom, and 150px on the left. (Remember your shorthand order.)

   The 150px on the left will keep the logo from sliding beneath the flower image. The padding on the top and bottom will create the needed space. The shorthand should look like this:

   ```
   #header {
       background: #FFF;
       padding: 40px 0 20px 150px;
   }
   ```

5. Save your page and take a look at it in Live View.

FIGURE 3.20 The header and sides have really taken shape!

If you were linking to a real file, you would either type the name and path of that file into the input area or click the folder on the right of the input and navigate to the file you want to link to. Using a hashmark (#) causes Dreamweaver and browsers to style the element as a link for design purposes.

FIGURE 3.21 Ew! What's the ugly blue border?

Usability experts will tell you that users expect to have the site's logo link to the home page. We're going to give our users what they expect.

6. Click on the logo image. In the Property inspector, add the link by placing a # in the Link input below the Src input.

We've suddenly found a bright blue outline around our logo. We're betting both the designer and the client will be unhappy with this unsightly mess! Don't worry, there's a quick fix: we'll create a simple rule to get rid of it. Since we've not yet defined our link colors, the default blue still applies. The border on our image is simply the default blue link color indicating that the image is linked.

7. On the Related Files toolbar, click on your CSS document.

You'll notice the order of rules begins with the **body**, moves to **#container**, and then to each division on the page starting at the top with **#header**. In the header area, you'll see a rule called **#header h1** that is no longer in use (remember, we removed the **h1** element in the **#header**). Let's completely remove that as we create the rule needed for the blue border.

8. Find the **#header h1** rule, select the whole thing (including the ending curly bracket), and click delete.

Yes, we could have deleted it directly in the CSS styles panel before the element was removed from the page, smarty! Since we didn't, we're going to get our hands dirty in the code (our favorite place). Hey, it had to happen at some point!

9. Leaving our cursor in place, we'll create the new rule. Directly in your CSS code, type: **a img** (read by the browser as "any image that is a descendant of an anchor element)."

10. Type the opening curly bracket ({) and press Enter.

Dreamweaver presents us with a helpful drop-down list of possible properties. As you start typing the border property name, the list continually gets more targeted.

11. When you see the `border` property highlighted, press Enter.

Dreamweaver adds the property name along with the colon separating it from the value.

12. Type n and the code hinting list will jump to `none`. Select `none` by pressing Enter. Add the semicolon, press Enter, and add the closing curly bracket:

```
a img {
   border: none;
}
```

Though we love Dreamweaver's CSS Styles panel, sometimes it's just quicker to work directly in the code. Dreamweaver's code-hinting tools make it painless.

N   *It's not necessary to have a semicolon at the end of the last declaration of a rule. However, we've learned the hard way that good habits are worth having. Adding a semicolon at the end of every declaration keeps you from having a situation where a declaration is skipped by a browser due to improper formatting.*

Our header is now complete with the blue border removed. We're really crankin' now! If you'd like to check your work against ours (in case of any discrepancies), look in the builds directory for index_2.html.

Rounding the Side Column

We're sure it didn't slip by your keen eye that our side column actually has a rounded corner at the top and the bottom. Like all CSS techniques, there's more than one way to skin the proverbial cat. In our case, the upper-left and lower-right corners are rounded. (With a fixed-width layout, however, the method would be similar even if the entire box were rounded since we can anticipate the exact width of the column.)

We want to keep presentation and structure separated, so we're not going to place the image directly into the code for the top and bottom of the column. In fact, placing the bottom rounded graphic into the column itself would display that graphic where the right column content *actually* ends. Since our column background is "painted" on the container, the rounded corner could end up sitting somewhere in the middle. Yuck!

FIGURE 3.22 The top-left rounded corner of the sidebar, in Fireworks.

N *Be sure when you're slicing your own corners, to slice all the way to the area where the box becomes completely straight. This will ensure that you have perfect graphic/background color blends every time.*

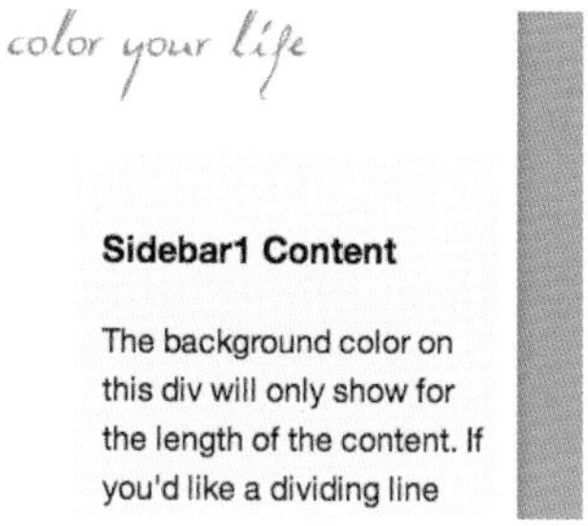

color your life

Sidebar1 Content

The background color on this div will only show for the length of the content. If you'd like a dividing line

FIGURE 3.23 Hmmm...the corner doesn't meet up perfectly, does it?

Let's Start at the Top

Let's think about our options. The top is simple, of course, because the top of the column will always be at the visual top of the column. The graphic we created for the top is a 28 x 28px slice containing only the left corner. We called it `corner_tl.gif` (tl stands for top, left in our personal shorthand).

1. Place the `corner_tl.gif` image into `sidebar1` as a background image using the CSS Styles panel. (We know you can do this yourself by now—just click the edit icon on the bottom of the CSS Styles panel.)

2. Set the Repeat property to `no-repeat`. Click OK and preview your page in Live View.

   We notice the border isn't sitting flush against the left side of our column graphic. That's because we haven't made any adjustments to our column size based on our designer's vision. We've still got our divs set to their defaults. In order to begin these adjustments, we'll first create a simple element selector for our **p** element. This will allow us to visualize more clearly the space available in the various divs.

3. In the CSS code, or using the CSS Styles panel New CSS Rule icon, create a simple element selector for the **p** element. Set the font-size to 85%.

   If you allowed Dreamweaver to create the rule, it has placed it at the bottom of your list of rules. We like to stay organized as well as keep later cascading issues in mind, so we're going to move that up—just below the **a img** selector we created.

4. Change to the All mode of your CSS Styles panel.

   If all you see is your CSS page name, you need to click the little arrow button to its left to view all the rules within it.

5. Click-hold the **p** selector at the bottom and drag it up the list, dropping it directly below the **a img** rule.

   This is an awesome feature in Dreamweaver that allows you to manage and reorder your style sheets and rules right in the All mode window. Since CSS is a *cascading* language, this is a great timesaver!

In our graphics program, we took some measurements. The width of the right column is 214px. It is sitting 10px away from the right edge of the page. 214 + 10 = 224. Our sidebar1 div is currently 200px. Let's make the adjustments to our padding and width on sidebar1 so the corner matches up.

6. Change your panel back to Current mode. Click into the sidebar1 div.

    Since we've added the **p** element selector, clicking into the sidebar1 div shows us the properties for the **p** element first. Use the Rules pane to move up the cascade to the **#sidebar1** rules.

7. In the Properties pane, change the side padding to 20px on each side.

    200px + 20 + 20 = 240px. This is too wide: we want that 224px width. Since we have to include the padding in this measurement, let's work backward: 224 - 20 - 20 = 184.

8. Change the width value for **#sidebar1** to **184px**. Save and view in Live View.

```
#sidebar1 {
    float: right;
    width: 184px;
    padding: 15px 20px;
    background: url(images/corner_tl.gif) no-repeat;
}
```

Sidebar1 Content

The background color on this div will only show for the length of the content. If you'd like a dividing line instead, place a border on the right side of the #mainContent div if it will always contain more content.

FIGURE 3.24 Ahhh—now this is more like it!

N *Remember that, currently, only one background element can be placed on each element. If the footer requires its own back-ground element, we could wrap a div around the mainContent and sidebar1 divs, and place the col-umn bottom on the bottom right of that wrapper div instead. There's always another way!*

Creating a Faux Bottom

We've re-created the top of our column, but now it's time to tackle the bottom. Whether we add the curved corner as a background image or into the sidebar1 div itself, unless the side column has more content than the main content area, we'll end up with an unsightly mess. The rounded bottom would end where the con-tent ends and the column would continue. What other options do we have?

Let's think about what elements meet up with the side column—visually at least. On the bottom, we have the footer. What if we placed the bottom graphic of the column into the footer as a background image? No matter where the column ends, it would have a rounded bottom.

In your sliced graphics, you'll find our version of the sliced bottom graphic—called **corner_br.gif** (yes, br stands for bottom right). If you're creating your own slice, slice from the right side of the white page area to the very left edge of the column. Make your slice as tall as the rounding of the corner—ours is 28px tall just like the top corner was.

FIGURE 3.25 The bottom slice of the column, in Fireworks.

We tend to edit background images within the dialog since we can more easily navigate to the graphics. For simple property additions or value changes, we more often work directly in the Properties pane.

1. Place your cursor into the footer div and in the Rules pane, select **#footer**. Click the edit icon to change the properties.

2. In the Background Category, change the background color to white (#FFF or #FFFFFF). Add the Background image by navigating to the **corner_br.gif**. Set it to **no-repeat**. Click Apply.

   Notice that our graphic is in the footer, but it's on the top left, not the top right.

Footer

FIGURE 3.26 Our image is in the footer, but in the default position.

By default, background images are applied beginning at the top-left corner of an element.

3. Add Horizontal position (X): **right** and Vertical position (Y): **top**. Click OK.

```
#footer {
    padding: 0 10px 0 20px;
    background:#FFFFFF url(images/corner_br.gif) no-repeat right top;
}
```

FIGURE 3.27 We've got the entire column looking just like our comp!

Adding the Bottom of the Page

Well, heck. While we're down here working in the bottom of the page, it might be a good time to add that page bottom graphic, the one that makes the edges look finished like a three-dimensional object.

But we don't seem to have an element on which to place the background image, do we? The page container has the background image of the column and the footer has the bottom of the right column. Since background images are one per customer, it would seem we're out of luck. Never fear, this sounds like a job for the multiple wrappers trick mentioned in the sidebar note of the previous *Creating a Faux Bottom* exercise. It's a handy CSS technique to have in your arsenal of tricks. If you've had any challenges while following along in the previous parts of the chapter, you can check your work with the index_3.html file in the builds directory.

Adding an Outer Page Wrapper

The simple theory behind this technique is that by placing a second wrapper around our page, we can add a second background image. This can be handy for a variety of design challenges.

One important point to note is that a wrapper inside another wrapper, unless molded into shape using padding and margin, will be the same size as the outer, parent wrapper. So the precise technique depends on the design you're working with.

In our case, it's a simple bottom graphic. We sliced the graphic at exactly the same width as the body_back.jpg image that creates the page sides, as the two must precisely meet. We sliced the height from the white page area to just below the glow. Our image is 10px tall and we named it something really original: page_bottom.jpg.

FIGURE 3.28 The page bottom graphic to be added to our new wrapper.

1. Click anywhere in the document and select `<div#container>` from the tag selector.

   Dreamweaver will highlight the whole page in Design view.

2. In the Common category of the Insert bar, select Insert Div Tag (the sixth icon from the left).

   Dreamweaver opens the Insert Div Tag dialog.

3. Make sure the drop-down list is set to "Wrap around selection." Leave the class field blank and in the ID field, type wrapper. This will be the name of the outer div we're adding. Click New CSS Rule.

   Dreamweaver opens the New CSS Rule dialog with the name we typed pre-filled into the Selector Name field.

4. Make sure the rule will be created in your external style sheet and click OK.

5. From the Category list, go to Box. Set the width value to 700px (the same width as our graphic). Uncheck the "Same for all" box in the Margin property and set the Top field to zero. Use the drop-down list for the Left and Right fields and choose auto. Choose 15px for the bottom margin.

The bottom margin simply creates some space around the container so the page bottom, once applied, will be more apparent.

6. From the Background Category, browse to the `page_bottom.jpg` image. Set it to background-repeat: `no-repeat`, Background-position (X): `center`, and Background-position (Y): `bottom`. Click OK.

    The dialog will close, revealing the Insert Div Tag dialog still open behind it.

7. Click OK in the Insert Div Tag dialog.

    It's possible we're a bit *too* organized about our CSS rules, but it's never hurt us any.

8. Change your CSS Styles panel view to the All mode. Drag the `#wrapper` rule from the bottom, where Dreamweaver just created it, to the space between the `body` and `#container` rules. Switch back to Current mode.

    We've got just a couple more tweaks to make before this works as expected.

9. Select your container div. In the Properties pane, right-click the margin property and choose Delete. Do the same with the width property.

    The `#container` is now contained in the `#wrapper`. The `#wrapper` now has the auto centering properties, so we really don't need them on this selector anymore. The width is also unnecessary since the inner div will be as wide as its parent div unless otherwise constrained.

10. Right-click and delete the `position: relative`.

    We're going to move that to the containing div as well.

11. In the Rules pane, select `#wrapper`. In the Properties pane, click Add Property and type `position`. From the drop-down list, select the value `relative` as we had before on the `#container`. Save and preview in Live View.

    Oddly, our bottom graphic still isn't showing. We've created the surrounding div and given it the right width. We've placed the background image and positioned it at the bottom.

As we mentioned earlier, the outer and inner divs will be the same size except where they are changed by padding and margin. Think of it as clay building blocks. Our wrapper is hugging up exactly around our container div. We need to create 10px of space at the bottom so that our page bottom graphic can show between them. That's easy enough!

12. With the wrapper selected, add the `padding-bottom` property. Give it a value of 10px.

We use 10px because that's the height of the graphic we're using. Too much padding and we'd be able to see the body background showing between the container and the bottom graphic in the wrapper, causing an unsightly gap.

```
#wrapper {
  margin: 0 auto 15px;
  width: 700px;
  background: url(images/page_bottom.jpg) no-repeat center
bottom;
  position: relative;
  padding-bottom: 10px;
}
```

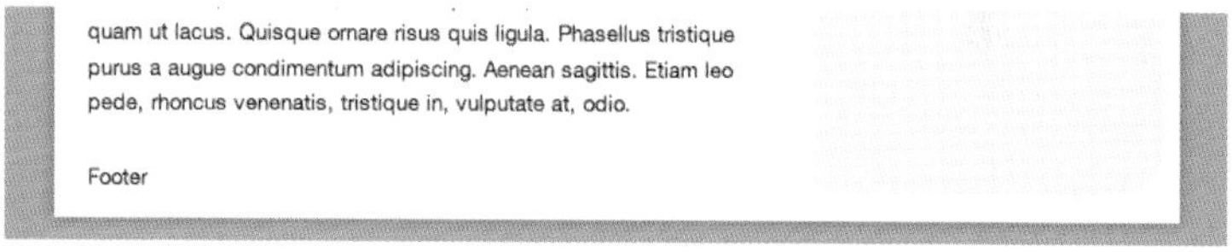

FIGURE 3.29 The footer with the nice, finished, bottom-page border.

quam ut lacus. Quisque ornare risus quis ligula. Phasellus tristique purus a augue condimentum adipiscing. Aenean sagittis. Etiam leo pede, rhoncus venenatis, tristique in, vulputate at, odio.

Footer

Positioning the Bottom Flower Graphic

We had to consider a few issues when we were envisioning how to handle the overhanging bottom flower graphic. First and foremost, it's sitting on three colors. Yes, we could actually create a slice as a jpg leaving all the background colors intact, and position the image (just as we did at the top). But right now, we'd like to demonstrate a technique that would be more flexible in a variety of layouts—especially if the color the graphic needs to sit on may vary from page to page.

True, clean transparency has always been elusive. We all know you can't create a transparent jpg. A jpg is best used when you have a photo-type image or an illustration with drop shadows, gradients or glows. The gif format *can* be transparent, but with irregular edges, it must be matted with one color in order to blend the edges smoothly. It's the best choice for flat, simple color but doesn't do well with the types of images the jpg format is best at. But those are the choices we've had for many years.

However, for the past few years, standards-compliant browsers like Safari and Firefox have offered support for a format called Portable Network Graphic, or png. The png format offers alpha transparency in a separate channel of information. This channel can be adjusted from opaque to fully transparent. It allows us to have beautiful jpg-quality images with better, halo-free transparency than a gif. So why haven't we all switched to the png format? Three guesses and the first two don't count. Yup, Internet Explorer, prior to version 7, did not support alpha transparency in pngs (yes, they did support non-transparent png images). Since IE was the dominant browser, most of us didn't bother.

To png or Not to png—
That Is the Question

The png format online is not the same as the png files that Fireworks creates. Fireworks png files are not intended to be placed online and png is simply Fireworks' native file extension (like Photoshop's .psd). You must still export an image into the online png format for use on the web.

With Microsoft's move to support pngs with alpha transparency in IE7, there's renewed interest in using this powerful format. But what to do about the older versions of IE? They're not going completely away anytime soon, and a transparent png appears to have a light blue-gray background in unsupported versions of IE. It can look pretty gross.

There are a variety of ways to use a png while still supporting all browsers, each with its own pros and cons. Many of them use JavaScript. But we're going to use a simple technique that uses no JavaScript and takes advantage of Internet Explorer Conditional Comments (IECC). This technique *cannot* be used on an image sitting directly in the page, but it works quite well for background images.

There are two images in your images directory you'll need for this technique: `sm_flower.png` and `sm_flower.gif`.

FIGURE 3.30 Looking at the placement of the flower from our comp, we don't see a nearby element on which to place the background image.

If this image has to be placed into our page as a background, what element should we use? The overhang design challenge makes our choice a bit more complex due to the placement of the elements. However, we can put an empty div in our footer and give it height, width, and a background image. Then we can position it.

1. Place your cursor into the footer and select the p element on the tag selector. Press your right arrow key once to move outside the p element.

2. Select Insert Div Tag from the Insert bar. In the dialog, choose At insertion point and Class: overhang. Click OK. Click the New CSS Rule icon at the bottom of the CSS Styles panel.

   The New CSS Rule dialog will open with our class inserted as well as the full path to the element. For reasons we'll discuss in a moment, we want to use a more complex descendant selector, but not *quite* as complex as the dialog filled in for us.

3. In the Selector Name area, click the Less Specific button one time, leaving `#container #footer .overhang` as the name of your selector. Leave the Selector Type set to Compound (based on your selection), and set Rule Definition to your external style sheet. Click OK. In the Background category, browse to the `sm_flower.png` image. Set Background-repeat to no-repeat.

FIGURE 3.31 Dreamweaver CS4 makes it easy to make your rules as specific as you need.

New CSS Rule

Selector Type:
Choose a contextual selector type for your CSS rule.

Compound (based on your selection)

OK

Cancel

Selector Name:
Choose or enter a name for your selector.

#wrapper #container #footer .overhang

This selector name will apply your rule to all HTML elements with class "overhang" that are within any HTML elements with id "footer" that are within any HTML elements with id "container" that are within any HTML elements with id "wrapper".

Less Specific   More Specific

Rule Definition:
Choose where your rule will be defined.

twoColFixRtHdr.css

Help

You'll recall that we defined a rule for the **#container .overhang** selector. Unless changed, those same properties will cascade through to this selector. That means absolute positioning is already applied, so we just need to override the top and left values.

   Notice that Dreamweaver allows you to set the width and height in both the box and positioning categories. Though there are two different places to set it, the resulting declarations are the same. Use whichever is most convenient as you work.

4. In the Positioning category, set the width to 84px and height to 100px to match our image. Set the top to 10px and left to 611px. Click OK.

    If you view your page in Live View right now, you'll notice the div with the small flower up at the top-right side of our layout. The parent element in which this div is being positioned is the footer. But it doesn't have any positioning yet. We want our top and left values to be relative to the footer div.

    ```
    #container #footer .overhang {
        background: url(images/sm_flower.png) no-repeat;
        height: 100px;
        width: 84px;
        top: 10px;
        left: 611px;
    }
    ```

5. Place your cursor in **#footer** and, making sure it's your selected element, add **position: relative**.

    Now that the footer has position, our div has positioned itself within it. But it's hanging off the bottom of the page.

    Since an element with absolute positioning is taken out of the flow of the document, we need to add padding to the parent to provide space for the positioned div. Since there is no text within the absolutely positioned element, we don't have to worry about resizing issues.

6. In the **#footer** selector, change the padding to **top: 70px**, **left** and **right: 0**, and **bottom: 30px**. Remove the text that says, "Content for class "overhang" Goes Here."

FIGURE 3.32 The bottom looks great in most browsers, but in IE6—ewwww!

Footer

N *If you prefer to use JavaScript to fix Internet Explorer's lack of alpha channel png support, Dean Edwards has a simple fix. He created a JS library called, appropriately, 1E7. It causes IE6 and earlier to work like IE7. You can read more about it at this page of his site: http://dean.edwards.name/ weblog/2008/01/ie7-2/*

N *As mentioned in Chapter 2, Community MX has an extension written by Paul Davis that will place the IECC into the document for you, saving you from remembering the syntax. For non-members, the extension costs $10.00. See http://www.communitymx. com/abstract.cfm?cid=C433F*

We took a quick glance at IE6. From the image here, you can see that the light blue background that IE 6 and earlier gives to a png image is very unsightly indeed! (If you decided to have a look in IE6 for yourself, just ignore the rest of the issues you'll see there. Remember, right now we're coding for standards-compliant browsers. We'll fix the rest of the IE problems when we're all done.)

We do need to fix the png issue right now, though—using an IECC. But currently, our page has an IECC for version 5 browsers (`<!--[if IE 5]>`) and another for all versions of IE (`<!--[if IE]>`). We need this code to apply to IE6 and earlier, but not to IE7, which supports the transparent png format. We'll create a new IECC in our page to apply to IE6 and earlier. The syntax will be slightly different than those we have already, but along the same lines. Dreamweaver has no native way of adding an IECC to the page, so we'll hand-code this into our page.

1. In the code portion of the page, place your cursor between the two IECCs already in the head of the document. Press Enter twice to create a space.

   ```
   <![endif]-->(Place cursor here)<!--[if IE]>
   ```

2. Type the following block of text into your page:
   ```
   <!--[if lte IE 6]>
   <style type="text/css">
     #container #footer .overhang {
       background: url(images/sm_flower.gif) no-repeat;
     }
   </style>
   <![endif]-->
   ```

   The syntax `lte` means that versions of IE that are less than or equal to version 6 of Internet Explorer should render the rule shown within the IECC.

   Notice that the selector name is the same selector name we created in the main style sheet. The only difference is that we've specified a gif file to be shown for IE6 and earlier, instead of the png we showed the other browsers. We don't need to override any other properties in that selector, so the rest will cascade through to IE6 as well.

You could use a jpg as well as a gif but either way, exporting two files (either a png and gif or a png and jpg) is required to create this effect. The standards-compliant browsers will see a lovely, halo-free transparent image, and IE6 and earlier may see something not quite as nice but acceptable.

FIGURE 3.33 The bottom is nicely arranged now.

A Bit About Floating and Clearing

In Chapter 2, we discussed the basic principles of floating and clearing: now let's develop these principles a little more, and add containing floats, as well as clearing within a non-floated container. Many designs require a floated self-contained area of some sort, commonly referred to as a pod. A pod may contain an image floated within and some text. In this exercise, we'll add a bordered div to our page, float an image and text in it, and then look at various effects with floating and clearing. To check the last portion of the chapter or to simply start with this one, use the file index_4.html in the builds directory.

Creating a Pod in the Page

1. First, to make the effect more apparent, copy one of the paragraphs in your side column and paste it below to make the column longer. Place your cursor about midway into the first paragraph of your `mainContent` div and hit Enter to create a new paragraph.

    We'll be inserting our pod, or callout box, here.

2. Place your cursor in the first paragraph of the `mainContent` div and select the **p** element on the tag selector. Arrow to the right (or, in Code view, place a **div** element between the two **p** elements). From the Insert panel, place a **div** element with a class of **pod** into the page and click New CSS Style.

Let Dreamweaver simply name the class `.pod` and place it in our external style sheet.

3. In the box category, set the padding to 10px on the top and 0 on the bottom. Set 5px on the right and 15px on the left. In the border category, create a border all the way around the box: 1px solid #628958. Click OK in both dialogs.

```
.pod {
  padding: 10px 5px 0 15px;
  border: 1px solid #628958;
}
```

We've just created a nice little padded box to place our content in. If you haven't moved your cursor yet, Dreamweaver still has the text selected.

4. Choose Paragraph from the HTML pane of the Property inspector. Add about two lines of text. (Anything will do.) Place your cursor at the beginning of the paragraph you just created and insert the `orangedaisy.jpg` image from your images directory.

5. With the image still selected, apply the `fltrt` class from the Property inspector.

Using the float classes that come in the CSS layout's default style sheet, we can float our image to the right side of our pod. But what's up with the border? It's appearing beneath the flower image.

FIGURE 3.34 Our flower is falling out the bottom of our pod!

quam ut lacus. Quisque ornare risus quis ligula. Phasellus tristique purus a augue condimentum adipiscing. Aenean sagittis.

This is text that will be used to demonstrate this technique. Quisque ornare risus quis ligula. Phasellus tristique purus a

Etiam leo pede, rhoncus venenatis, tristique in, vulputate at, odio. Donec et ipsum et sapien vehicula nonummy. Suspendisse potenti. Fusce varius urna id quam. Sed neque mi, varius eget, tincidunt

Avoiding Float Creep—or How to Force a Div to Contain Its Floats

Remember how absolutely positioned elements are invisible to the other elements? The container won't enclose them and the other elements can run right underneath, because they're taken out of the flow of the page. Floats work in a similar way: they're somewhat taken out of the flow, since their containing element doesn't know where they end. But unlike absolutely positioned elements, other elements can still react to them and the float's container can be forced to see where the float ends if you use a clearing element.

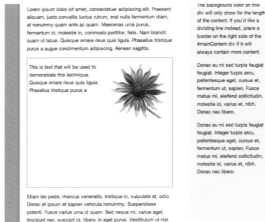

In this chapter, we're either using a clearing element or floating the parent element, as our clearing method of choice. There are a variety of ways to clear, however—each with its own pros and cons. Using overflow:auto or a .clearfix class are two of the more popular. Many times they work well. In some situations, with certain browsers, they do not. We've chosen to use a method that does add an element to the page, but that works consistently well for older browsers.

In Chapter 2, we discussed the clearing element that comes with the CSS layouts: `clearfloat`. It is placed on a break element as the last item before the footer in all the CSS layouts. This clearing element lets the container div know where `mainContent` and side columns end and contain them properly. We're going to reuse `clearfloat` here to force our pod container to see the image floated inside it.

- Place your cursor in the **p** element inside the **.pod** div. Select it on the tag selector and press the right arrow. Press Shift-Enter to insert a break element. In Code view, using Dreamweaver's code hinting feature, add the **clearfloat** class to the break.

Dreamweaver won't let you right-click to add the class directly to the break element. It will attempt to apply it to the parent element. Either type directly into Code view or copy/paste the clearing element that precedes the footer div.

FIGURE 3.35 Whoa! What just happened to our pod?

Space, the Final Frontier

We've just run into the next "little issue" with floating and clear-ing. If you clear within a *non-floated div*, it will clear *all* floats. What we're witnessing here is not a train wreck: it's the browser obeying the specs. You'll notice that the bottom of our pod ends where the content in the right column ends. That's because the break ele-ment with the clearing class is looking for the last floated element and clearing it. It's going all the way down to the end of the side content. If `sidebar1` were longer, the space in our pod would be bigger. What to do?

As we said earlier, this only happens when clearing in a non-floated div. Remember the `mainContent` div is margined away from the column next to it rather than floated itself. This was done so that all the CSS Layouts were consistent.

We have three choices. What you choose to do on your own will depend on your layout and the requirements of your client, but all of these choices will allow you to clear without clearing the side column as well.

- You can add a `float` property with a value of `left` to the `.pod` rule. This will allow you to clear within the pod, but will also require you to add some bottom margin to the `.pod` class since the `p` element following it will sit rather snugly up to it.

- You can float the `mainContent` div left. This will require some adaptation in the source order and CSS, but this is the method we'll use below.

- You can add a div right inside the `mainContent` div with no width—only a `float:left` declaration. You can do this by high-lighting all the content within the `#mainContent` div and choos-ing Insert Div Tag from the Insert bar (choosing the "Wrap around selection" option). This will allow you to choose New CSS Rule from the dialog and add the float declaration. Or, in Code view, type `<div class="left">` right inside the opening of the `#mainContent` div with a closing tag right before the closing `#mainContent` tag (which is marked by a comment). You'll then need to create the `.left` rule, with only the `float:left` declaration.

```
.left { float: left; }
```

Since a float requires a width, and the hybrid layouts (dis-cussed in Chapter 6) could not be given widths, none of the CSS lay-outs have a floated `mainContent` div. This doesn't mean you can't change that if necessary. You can, and it's simple!

N *The hybrid CSS layouts—percentage-based container with em-based columns—cannot be fully floated. That is, the width of the mainContent cannot be dependably calculated in order to float it as needed. The div inside a div trick is a great way to get around the issue of clearing in the mainContent div of the hybrid layouts.*

Though we didn't float the #mainContent div itself, placing a child div directly inside with no properties save float:left solves our clearing issue. Our pod is now seen as sitting inside a floated div (so we can clear within it) and the div it's in is 100% of the width of the parent element (#mainContent). So for all practical purposes, we're clearing within #mainContent. Yes, it's cheating—or adding a non-semantic element which raises the ire of some—but there are times when this trick is handy and it really doesn't add any weight.

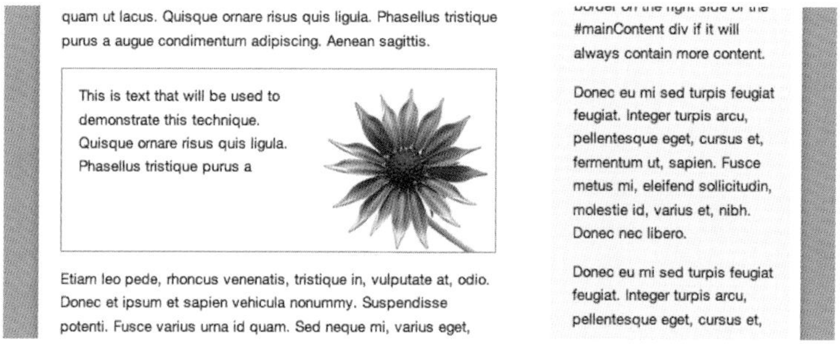

FIGURE 3.36 Using any of the three methods, the pod will enclose its content without clearing the side column.

Let's look at our second option—floating the mainContent div—in more detail.

The Issue of Source Order

N *You'll see a comment right before the footer div that says:*
<!-- This clearing element should immediately follow the #mainContent div in order to force the #container div to contain all child floats -->
What that means is the clearing div should be the last thing in #container before the footer. So if you change the order, you'll still leave the clearing element where it is.

Search engines are a concern for many web sites. Everybody wants to feed the spiders properly so they'll come back for more yummy words. For search engines, words closer to the top of the page (and thus, higher in the source order) hold more "weight" than words *way* down the page. On a page the size of ours, it's likely not going to make a lot of difference, but on a page where the sidebar holds a lot of content, there can be advantages to putting the mainContent area first.

Changing the source order of our page requires a bit of copy-paste and the changing of a couple of rules. But for some sites, it's worth it to support search engines—and conveniently, it allows us to clear content within the mainContent div to boot!

1. Select the sidebar1 element. Cut and paste it directly after the mainContent div (and before the clearing element).

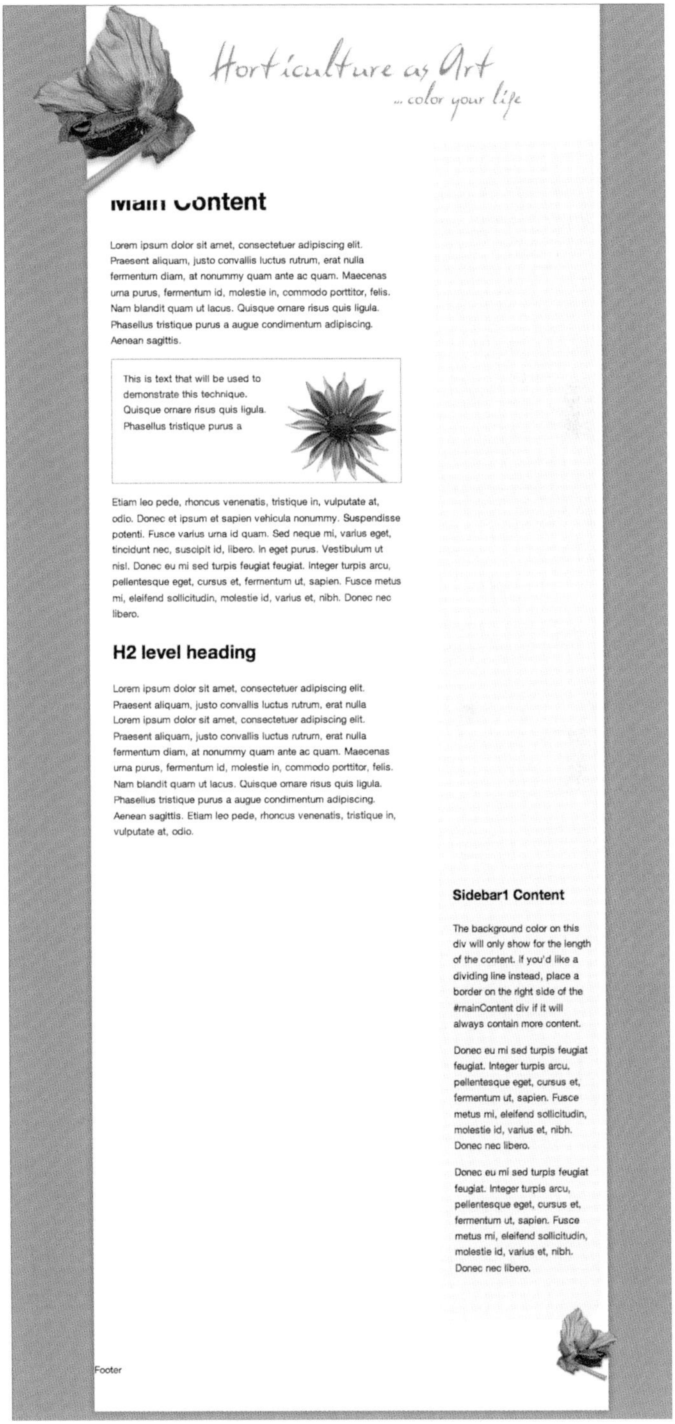

FIGURE 3.37 Whoa! Source order matters!

Horticulture as Art
... color your life

Main Content

Lorem ipsum dolor sit amet, consectetuer adipiscing elit. Praesent aliquam, justo convallis luctus rutrum, erat nulla fermentum diam, at nonummy quam ante ac quam. Maecenas urna purus, fermentum id, molestie in, commodo porttitor, felis. Nam blandit quam ut lacus. Quisque ornare risus quis ligula. Phasellus tristique purus a augue condimentum adipiscing. Aenean sagittis.

This is text that will be used to demonstrate this technique. Quisque ornare risus quis ligula. Phasellus tristique purus a

Etiam leo pede, rhoncus venenatis, tristique in, vulputate at, odio. Donec et ipsum et sapien vehicula nonummy. Suspendisse potenti. Fusce varius urna id quam. Sed neque mi, varius eget, tincidunt nec, suscipit id, libero. In eget purus. Vestibulum ut nisl. Donec eu mi sed turpis feugiat feugiat. Integer turpis arcu, pellentesque eget, cursus et, fermentum ut, sapien. Fusce metus mi, eleifend sollicitudin, molestie id, varius et, nibh. Donec nec libero.

H2 level heading

Lorem ipsum dolor sit amet, consectetuer adipiscing elit. Praesent aliquam, justo convallis luctus rutrum, erat nulla Lorem ipsum dolor sit amet, consectetuer adipiscing elit. Praesent aliquam, justo convallis luctus rutrum, erat nulla fermentum diam, at nonummy quam ante ac quam. Maecenas urna purus, fermentum id, molestie in, commodo porttitor, felis. Nam blandit quam ut lacus. Quisque ornare risus quis ligula. Phasellus tristique purus a augue condimentum adipiscing. Aenean sagittis. Etiam leo pede, rhoncus venenatis, tristique in, vulputate at, odio.

Sidebar1 Content

The background color on this div will only show for the length of the content. If you'd like a dividing line instead, place a border on the right side of the #mainContent div if it will always contain more content.

Donec eu mi sed turpis feugiat feugiat. Integer turpis arcu, pellentesque eget, cursus et, fermentum ut, sapien. Fusce metus mi, eleifend sollicitudin, molestie id, varius et, nibh. Donec nec libero.

Donec eu mi sed turpis feugiat feugiat. Integer turpis arcu, pellentesque eget, cursus et, fermentum ut, sapien. Fusce metus mi, eleifend sollicitudin, molestie id, varius et, nibh. Donec nec libero.

Footer

2. In `#mainContent`, adjust the padding to 30px on the left to create the space and alignment we want down the page. Leave the
20px on the right.

To float the `#mainContent`, we'll need to give it a width. In the
case of this layout, due to the fixed overall width, that's not
too difficult. We're geeks—surely we all aced math class, right?
Start with the overall width and begin subtracting anything
that will affect the box model to see what we have left.

700 - 9 - 9 = 682px.

(That's the wrapper width minus the padding on the container
that holds the rest of the page elements). Then we'll subtract
the side column space (don't forget the padding and border),
giving us 682 - 184 - 20 - 20 = 458px.

Finally, we'll subtract the padding we're placing on `#mainCon-
tent` itself, 458 - 20 - 30 = 408px.

In the CSS code, a comment next to the margin declaration
on the `#mainContent` div partially reads, "the right margin on
this div element creates the column down the right side of the
page—no matter how much content the **sidebar1** div contains,
the column space will remain." The comment is referring to
creating the space *for* the right side column. But we won't need
this space anymore when we float the column. We'll be giving
the column a width instead of creating the space with a margin, so the margin will be set to 0 all the way around. Lastly,
we'll float the side column to the left.

3. To the `#mainContent` div, alter or add these properties:

margin: 0

width: 408px

float: left

```
#mainContent {
  margin: 0;
  padding: 0 20px 0 30px;
  width: 408px;
  float: left;
}
```

The page looks just like it did before. But our source order is
different. Sweet!

Fonts and Final Styling

N *For those of you who have been using CSS for styling only, this may be old hat. Consider this a review.*

Now that the markup, structure, and background images are in order, it's time to turn our attention to the styling.

Anchors and Links

Anchors, commonly referred to as links, are likely the most commonly used CSS selectors. The big thing to remember with anchor styling is LVHA—or LoVe HAte—link, visited, hover, active. This is the order in which our selectors must come if they are to work as we expect.

- **Link:** Unvisited links

- **Visited:** Applies when a user has already visited the destination link

- **Hover:** Links are designated with a pointing device but not activated

- **Active:** Applies while activated by the user

- **Focus:** Applies while an element has focus (is able to accept keyboard events)

The above list includes one state that's not in our love-hate mnemonic. Focus is an often-neglected pseudo-class that's important for users who navigate with keyboards. As you know, a pointing device activates the hover state but keyboard navigators can't point: instead, the focus pseudo-class lets the keyboard navigator know where the keyboard focus resides so he or she can click to navigate to another page. Perhaps you don't think this is a common way to navigate—but for many people with carpal tunnel and other physical limitations, it's the only way.

Because hover and focus serve the same purpose, we like to group them when creating our link rules. We also group active in the same compound grouped selector. You may be wondering why, since active should be showing a different state when the link is clicked on, we grouped it with the others? For users who are navigating with the keyboard using Internet Explorer, `active` actually shows them the keyboard focus instead of `focus`. Thus, by giving the `:hover`, `:active`, and `:focus` states the same properties, the majority of users get to see the styles we've chosen to let them know it's possible to activate a link. (And yes, we're sacrificing the ability to show a different state as the link is clicked, but that's the choice we have to make!)

1. Create a new rule for `a:link` by clicking the New CSS Rule icon. Depending on where your focus is within Dreamweaver, the selector autofilled in the Selector Name field will vary. What is consistent is clicking the drop-down list next to the input. No matter where it starts, it will end with four of the pseudo-classes (the a:focus is missing). Choose `a:link` from the drop-down list. Click OK.

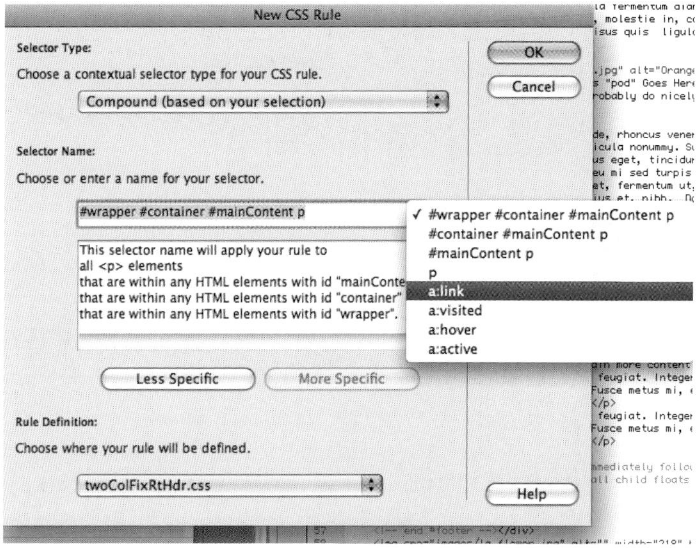

FIGURE 3.38 The drop-down list by the Selector input contains most pseudo-classes.

2. In the Type category, let's choose a dark green: #628958.

3. In the same way, create a new rule for the `a:visited` pseudo-class. This time, choose a more faded-out color, perhaps #666.

4. Finally, create a compound selector for `a:hover, a:active, a:focus`. Set the text-decoration to none and change the color to the orange sampled from the daisy: #CE5441.

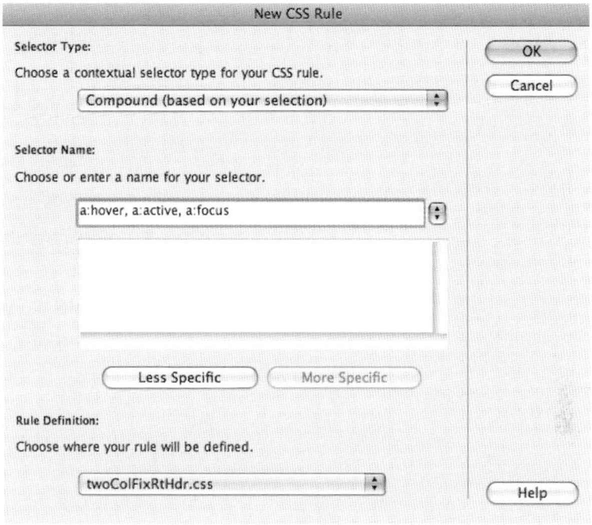

FIGURE 3.39 Creating a grouped selector is simple using the Compound contextual selector drop-down list.

N   *Many times, developers remove underlines from the links and style them using different colors and styles. If you're making your links very different from the other text, this may be fine, but studies have shown that users expect underlines on their links. This means you should never underline text that is not a link. Users will be annoyed when clicking the underlined text doesn't take them to another page.*

Yes, the color could have been anything, but we find that using a highly contrasting color is best. Since orange is the complement to blue (the dominant color on our page), we used Dreamweaver's eyedropper to sample the color from the daisy. We removed the link underline so that if the user was color-blind or had difficulty seeing, the disappearing underline might make the link more apparent.

5. In the `mainContent` and `sidebar1` divs, create a sample link to view the styles we just created. Highlight a word or two in your text and on the HTML portion of the Property inspector, place a hash (#) in the Link input to make it render as a link.

   We notice on previewing in Live View (and notice how you can trigger the hover state right there) that the initial link state in the side column isn't quite as apparent due to the light gray/blue background. We can remedy that with a descendant selector.

6. Create a new rule called `#sidebar1 a`. Either type the selector name in directly as a compound selector or, with your cursor in the `sidebar1` link, allow Dreamweaver to auto-fill the Selector Name input and click Less Specific until it says `#sidebar1 p a`. Remove the p, leaving `#sidebar1 a`. In the Type category, give the weight property the value of `bold`.

The **a** selector without a pseudo-class will apply to, and cascade to, all the **a** pseudo-classes. The rest of the selectors will be inherited from the pseudo-classes we just created. Let's make sure they're in the right order.

7. Change your CSS Styles panel into All mode, select the rules we just created (by shift-clicking them), and drag them up under the **a img** rule. Make sure they're in the proper order: LVHA.

```
a img {
   border: none;
}
#sidebar1 a {
   font-weight: bold;
}
a:link {
   color: #628958;
}
a:visited {
   color: #666;
}
a:hover, a:active, a:focus {
   color: #CE5441;
   text-decoration: none;
}
```

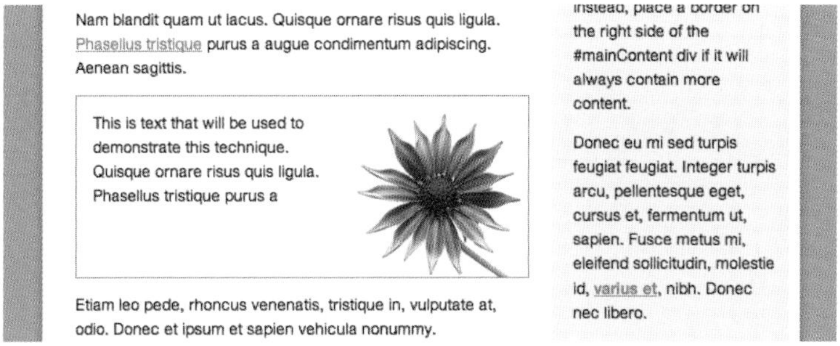

FIGURE 3.40 Using a descendant selector for the links in the side column gives it a heavier weight.

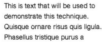

Nam blandit quam ut lacus. Quisque ornare risus quis ligula. Phasellus tristique purus a augue condimentum adipiscing. Aenean sagittis.

This is text that will be used to demonstrate this technique. Quisque ornare risus quis ligula. Phasellus tristique purus a

Etiam leo pede, rhoncus venenatis, tristique in, vulputate at, odio. Donec et ipsum et sapien vehicula nonummy.

instead, place a border on the right side of the #mainContent div if it will always contain more content.

Donec eu mi sed turpis feugiat feugiat. Integer turpis arcu, pellentesque eget, cursus et, fermentum ut, sapien. Fusce metus mi, eleifend sollicitudin, molestie id, varius et, nibh. Donec nec libero.

Before we move on to the next section, feel free to check your work using index_5.html in the builds directory.

Styling the Headings

Be sure, as you create font cascades for headings, that the fonts look equally good in a normal or bold weight—whichever you've chosen to use. Also, be careful of using letter spacing since some fonts don't render it as well as others.

Headings, that is h1, h2, h3, h4, etc. elements, are important to search engine spiders. Many a developer or designer has made the mistake of using a p element, placing a class on it, and styling it *as if* it is a heading. But that's not *nearly* as yummy to a spider. They love those semantically marked headings. And after all, we really want to give them what they want!

Since all the headings on our site will use the same color, font, and letter spacing, we'll set those values in one simple grouped selector. (As you remember from Chapter 2, element (tag) selectors save a lot of weight in our CSS when properly used.)

1. Create a grouped selector for headings 1 through 4. In the Type category, set them all to use the **Font-family** (pre-made in the Dreamweaver font drop-down list) that begins with Georgia. Set the **Font-weight** to normal, the **color** to #628958. In the Block category, set the Letter-spacing to -.04em.

    ```
    h1, h2, h3, h4 {
        font-family: Georgia, "Times New Roman", Times, serif;
        font-weight: normal;
        color: #628958;
        letter-spacing: -0.04em;
    }
    ```

    All headings, whether in the #mainContent or #sidebar1, will get the font cascade starting with Georgia, and will be green with a close letter spacing, and a normal weight font.

If you look at the page, you'll see that although we've got our nice green styled headings, our first mainContent heading is hiding under the absolutely positioned flower at the top of our layout. This is obviously one of the treacheries of absolute positioning— the other elements are blind to the positioned element's placement. But we can easily work around this issue. First, we'll make the header the proper size using additional padding.

FIGURE 3.41 The flower has overlapped the heading in the mainContent area.

2. Click into the **header** div and change the bottom padding to match the top: 40px.

   This will shift the entire area below the header down, including the side column. If we shifted the side column itself down with top margin, the faux column would show above it and ruin the look of the rounded corner. So the side column must remain snug against the header—and be moved down using the header.

   Though our designer has specified that headings in the **mainContent** div should be right aligned (which will take care of the overlapping problem as long as the headings are short), we're going to add a fix now for left-aligned designs or longer headings.

3. Place your cursor into the h1 in the **mainContent** area. Create a selector and click Less Specific until you have **#mainContent h1** left as the selector name. In the Positioning category, set the **Position** to relative and the **Z-index** to 2. In the Type category, give it a **Font-size** of 180%. Click OK.

   Adding positioning to the heading, even without shifting its placement, allows us to set the position and stacking order. By adding a positive z-index value, we have actually placed the heading on top of the absolutely positioned flower.

FIGURE 3.42 The heading now overlaps the flower in the mainContent area.

4. Add to the **#mainContent h1** rule, Text-align right from the Block category and 20px of right margin in the Box category.

   Now we'll define the size and alignment of the **h2** selector and create some space above it.

5. Create a selector for the #mainContent h2 rule. In the Type category set a font-size of 150%. In the Box category, give it a top margin of 35px and 20px of right margin. In the Block category, choose Text-align right.

   Since the element selectors have been created for h1-h4 with color, font and style, it's not necessary to re-create these declarations.

6. Create an element selector with a font-size of 130% to size the h3 element in any div.

   Your final outcome for the above selectors should appear as follows:

```
#mainContent h1 {
    position: relative;
    z-index: 2;
    font-size: 180%;
    text-align: right;
    margin-right: 20px;
}
#mainContent h2 {
    font-size: 150%;
    margin-top: 35px;
    text-align: right;
    margin-right: 20px;
}
h3 {
    font-size: 130%;
}
```

Evening the Side Column

One of the common issues many of us struggle with is margin collapse (or margin escape). We discussed it at the end of Chapter 2. In the IECC included in this, and several other, CSS layouts, padding is added at the top of #sidebar1 or #sidebar2 to force IE to render the same as the other browsers. But we're going to solve the problem using a different technique here: we will zero the top margin of any element that is the first element inside a div where there is *not* a border (if there is a border, it's unnecessary).

First, we'll create a class we can use to remove the margin at the top, then we'll remove the selector in the IECC that created the padding at the top of the div.

1. Create a class called `.noTop` and give it a top margin of 0.

   ```
   .noTop {
     margin-top: 0;
   }
   ```

N   *The same technique can prevent margin collapse and escape at the bottom of an element. Simply create a class called .noBott and give it a margin-bottom: 0. Apply it to the last element in the div. If you don't have that much control (i.e., dynamic content), read the sidebar at the very end of Chapter 2 called Margin Collapse for an explanation of other methods that can be used as well.*

2. Apply the class to both the `h1` in `#mainContent` and the `h3` in `#sidebar1`.

   You'll notice that the headings move up substantially. This evens various browser defaults on the heading elements, avoids margin collapse and escape, and makes things work evenly across browsers. Since we removed the top margin for the top headings, we can re-create the space needed with top padding. Padding does not collapse and escape like margin.

3. Place your cursor into the `h1` in `mainContent`. In the CSS Styles panel, click Add Property and choose `padding-top`. Set the value to .05em.

   It's best to use em units, sizing based on the font size, to set the padding. This way if the text size is scaled up, the padding will scale in the same proportions. (Read more about em units in Chapter 5.)

4. Create a descendant selector for the `sidebar1 h3` selector. We currently have a rule for *all* h3 elements. Since we may have an h3 in the `mainContent` area as well, we want to specifically target only the h3 in the side column. Give it a top padding value of 1em.

   All h3 elements on our page will have their default padding. Only an h3 in the side column will be changed. Since the side column comes with top padding, the side column has more space than we need.

   ```
   h3 {
   font-size: 130%;
   }
   #sidebar1 h3 {
   padding-top: 1em;
   }
   ```

5. Place your cursor into the **sidebar1** div and change the top padding to 0 so that it matches the top padding in the **mainContent** div. Give the bottom padding a value of 0 since it's not needed.

With the bottom rounded corner graphic in the footer, there will always be a little bit of extra space between the text and bottom graphic, so no additional padding is needed there.

```
#sidebar1 {
    float: right;
    width: 184px;
    padding: 0 20px;
    background: url(images/corner_tl.gif) no-repeat;
}
```

6. Find the IECC rule in the page head (within the if IE conditional comment) called **#sidebar1** and delete it.

```
#sidebar1 { padding-top: 30px; }
```

FIGURE 3.43 Nice, even top elements!

Drop Caps—Simple Page Interest

If you don't need to support IE6 and earlier, still at about 25% market share at the time of this writing, you can explore using the pseudo-elements to create a drop cap to keep your (X)HTML clean.

The print world has used drop caps, those large first letters that span 3-4 lines of text, to their advantage for years. But before CSS, it was difficult to pull drop caps off on the web unless you used images. Although the `first-letter` and `first-child` pseudo-elements were created for CSS 2, we still have to deal with lack of support in older browsers. Now, with a small amount of markup, drop caps are a snap.

A great chart that shows browser CSS selector support is at Estelle Weyl's blog, Evotech. http://www.evotech.net/ blog/2008/05/browser-css-selector-support/

The secret is in the span element. Spans, which render inline by default, are handy elements for styling. In this case, we'll create a class called `.dropcap` and apply it to the first letter of any paragraph we want styled this way, using a span.

1. Create a `.dropcap` class and set it to float left.

   This allows the text that follows the drop cap to appear in lines next to the drop cap until the text runs out of space, then wrap around the drop cap.

2. In the Type category, use the same Font-family cascade as the headings: Georgia, Times New Roman, Times, and serif. Set the Font-size to 5em with .85em in the Line-height input. Choose the blue color (**#7F98C3**) of the page background as the Color.

   This gives us some continuity with the rest of the page in the styling, but uses a really large font. The line-height allows us to snug things up around the letter and remove some of the white space around it. It's better not to decrease it below .8em. If you do IE 6 will sometimes cut part of the letter off.

There are a variety of ways to style a drop cap. You can use a border and background color, creating a box around the span. Fantasy and cursive fonts can also be used. Experiment!

3. In the Box category, set the padding on the top to .03em with .1em on the right. Leave the bottom and left set to 0.

   This simply allows a little breathing room around the letter.

```
.dropcap {
    font: 5em/.85em Georgia, "Times New Roman", Times,
serif;
    padding: .03em .1em 0 0;
    float: left;
    color: #7F98C3;
}
```

4. In your HTML document, highlight the first letter of the first paragraph under the **h1** element. Right-click and choose CSS Styles > **dropcap**. If you'd like to see another letter styled (not another L from Lorem), remove the first few words of the first paragraph below the **h2** heading and apply the span again.

FIGURE 3.44 A large drop cap for visual interest.

Completing the Footer

Typically, footers contain information that needs to be included on each page, such as copyrights. They tend to be a little less obvious with smaller font sizing.

1. Add some fake copyright text to the **p** element in the footer div.

2. Change the **#footer p** selector so that there's 70px of padding on the right and 20px on the left with 0 on the top and bottom. Set the text alignment to center.

   Adding the padding to the right side allows the text to miss the flower that's absolutely positioned on the right.

3. Give the text a medium gray color (#666) and decrease the font-size to 70%.

   ```
   #footer p {
     margin: 0;
     padding: 0 70px 0 20px;
     text-align: center;
     color: #666;
     font-size: 70%;
   }
   ```

Bust the Bugs

Now that our page is exactly as we'd like it in standards-compliant browsers, it's time to turn our attention to the browser with a mind of its own, Internet Exploder...errrr, Internet Explorer. If you're on a Mac, you'll need to access the page using your favorite way to view on the PC side so you can see what we're looking at here. The last exercise ended with index_6.html in the builds directory if you need to check your work before you get started.

Adjusting Values for IE5—Quirks Mode

First, in Internet Explorer 5-series browsers, we're dealing with the broken box model. This means that items that have width plus padding and/or border have to be recalculated and different values fed to IE using an IECC. Currently in our page, there's an IECC for IE5 which holds a different value for the **#sidebar1** width only.

We need to change the width of **#sidebar1** to be 224px. This is the declared width (184px) plus the padding for the sides (20px + 20px). The quirks mode box model width is placed in the IECC.

We'll also change the source order and declared a width on the **#mainContent** div. In the IE5 IECC, add a selector for **#mainContent** with the width set to 458px. (That's 408px + 20px + 30px = 458px.)

Your code should look like this:

Place CSS box model fixes for IE5 in this conditional comment.

```
<!--[if IE 5]>
<style type="text/css">
  #sidebar1 { width: 224px; }
  #mainContent { width: 458px; }
</style>
<![endif]-->
```

hasLayout Issues Abound

If you don't have access to IE6, look at Figure 3.45 to see what is going on. The header isn't showing its background color. Since the header had a gray background color by default, and that showed just fine, we can be sure that the problem is caused by some interaction that we've created as we changed things.

FIGURE 3.45 Business as usual. Internet Explorer 6 has issues in the header area.

By sleuthing and commenting out the **position:relative** on the **#wrapper** div, we find it's the typical IE **hasLayout** problem. (You can read more about this in Chapter 2.)

Since we can't remove the `position:relative` (it's needed to allow the top flower to be positioned properly), we can simply add the `#header` to the rule that gives the `zoom:1` declaration to the `#main-Content` in the IECC that targets all versions of IE (`<!--[if IE]>`).

In fact, we can also remove the `#mainContent` from that rule since we've changed the source order and given it a width. (A width is one of the properties that triggers layout for an element.) We no longer need to include `maincontent` in that IECC.

We've got a small issue with the pod we placed on our page. It's not containing the float—and we've got a clearing element included. Rather than spend a lot of time on it, why don't we just try the `hasLayout` fix right off the bat?

FIGURE 3.46 Another issue with our pod.

This is text that will be used to demonstrate this technique. Quisque ornare risus quis ligula. Phasellus tristique purus a

Etiam leo pede, rhoncus venenatis, tristique in, vulputate at,

You may have noticed the `zoom:1` declaration fixes a whole host of IE sins. Before the advent of IE7, we used the holly hack in a similar way— `* html .targetElement { height: 1px; }`. *That is no longer recommended.*

Adding the `.pod` class to the `zoom:1` rule in the IECC causes the `.pod` to contain its content.

Lastly, both IE6 and 7 show some rendering quirkiness at the footer (IE7 doesn't quite meet up with the bottom shadow and IE6 seems to lose some of the outer glow). Again, the first fix we try is `zoom:1`. And once again, we find that adding the #footer rule to our IECC has fixed the rendering issue.

Place CSS hasLayout fixes for all versions of IE in this conditional comment.

```
<!--[if IE]>
<style type="text/css">
#header, #footer, .pod { zoom: 1; }
</style>
<![endif]-->
```

Using Check Browser Compatibility

As far as we can tell, our page is peachy keen. But let's try one more thing. Dreamweaver has a new feature that will help you track down the most common bugs—and give you the fix for them as well. It's called Check Browser Compatibility and it's accessed through the Check Page icon in the Standard toolbar. We'll run it now to see if there are possible bugs we've not run into in our testing.

FIGURE 3.47 The Check Page icon in the Standard toolbar.

N *Dreamweaver currently has no way of "seeing" the rules in your IECC. They appear to Dreamweaver to be comments and thus are not manageable in the CSS panel or seen by Check Browser Compatibility. If you have added the proper fix to an IECC, rest assured that even if Dreamweaver continues to show it, it's fixed.*

Check Browser Compatibility has determined there are three possible bugs on our page. It gives us a description of them, which browser or browsers they affect and the likelihood of encountering them. It also gives you a View Solutions link at the bottom right so you can read more about the bug and its solutions at Adobe's CSS Advisor site. CSS Advisor is a moderated wiki where you can add issues and bugs you've found as well. Though it contains information on the most common bugs that Dreamweaver can spot and report, it also contains loads of details on many, many other bugs—and it grows all the time.

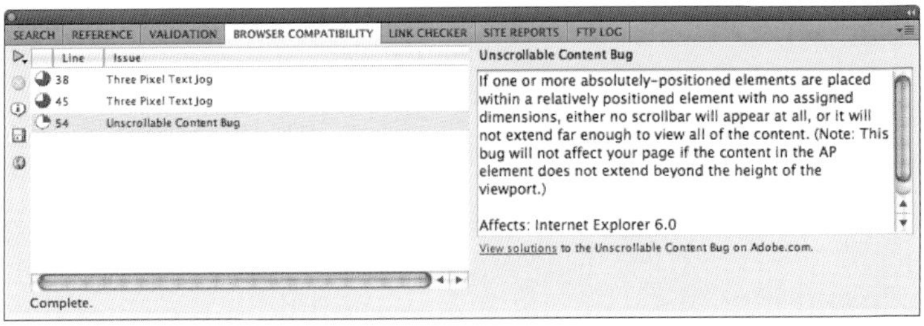

FIGURE 3.48 Check Browser Compatibility has reported three possible bugs.

N *When using IECC to fix bugs or override styles, it's best to have them as the last element, or at least the last CSS element, inside the head of your document to make sure that they are applied properly. It's also best to remove all the rules from each IECC and place them into their own style sheet and link it from within the IECC. This allows you to change values sitewide (instead of having the selectors embedded in the head of each page).*

For our page, the first two in the report are related to the Three Pixel Text Jog. Double-clicking the line number takes us to our drop caps in both cases, so we're not too concerned about the issue. However, the Unscrollable Content Bug, though we don't necessarily see it with our large browser, could be a problem for some users. Fortunately, the fix is simple. Once again, apply `zoom:1` to the affected element.

When double-clicking the problem line in the reporting window, Dreamweaver gives focus to the `#footer` as well as highlighting the possible trigger, `position:relative`, in the CSS Styles panel. Since we already added the `#footer` div to the IECC containing the compound group of rules for `zoom:1` previously, we're good to go!

Looks like all our bugs are squashed flat!

Declaring Media Types

N *If you don't see the Style rendering toolbar at the top of your document, right-click on the top of the document and select it (or go to View > Toolbars). If you previously used Dreamweaver CS3, you may notice the icon that toggles styles on and off has changed.*

CSS gives us the ability to declare a media type in relation to a rule or an entire style sheet. Media types allow the author to specify how a document should be presented for a variety of media. From screen to print, from handheld to aural—it all sounds so useful. Sadly, the reality of the situation, at least at the printing of this book, is that many user agents don't support media types well, if at all.

The handheld media type may become more useful as pressure is placed on the industry to support it. Until then, the two basic media types of which to be aware are screen and print.

Be default, if no media type is specified, a style sheet is applied to all media. If you want the media type to only apply to a single media type, you can declare only one. But you can also declare more than one media type by creating a grouped list of media types, separated by a comma.

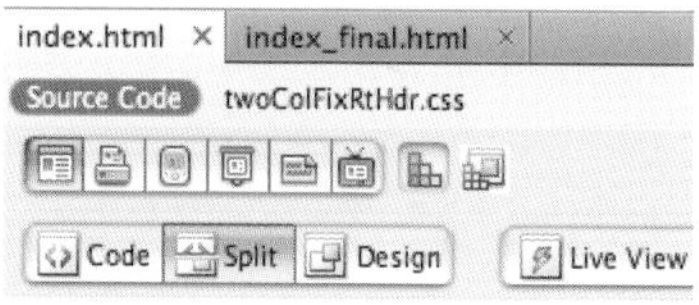

FIGURE 3.49 Dreamweaver allows us to preview media types directly in Design view using the style rendering toolbar.

A typical linked style sheet with a media type of screen looks like this:

```
<link href="main.css" rel="stylesheet" type="text/css" media="screen" />
```

Rules for Creating a Simple Print Style Sheet

There are two basic methods of creating a print style sheet. Using your browser's print preview will give you an idea of what your user will see, but not all browsers print the same way, so checking a variety of browsers is always a good idea.

- Give your main style sheet a media type of `all` (or leave it with no media type, which will default to `all`). Then, override all the styles you need to with a second style sheet with the media type of `print`.

- Give your main style sheet a media type of `screen`. Then, create a second style sheet with the media type of `print` that gives basic styling to the flow of your page.

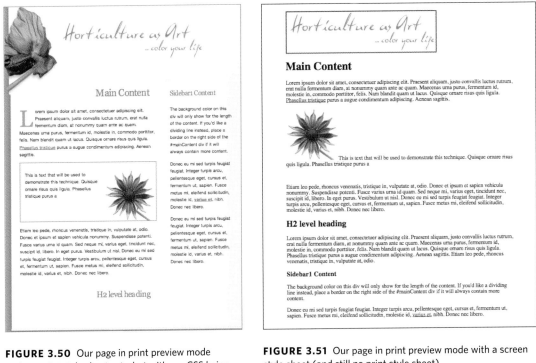

FIGURE 3.50 Our page in print preview mode with no print style sheet yet—but with our CSS being applied.

FIGURE 3.51 Our page in print preview mode with a screen style sheet (and still no print style sheet).

Both methods work: choosing which one to use basically depends on the way your site is coded. Often there are simply a few items to hide—such as unnecessary images—and some background, font, and color changes. If your information is marked up semantically, you're 75% of the way there.

If you're using the File > New dialog, you do not have the option of declaring the media type at that time. When attaching a style sheet, Dreamweaver has a media type input where you can choose the media type. But once the CSS file is attached to the page, the best way to declare the media type is to type directly into the link code (in the head of your (X)HTML document) and use Dreamweaver's code hinting.

But let's face it, when someone prints a web page, it's rarely because they're in love with the design and want to remember it. Typically, it's because there's some information there that they want to keep. So giving them neatly formatted text, in black, white and gray (to save their color ink) is usually all you need.

We won't go through the entire creation process here, but we'll give you the principles to use as you create your own.

- When allowing the main style sheet to apply to `print` as well as `screen`, you'll likely want to hide some elements. Use `display:none`, not `visibility:hidden`. The former creates no box, or space, on the page. The latter *will* hide the element, but the space for the element will be reserved. Likely elements to be hidden include unnecessary navigation, search forms, and interactive elements with no functionality in the print medium.

- Perhaps a client has a busy, colorful logo on their site, but for print, they have a black and white version. You can actually place both logos into the HTML. In the screen page, show the colorful one and set the print logo to `display:none`. In the print style sheet, set the print logo to `display:block` and set the screen logo to `display:none`.

- Use grouped rules to hide elements using `display: none`. A list of selector names separated by commas may save a good deal of space.

- Hide unnecessary background colors and images in your print style sheet using the declaration `background: none`. In print, the user has control over whether or not background images print from their device. It's best to remove them to make sure proper contrast exists between background and text.

- For the same reason, if you've used background images as list markers in your site, place the list markers back on your lists for print.

- Change your body fonts to serifs as they are more legible in print. Feel free to use points instead of pixels. This *is* print, after all.

- Change your headings and links to black or grays to save your user's color ink.

- Hide any unnecessary images. Obviously, you don't want to hide all images if you're dealing with a site selling homes or art. People may want to print those photos. But for many sites, decorative images are not necessary for print. If you choose to hide all images, you can add the `img` tag to the grouped selector that you created for the `display:none` declaration, or alternatively, add a class that you can then place on any images that need to be hidden.

- You may want to allow the information to flow instead of keeping it floated. Floats and absolute positioning are sometimes problematic in printing—edges can be cut off. Adding `float: none` or `position: static` will reset these values.

- Setting a width and margins using inches or centimeters on the body can sometimes be helpful for rendering.

- Since links can't be clicked in a printed document, it's best to either remove the underline or add the full path for the URL if it's important. Though it won't work in all versions of Internet Explorer, you can show your URL paths for compliant browsers by using generated content and the `:after` pseudo-element. We won't get into detail here, but adding the following code will allow the href attribute of your links to be shown as their full paths in the print style sheet:

```
a:after { content:" [" attr(href) "] "; }
```

Wrapping It Up

In this chapter, you've looked at some advantages and disadvantages of a fixed-width layout. You set your preferences in Dreamweaver and learned about using shorthand with CSS. We looked at a variety of ways to create faux columns, discovered source order, got some more detail on floating and clearing, and spent some time exploring when it's safe to use absolute positioning.

Finally, we looked at print style sheets and media types.

CHAPTER 4

Using the Liquid CSS Layouts

WITH THE PROLIFERATION of large monitors, creating a layout that serves the same fixed width (typically either 800 x 600 or 1024 x 768) to all browsers may leave a good deal of empty space on some screens. Clients often question this unused space, since using more of the viewer's screen *must* give the client more bang for their buck, right? Liquid layouts, based on a percentage of the size of the browser's window (or viewport), are one way to create flexible sites that work for a variety of users.

In this chapter, we will look at the pros and cons of creating a liquid layout using our fictional client, the Pleasantville Regional Chamber of Commerce. Their in-house designer has sent us a Photoshop comp and has requested that the blue portion of the design fill the browser window. They want no space on the sides.

FIGURE 4.1 The design comp from their in-house designers shows their vision of the site.

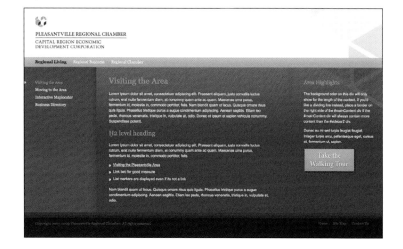

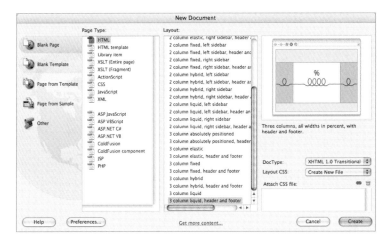

Before proceeding, define a site within Dreamweaver CS4 and create a folder called Pleasantville to contain your files (and the images from this chapter's download if you're not going to slice the comp yourself).

The easiest way to fill the browser window and remain flexible is to use one of Dreamweaver's three-column liquid layouts with header and footer. The liquid layouts are composed of percentage-based columns contained within a percentage-based container. We'll need to make a few modifications to achieve the desired effect, but we'll discuss that as we go.

1. Create a new page using File > New.

2. In the Blank Page section of the dialog, select the 3 column liquid, header and footer layout.

3. Set the DocType to XHTML 1.0 Transitional and make sure that Create New File is selected in the Layout CSS drop-down list.

FIGURE 4.2 Choose the 3 column liquid, header and footer layout.

To work efficiently with CSS, most of the time you'll establish your rules in an external CSS file, not in the page itself as is done here. As a general rule (no pun intended), even if you develop the rules locally, you should move them to an external style sheet. But, of course, the exception proves the rule (pun intended); on rare occasions, you'll have an instance of a rule designed to override a style on one single, solitary page in a site. In that case, it's perfectly acceptable to define the rule within the head of the page.

4. Click Create.

   Dreamweaver allows you to name the CSS file as well as determine where it will reside in your site structure. If you use the defaults, your file will be called thrColLiqHdr.css and will reside in the root folder of your site.

5. Save the (X)HTML file as index.html into the root of your site.

Simplifying the CSS Selectors

Since our pages will all contain three columns in this site, we won't need to mix different types of CSS layouts. As we discussed previously, if you don't need to mix layouts, you don't need to keep the class on the body that precedes the selectors. For simplicity's sake, and to make the selectors more readable in the CSS panel, let's strip out all the `.thrColLiqHdr` classes.

1. At the top of your index.html page, click the thrColLiqHdr.css on the Related Files toolbar.

    If you were working in another view, you'll be placed in Code and Design view. Remember, if you have the monitor space, you can split your views vertically on the new Application Bar.

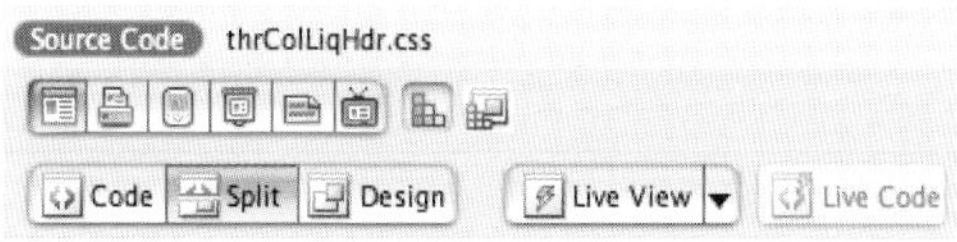

FIGURE 4.3 The Related Files toolbar showing both the Source Code and the linked CSS document.

2. Highlight a class that begins with `.thrColLiqHdr` in the CSS of your document (as well as the space behind it) and use Ctrl+F to open the Find and Replace dialog.

    It opens with the class you highlighted in the Find portion of the window. Make sure Find in is set to Current Document and leave the Replace area blank.

3. Click Replace All.

    Dreamweaver quickly strips those classes right out of the CSS document.

FIGURE 4.4 The Find and Replace dialog with the `.thrColLiqHdr` class highlighted.

4. Move back to Source Code on your Related Files toolbar and repeat the process. Also, place your cursor anywhere in the page and right-click on `<body.thrColLiqHdr>` in the tag selector. Choose Set Class > None from the drop-down list.

    This removes the class applied to the body selector.

N *Remember that when using the Related Files toolbar, Dreamweaver will save the document that has the focus. Placing your cursor into the CSS or Source (design or code space) will save the respective file. In fact, if you want to put a file to your server, the same holds true. The file put is the file that has focus.*

N *In order to determine the color value of a given element in a Photoshop or Fireworks comp, you'll need to arrange your screen so that both documents are visible. Then click on Dreamweaver's color picker in the CSS Rule dialog or in the CSS Styles panel's Properties section for any property that uses color. On the Mac, simply move the eyedropper over the section of the comp you are interested in sampling and click to confirm the choice. On the PC, hold the mouse button down as you drag out of the color picker and release the mouse when you are over the desired section of the comp.*

5. Save both documents.

We're ready to begin the process of modifying the page for our intended layout.

Since our design uses 100% of the browser window, the background color on the body element will no longer be visible on the sides. But if we are working in a short page (which might happen if a user is working on a high-resolution monitor with their browser viewport quite large), the space below the footer will show the background color, or lack of color if none is defined. A white space below the footer will be visible, and with this design that could be quite jarring. Sampling the footer color and using it for our overall background color allows us to leave the footer background transparent and ensure we have a seamless transition when our page ends. The dark blue will simply continue to the bottom of the user's browser viewport.

1. Open the CSS Styles panel in the Current view. Select <body> on the tag selector. Click the edit (pencil) icon at the bottom of the CSS Styles panel.

2. In the Background category, change the Background-color to #1b1a52.

Notice that in the comp from our designer, all the fonts except those in the main body are rendered in Georgia.

3. While you're in the CSS Rule dialog, change the font property to the preset font set of Georgia, Times New Roman, Times, serif and click OK.

Viewing the CSS document, you'll notice the body selector is now changed to:

```
body {
  font: 100% Georgia, "Times New Roman", Times, serif;
  background: #1b1a52;
  margin: 0;
  padding: 0;
  text-align: center;
  color: #000000;
}
```

For some designs, we'd want the container (the div that contains all other divs) to be a percentage of the total browser width, and centered. In this case, we want the design to fill the entire window, so we'll adjust the width.

4. Click anywhere in the main layout and select `<div#container>` from the tag selector.

   In the Properties section of the CSS panel, you'll notice that this layout, by default, is 80% of the browser window (based on the body rule which is left at its default 100%).

5. Change the width value in the Properties pane to 100%.

   We also won't need the border, nor will we need to center the div using the value of auto assigned to the side margins since it will completely fill the browser window. Later, we will be bringing our colors and images in through other divs, so the background can go as well.

   Many times, when you're dealing with a layout that is predominantly white (or any other color), it's simplest to define that color in the overall #container rule.

6. Delete the border and margin properties by right-clicking each property in the Properties pane and choosing Delete or by selecting the property and clicking the trashcan icon at the bottom of the panel.

   Finally, let's scale all our fonts down since the 16px size most browser defaults are set at is rather large.

7. With `<div#container>` still selected in the tag selector, click the Add Property link in the Properties pane of the CSS Styles panel and type (or choose from the drop-down list) font-size. Tab to the next input field and type 80%.

   Our #container rule is now:

```
#container {
  width: 100%;
  background: #FFFFFF;
  text-align: left;
  font-size: 80%;
}
```

We've now completed the preliminaries and we're ready to move on to creating our client's actual page.

Creating the Header

In this chapter, we will be using Photoshop as the basis for our comp. If you prefer to use Adobe Fireworks, that's fine—simply substitute Fireworks for each of our references to Photoshop. We're also not going to give true step-by-step instructions for the tasks you need to complete in your graphics program, since we can't know what software you're using, and it's beyond the scope of the book. If you prefer not to complete the graphics-related tasks, you can always use the files you've downloaded from the book's web site. They can be found in the images directory for the site.

FIGURE 4.5 Opening a Photoshop file with Fireworks gives you a dialog box with many options.

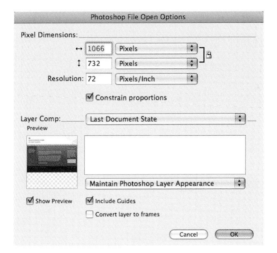

With each version of the Creative Suite, Fireworks and Photoshop understand each other a little better. We find that these days, there's very little Fireworks can't render from Photoshop. Feel free to use Fireworks if you're more comfortable slicing and exporting there.

Open the comp from the source folder in either Photoshop or Fireworks. Since the logo is created using the Minion Pro font, and this is not a common font, we'll slice and export the entire logo area. Create a slice around the little box image and the words in the logo. Export it into the images directory of your site as a transparent gif matted to white. We named ours logo.gif, but feel free to use any naming convention you commonly use.

We also need to slice the triangles on the right side of the header in the comp. Slice them as close as you can to the left side and export as a transparent gif (or png) matted to white. Name the file logo_background.gif.

Inserting the Background Image

N *Though there are many ways to edit CSS within Dreamweaver, we find that using the CSS dialog is simplest when dealing with background images.*

1. In Dreamweaver, select the XHTML file and click in the **header** div. Click **<div#header>** in the tag selector so that the CSS panel shows the properties of the header and not the header **h1**, and click the pencil icon at the bottom of the CSS styles panel to edit the header.

   If you look at the Box category, you'll notice that there is 10px of padding on the right and left sides of the header in this starter layout. We're not going to need this padding.

N *A quick way to get rid of margin or padding values that vary is to click the "Same for all" checkbox, then delete the top value. All values will be removed.*

2. Delete the values in the padding fields. In the Background pane, change the Background-color: to #FFF.

3. Click Browse and navigate to the logo_background graphic you just exported. Click Choose.

4. Select **no-repeat** in the Background-repeat drop-down list. Click Apply.

   Notice that our graphic is showing in the header, but it's on the left. This is because, unless we position it otherwise, a graphic always positions itself from the top left of the element it's placed on. Let's move ours to the right.

FIGURE 4.6 Backgrounds on elements begin by default at the top left.

N *If you prefer to use short-hand, as we do, the white background can be written as #FFF. Color shorthand uses the first (r), third (g) and fifth (b) digit of the color, as long as they're identical to the second, fourth, and sixth. So, for instance, #FF0066 is written as #F06, #CC3333 is written as #C33, and #000000 is written as #000.*

5. In the Background-position (X), choose right. In the Background-position (Y), choose top for the positioning. Our code looks like this:

```
#header {
  background: #FFF url(images/logo_background.gif)
no-repeat right top;
}
```

Back in Design view, notice that the word Header (as an **h1** element) is sitting boldly on the left, with only a tiny bit of the background image we just placed within apparent on the right. Don't worry—the header simply has no idea that graphic is there, or how large it is, since it's a background image. The amount of graphic showing depends on the amount of content in the header, and we're about to replace that content as well. Though it's going to get ugly for a minute, we'll be fixed up in no time.

N *We also keep our preferences set to write shorthand for
all other properties as well. This
means that rather than having four
property/value pairs for the background, we have one declaration
as seen in step 4.*

6. With your cursor in the header div, right-click the `<h1>` on the tag selector and choose Remove Tag. The word Header will become highlighted. Simply hit the Delete or Backspace key to remove it completely.

   With no content in the header div, this will remove all but the smallest trace of the background image for the moment.

   Since we won't be using any **h1**s in the header within our site, go ahead and delete the **#header h1** rule.

7. Switch to the All pane of the CSS Styles panel, right-click the rule for the **h1**, and choose Delete.

Inserting the Logo

N *The alt attribute is not only
an important accessibility resource
for screen readers and those navigating with images turned off, but
it is also a required attribute when
writing your document in XHTML.*

Making graphics as small as possible keeps the page weight light, so we sliced right around the logo. In the original Photoshop comp, the logo sits 20px from the top and 40px from the left so we'll position it in the same place in Dreamweaver. (If you sliced your logo differently, you'll need to adjust your values so that the alignment of the logo matches the navigation and sidebar below it).

1. Place your cursor into the header and, on the Common tab of the Insert bar, click the image icon. Navigate to your logo.gif and click Choose.

   The Image Tag Accessibility Attributes dialog will appear, where you can give your image an alt attribute and, if necessary, a long description.

2. Fill in the descriptive text for your image (exactly what it says in the graphic) and click OK.

   Most users expect to click the logo to link back to the home page. This is a good reason *not* to place the logo into the header as a background image. A CSS background image has no alt attribute, so a non-visual user agent would not even know it existed; background images are best left for decorative, unimportant graphics.

N *Placing a hash mark or octothorpe into the Link field will cause it to render as if it were a link. If you don't know what your exact link location will be, it's easy to use this trick to get the rendering you need.*

3. With the logo image selected, use the Property inspector to link it to your site's index page (or the URL where your index page will eventually reside).

Viewing in Design view with the image deselected, you'll see we now have a lovely blue border around the image. Dreamweaver (and some browsers) use this border to indicate a link. But it spoils our design. We can quickly remove that blue indicator, as well as the blue around any images we may link later.

4. Add the following code to the end of your CSS document:

```
a img {
border: none;
}
```

Our image is 114 pixels tall—yours may vary based upon how you sliced it. The header area as designed is about 175 pixels tall. Go ahead and give some thought to how we should best make up for that discrepancy so that the header is held open the full height to show the entire background image. And you can't use a height on the div, that's cheating. We'll wait for a moment till you decide…

If your idea was to use a top margin to position the image properly, give yourself a gold star. If you developed the thought a little more and decided you could use a descendant selector as opposed to a class on the image itself, you get even more credit. Kudos to you! That's exactly what we decided.

Since there are no other images directly in the XHTML in our header div we can write a selector that targets *only* the logo image within that header.

N *If you type directly into the CSS document, you'll see that Dreamweaver begins to auto-complete quite quickly after you start typing the first couple of letters of each property. Simply hitting Enter will then complete the property so that you can type the value.*

1. Click the New CSS Rule icon at the bottom of the CSS Styles panel, or type directly into the CSS document, and create a rule called `#header img`.

2. In the Box category of the CSS Rule Definition dialog, use these values for the margins:

top: 30px

right: 0

bottom: 30px

left: 40px

The height of the image (as supplied), plus the 30 pixel top and bottom margins, gives us the height we need for our header. We've also moved it away from the left edge of our page. This holds the header div open and shows the whole background image as designed.

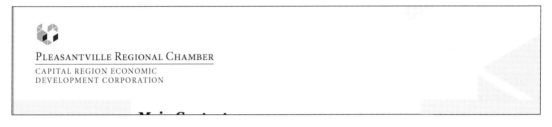

FIGURE 4.7 The header now looks just like the comp we were given.

Paragraphs, Headings, and Lists

Let's begin by dealing with our basic typography styling. Looking at the page with the overall serif font is making our eyes burn! If you need to check your work, or simply want to start in this section, you can use the index_1.html file in the builds directory.

Sometimes, it helps to size and visualize the headings if we change the text to match the comp.

1. Change the text in the `<h1>` in the `mainContent` div to say "Visiting the Area." Change the text in the `<h3>` in `sidebar2` to say "Area Highlights."

   Because sidebar1 will contain our navigation, we won't worry about that heading for now.

   Since our designer gave all the headings a normal weight and orange color, we can create a `font-weight` selector for the entire group of headings. The sizing will have to be changed separately.

2. Place your cursor into one of the headings. On the CSS area of the Property inspector, choose Targeted Rule <New CSS Rule>. Click Edit Rule. (Or create a new CSS rule by clicking the New CSS Rule icon at the bottom of the CSS Styles panel.)

   The New CSS Rule dialog appears auto-filled with the path to your element.

3. Choose Compound Selector Type. In the Selector Name input, type in h1, h2, h3, h4 and click OK.

    This will create a grouped selector where we can place the color and weight.

4. In the Type Category, choose #FF9F00 for the color and set the font-weight to normal. Click OK.

    ```
    h1, h2, h3, h4 {
      color: #FF9F00;
      font-weight: normal;

    }
    ```

    We'll similarly define the font-family and line-height for the para-graphs in our page as well as the lists in the main content area. We're keeping the lists in the main content area separate because our horizontal and vertical menus will be lists as well and we want these properties to be specific and not cascade to the menus.

5. Open the New CSS Rule dialog. Choose Compound selector and type in the grouped selector, p, #mainContent ul, #mainContent ol. In the Type Category, set the font-family to the font group starting with Arial. Set the line-height to 1.5 and select multiple from the list. Click OK.

    This gives us a nice sans-serif font with a bit more breathing room for p elements anywhere in the document and list items in the main content area only.

FIGURE 4.8 Comparing our headings to the comp.

We'll turn our attention the header sizing now. Comparing our comp to our page, we see the h1 in the main content area and h3 in the sidebar are smaller than the designer envisioned. We'll adjust those now by creating simple element selectors for h1-h4 level headings.

6. Place your cursor into the h1 element in the mainContent div. On the CSS area of the Property inspector, you'll see the grouped selector you made for the headings showing in the Targeted Rule select. Change that to <New CSS Rule>. In the Size input you'll see 80%. Type 225% into the text field and press Enter.

N *Though you can get as specific as you like with your selectors, we find that keeping the specificity as low as you can when creating them gives you much more freedom to override selectors later in the game.*

The New CSS Rule dialog will open showing the full path to the element—`#container #mainContent h1` in the Selector Name input. We don't really need to be that specific here.

7. Click Less Specific twice so that only **h1** is showing. Click OK.

   A new rule is created for the **h1** element with the larger font-size.

8. Repeat the process for the **h2** and **h3** selectors. Give the **h2** a font-size of 175% and the **h3** a font-size of 150%.

   Since there is no **h4** element in the page, you will have to create that one using the CSS Styles panel or directly in the CSS document using the Related Files toolbar.

N *If the sizes of your headings are consistent within the various divs, writing a simple type selector works nicely. If you want the size of the side column's h3 to be different than an h3 within your mainContent area, using a descendant selector works better.*

9. Create a rule for the **h4** and give it a font-size of 135%.

   Your new rules should be at the bottom of your CSS document and look like this:

```
h1 {
  font-size: 225%;
}
h2 {
  font-size: 175%;
}
h3 {
  font-size: 150%;
}
h4 {
  font-size: 135%;
}
```

Resetting and Styling the Lists

Lists, left to their defaults, show a good deal of difference in styling from browser to browser. You may have found their spacing odd and hard to control. This is because some browsers use padding and others use margin to indent the list. The easiest way to level the playing field is to create an element selector that zeros the list defaults. Then, place the margin or padding values we need for various lists, including menus.

In the comp at the middle bottom of the `mainContent` area, there are two links styled with the same little triangle indicator graphic as we see on the vertical navigation. In times like these, we need to find out what our graphic designer had in mind. Does she want a specific link style? Or is she indicating that all the unordered lists should have this indicator instead of a regular bullet? After discussion, we found that all unordered lists should be styled with the graphic instead of a bullet.

This means we're safe to remove the bullet from all lists in our site since the menus won't need bullets either. Let's place an unordered list into the middle of the main content area of our page.

1. Place your cursor about halfway through the text below the h2 level heading. Hit Enter twice to break the paragraph as well as create a new one. Arrow up into the empty space. Type some text.

   If you're looking at Source Code in Code and Design view, you'll see you're in a paragraph.

2. On the HTML area of the Property inspector, choose the Unordered List icon (top row, first of the four at the right).

FIGURE 4.9 The Unordered List icon in the HTML area of the Property inspector.

You'll see an indentation and bullet appear in front of your text.

3. Hit Enter and create two more list items. Make one or two of them links as well.

   Many times, especially when dealing with legacy code, designers create something that *appears* to be a list with a fancy bullet by using a two-column table. They place the bullet image in the left column, the text in the right column, and each so-called list item is in its own row. We created a demo that contrasts this common technique with the proper, semantic method that you should be using. You'll find it in the listDemo folder in your source files for this chapter.

   Let's build a properly formatted list with decorative bullets. First, we'll create a selector that will zero the list defaults sitewide.

4. Create a new CSS Rule for the ul element. (You know how to do this by now!) In the Box Category, give it a 0 margin and 0 padding value. In the List Category, choose none in the List style type selector.

    We notice the list is now even with the edge of the paragraph on the left. There is no indentation at all. There are also no list markers. Viewing the CSS in the Related files toolbar, we see:

    ```
    ul {
      margin: 0;
      padding: 0;
      list-style: none;
    }
    ```

    Now it's simply a matter of adding the list graphic.

CREATING A BACKGROUND IMAGE FROM PHOTOSHOP

Obviously, we could create the arrow graphic as we have been doing—simply slice this image in an image editor and export it. But we're going to do something slightly different this time. (If you don't have access to Photoshop, please export the badge from the graphics editor of your choice or use the arrow.gif in the images directory.) In fact, this is a technique you can use to import background images from Photoshop into Dreamweaver—and take advantage of Fireworks' capability to create smaller file sizes.

1. Open the design in Photoshop, and Alt+click on the arrow on the left menu.

    This will find the layer for you in Photoshop.

2. Select Layer > New Layer Based Slice from the Photoshop menu.

    Photoshop creates a slice directly over the tiny arrow icon.

3. Choose Edit > Copy from the Photoshop menu.

    If you've somehow deselected your slice, choose the Slice Select Tool from the Tools bar and click onto the slice just created before copying.

4. In Dreamweaver, place the cursor anywhere in the page. Choose Edit > Paste.

N *Clicking the icon in the bottom right of the optimization dialog will allow you to see the 2-up and 4-up views and compare different compression settings side-by-side—just like exporting from Fireworks.*

N *When you copy/paste an image into Dreamweaver, destined to be a background image, there's no need to input the alt attribute.*

Dreamweaver recognizes that the content on the clipboard is not text but an image, and opens the built-in Fireworks optimization dialog. We can now set the optimization level for the image.

5. Choose to optimize the image as a gif and click OK. Name the image arrow.gif and save it into the images folder of the site.

6. The Image Description (Alt text) accessibilty dialog will open. This is one of the rare instances where we don't need to type anything inside. Click OK.

7. Delete the image from the page.

   The image is now available to us in the images directory, we didn't have to zoom in close to slice it properly and we got the added advantage of a smaller file using headless Fireworks. Groovy!

ADDING THE GRAPHIC TO THE LIST

Now that we have the arrow imported, there are two ways we can use it as a list marker. The first, you can experiment with on your own. Yes, you can place a graphic as a list marker using CSS and the list-style-image property. The problem is, you have no control over placement with that method. Instead, we'll use a much more reliable way—using the background image property and a little padding to keep the text away from the image.

1. Create a new CSS rule called `#mainContent li`.

   By now, you should know this has to be a compound selector.

2. In the Background category, Background image, navigate to the arrow.gif in the images directory. Set the Background repeat to no-repeat and choose left for Background position (X) and center for Background position (Y). Click Apply.

   We've positioned the background image so it will remain nicely centered on the text vertically. However, if we had lists that might have several lines of text, this could look awkward. In that case, we might want to set it to the top, or a couple pixels from the top (to get the proper alignment with the image we're using). Viewing the page, we can see we have a graphic there, but our text is overlapping it!

3. In the Box category, set the left padding to 15px. Click OK.

Don't be alarmed at the odd coloring. We'll attend to that in a bit. For now, we can see that the placement of our image is working just swell.

```
#mainContent li {
  background: url(images/arrow.gif) no-repeat left center;
  padding-left: 15px;
}
```

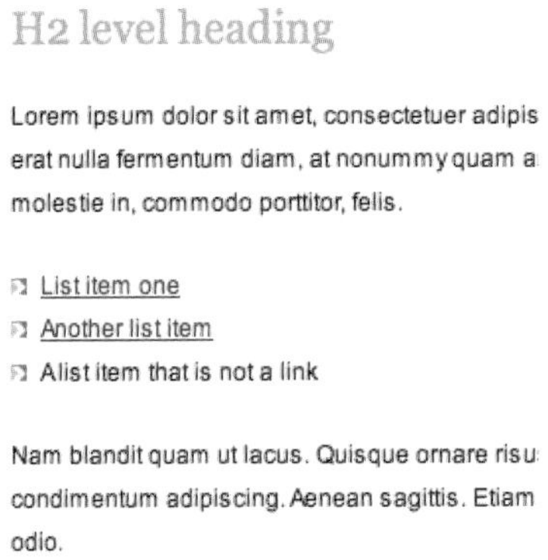

FIGURE 4.10 The Unordered List icon in the HTML area of the Property inspector.

H2 level heading

Lorem ipsum dolor sit amet, consectetuer adipis erat nulla fermentum diam, at nonummy quam a molestie in, commodo porttitor, felis.

▸ List item one
▸ Another list item
▸ A list item that is not a link

Nam blandit quam ut lacus. Quisque ornare risu condimentum adipiscing. Aenean sagittis. Etiam odio.

JUST A QUICK SWEEP!

Though it's fine to leave the rules at the bottom of the page, or to move them at the end of the build, we're kinda weird about staying organized (lest we lose control in a large style sheet). This would be a great time to switch your CSS Styles panel into All mode and move things around a bit. We're using our preferred method (discussed earlier).

1. Ctrl-click all element selectors and drag them up so they begin directly after the body element. We included the **an img** rule as well as the grouped selector that includes the **p** element in the rules we moved.

2. Move the `mainContent` and `header` descendant selectors under their respective divs.

The index_2.html file in the builds directory will allow you to check your work before moving to the next section.

FIGURE 4.11 The rules in their original state and in their organized state.

Creating the Horizontal Navigation Bar

Back in the old days, a horizontal navigation bar like the one in our comp would be created entirely with images. If we wanted to add functionality to show a hover state or which page a user was currently on, we'd use JavaScript. Using CSS, however, is much more lightweight and accessible. You can simply use text within a list to get the same image-like look.

The horizontal navigation is composed of a gradated orange horizontal bar. The designer used two single lines at the top and bottom of the bar to make it appear to have more depth. We'll discuss in a moment how the look will be re-created with CSS, but first, we'll build the semantic, XHTML structure for our navigation.

FIGURE 4.12 The horizontal navigation at 400%—notice the top and bottom lines.

Regional Business

Our header div visually matches the comp. Since we used margins on the image for proper spacing, we can add an unordered list of links after the image. The list doesn't need a class or ID or even to be housed within a separate div. Keeping it within the header lets us use a descendant selector to target *only* the unordered list we'll be styling as our horizontal navigation. We won't affect any of the other lists within the document as long as all our rules that pertain to the horizontal navigation begin with #header.

1. Place your cursor immediately after the logo image and tap the Enter key.

2. Type:

   Regional Living

   Regional Business

   Regional Chamber

3. Select all three entries and click the Unordered List button in the Properties inspector.

   We are not yet sure what page our navigation will actually go to, but we want to style them as links now; using a pound sign or hash mark (#) in the link field will make them display as if they were links.

   Our list looks like this in Code view:

   ```
   <ul>
    <li><a href="#">Regional Living</a></li>
    <li><a href="#">Regional Business</a></li>
    <li><a href="#">Regional Chamber</a></li>
   </ul>
   ```

   When we pressed Enter to move to the next line after the image, Dreamweaver wrapped the image in a <p> element. Since the <p> element is unnecessary in our semantic markup, we'll need to remove it.

4. Click to select the logo on the page, and on the tag selector, right-click on the <p> tag surrounding it and choose Remove Tag.

   Clean, simple, and straightforward, right?

PLEASANTVILLE

CAPITAL REGION
DEVELOPMENT CC

Regional Living
Regional Business
Regional Chamber

FIGURE 4.13 The semantically structured list of links.

Styling the Menu Container

In the world of menus, or any element for that matter, it's always better to allow an increase or decrease in size to happen organically. This allows a user with his or her browser's default set to a different font size to comfortably view the element. In the case of the menu, we could slice the orange bar from top to bottom and assign a height. But if the user's text was larger, the links within the menu could spread outside the orange bar, creating an unsightly mess. There is a creative way to get around this by including the top two lines with the overall image slice and using an orange background color for the rest. This creates a seamless transition between the image and the color. The bottom two lines are then created with CSS.

In your comp, slice from the very top edge of the orange bar down to the area where the gradation ends. We sliced nearly down to, but didn't include, the bottom two lines. Due to the gradient, this should be exported as a jpg. Name it nav_bar_back.jpg.

As we mentioned before, we like to keep our code clean, semantic, and as small as possible. For this reason, the container for our menu is actually the **ul** element itself. Why add an extra container, like a div, when you don't have to? The **ul** will have two other descendants contained within it and both give us styling hooks: the **li** element and the **a** element. Each of these will be given declarations that will, in the end, duplicate the look the designer wanted with no JavaScript or images within the XHTML.

Remember that previously we created an element selector that removed the margin, padding, and list markers for all **ul** elements in the site. Those values will cascade and be applied to this list in the header. Let's start the transition to a navigation bar look. This will require the background image we sliced.

1. Create a selector called **#header ul**.

    As we mentioned before, the principle behind creating this navigation bar so that it can adjust to the user's font size is to *not* limit the height. Remember we only sliced the image with the top two lines included? We'll set that background image to repeat on the x axis (across the page) and we'll use the orange

N *Always remember, there are a myriad of ways to get the same results using CSS. There's no right way for everything. Learning the principles and then making a decision based on the requirements of your design is always the best approach.*

N *Since we've already covered a variety of ways to edit your CSS, including directly in code, in the properties pane of the CSS Styles panel, the CSS area on the Properties inspector, or opening the CSS Rules dialog, choose the method you prefer and use it to modify your properties.*

color our graphic ends with as the background color. Wherever the repeating graphic ends, the orange that matches will show through seamlessly. We sampled the color using the techniques we discussed earlier and came up with **#FFAD00**.

2. For the Background color use #FFAD00. Navigate to the nav_bar_back.jpg and set the Background repeat to repeat-x.

Our rule now looks like this:

```
#header ul {
    background: #FFAD00 url(images/nav_bar_back.jpg) repeat-x;
}
```

Regional Living
Regional Business
Regional Chamber

FIGURE 4.14 The color runs all the way across, but it's too tall!

The color is now completely enveloping the li elements. But they're still stacked up like a regular list.

Choosing Our Horizontal Method

There are two ways to make list items display horizontally— setting their display to inline or floating them. We'll outline the general constraints of each. What you choose when creating your own menus will depend on the type of styling you need to create.

INLINE

When using inline formatting for your menu, the list items are laid out horizontally, one after the other from the top of their containing element. We can *only* set their horizontal margin, padding, and borders. Vertical margin, padding, and borders will be ignored. A width property will not be respected. Instead, the list item will be as wide as the text it encloses plus any side padding. It will be held away from other list items with side margin. A large line-height (200-300%) can be used to create vertical height on the menu item. This is a simpler menu to use, but it has its limitations.

FLOATED

When using floats to horizontally place the list items, they retain their block display. You may remember that a block-level element takes up 100% of the width of the parent element. However, when we float an element, the browser will shrink the float as small as it can and they will line up within the parent. Even though they're originally shruken down around their text, much like using the inline element, there is a greater number of properties that can be applied to them. Both vertical and horizontal margins, padding, and borders will be respected. A width can be set if desired. The text-align property can be set to the right or middle.

Using a floated menu can be slightly more complicated due to floating and clearing issues. Still, overall it's a more flexible method and thus more commonly used. Our menu in this comp isn't very complicated. We could likely use the inline method with some line-height and make it work nicely. However, for reasons of illustration and because you'll likely find this technique more useful, we'll use the floated method here.

1. Add a rule called #header li and float the list elements to the left. Adjust the font-size to match the comp by setting it to 110%.

```
#header li {
  float: left;
  font-size: 110%;
}
```

Regional LivingRegional BusinessRegional Chamber

Sidebar1   Visiting the Area   Area Highlights

FIGURE 4.15 Wow! What in the world just happened to our page?

Notice how our list items are sitting next to each other with no space at all. This is because when we float an element without a width, the browser will shrink the float as small as it can. We'll add other properties later to create the look our designer wanted.

This is one of those little float gotchas we talked about in Chapter 3. Now that the list elements are floated, the ul doesn't "see" them, and so it's not containing them. The list elements interact with each other, so they're not taken completely out of the flow of the document as they would be if they were absolutely positioned, but the container is unaware of their presence. This means the background color and image on our ul element no longer shows since the element believes there's nothing inside it. You'll also notice that the floats (the document's columns) that follow them in the flow of the document have moved up to the same line where the floated list items end. They believe there's room for them there and quite frankly, there is, but that's not where we want them.

N *Sometimes* overflow: auto *causes unsightly scrollbars on your element. Using* overflow: hidden *may solve the issue but sometimes it's simpler to use a clearing element or float the parent container itself. The elements on your page determine the best method. In the case of a horizontal list with a UL as the container, floating the UL (with a width of 100% and no padding within that would add to the total width) will force it to contain its floated children (LI). You will likely need to have a clearing element follow it as well.*

We could use a clearing element (as we discussed in Chapter 3) to force the container to "see" the floated elements within, or we could float the parent ul and give it 100% width since a float will contain child floats. In this simple case, though, we'll use a quick little remedy that won't require that we use a clearing element at all (yet another float clearing method for you to add to your arsenal). We'll add the overflow property with an auto value to the float's container. This causes the parent to expand and contain all the child floats. Overflow with the hidden value will work as well.

2. Add the overflow: auto declaration to the ul rule in the header and see what effect it has.

```
#header ul {
  background: #FFAD00 url(images/nav_bar_back.jpg)
repeat-x;
  overflow: auto;
}
```

FIGURE 4.16 Our floated list items are now contained in the ul, but we still don't see the background color.

Regional LivingRegional BusinessRegional Chamber

Sidebar1   Visiting the Area

Don't panic. There's nothing wrong with your code. What you're seeing is one of those rare occasions where Dreamweaver's Design view simply doesn't render the property correctly. That used to be a real pain, but these days, we have a new tool to fight the rendering bugs—Live View.

3. Click the Live View button on your toolbar and take a look at the page.

Regional LivingRegional BusinessRegional Chamber

FIGURE 4.17 We still have work to do, but in Live View we can see our background color.

Styling the Anchors as Buttons

Now that the navigation bar runs the full width of the page, we can complete the look our designer created. There are a few things to be aware of to make your links act like buttons and to avoid creepy, crawling bugs.

In menus, if you want the link to act like a button in Internet Explorer—activated by the mouse for its entire height and width, not only on the text itself —you'll need to add the `display:block` declaration to the rule for the **a** elements. Changing the **a** element to block display also allows us more styling control. We can place the padding on the link that then expands the shrink-wrapping float.

Right now, the links are all running together and that's certainly not the plan. There's a possible bug in IE that, with a little wise planning, we can completely avoid. It's called the doubled float margin bug and is caused by using a margin on the same side the element floats toward. We'll avoid using a margin by using padding instead.

Now, the amount of padding required is where the rocket science enters in. How do we determine the padding values to use for our **a** element? We could get out our ruler and measure the exact spacing, making allowances for font sizing and such—and if you have an advanced mathematics degree from Stanford or MIT this might be a choice. But we find that guessing at it works just as well. After all, we're using a method that will allow the text to expand if it's necessary for our user, so simply coming close to what our designer had in mind is what matters.

Our first guess is 10px, which, of course adds 10 pixels of padding to all sides of the element. In viewing our page in Live View and then comparing it to the comp, 10px seems to be slightly too tall and doesn't add enough space between each link. Using 8px for the top and bottom and 12px for the left and right sides does the trick in our eyes.

1. Create a new rule called `#header li a`. In the Block category, choose block from the Display values. In the Box category, set the top and bottom padding to 8px and the left and right to 12px. Finally let's remove the underlines from the links in the Type category.

   All links in our page, both menu and text, will be white, so we'll go ahead and create that rule globally. For a brief moment, until we place the background colors on our divs, any links in the page will appear to disappear. They'll be back in a bit.

N *Another common design mistake is to use a margin on the first element of a floated element on the same side as the float (for example, a left margin on a left floated element). You can avoid the dreaded IE doubled float margin bug by using padding instead. If you must use a margin due to design constraints, adding* `display: inline` *to the element will zap this bug. To learn more about the doubled margin bug, read up on it at Adobe's CSS Advisor site: http://www.adobe.com/cfusion/communityengine/index.cfm?event=showDetails&postId=785&productId=1*

N *So we can properly view the menu, we'll stay in Live View while we work on it. And yes, Live View will allow us to create new CSS rules.*

2. Create an element selector for the **a** element. Simply give it a white color.

The new selectors should look like this:

```
#header li a {
 display: block;
 padding: 8px 12px;
 text-decoration: none;
}
a {
 color: #FFF;
}
```

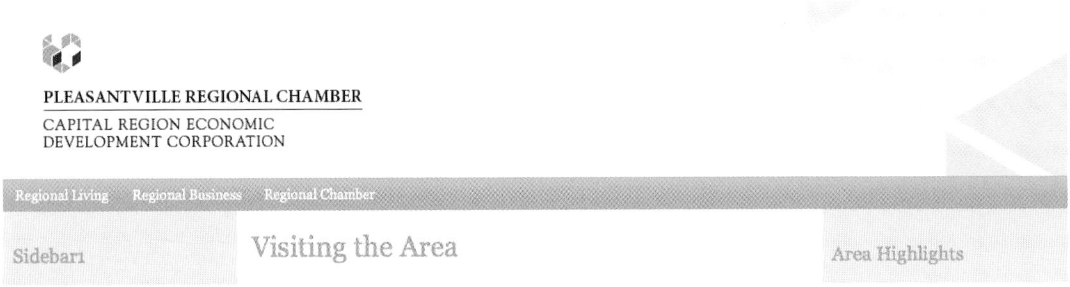

PLEASANTVILLE REGIONAL CHAMBER

CAPITAL REGION ECONOMIC
DEVELOPMENT CORPORATION

Regional Living   Regional Business   Regional Chamber

Sidebar1   Visiting the Area   Area Highlights

FIGURE 4.18 It's starting to shape up nicely!

Putting the Final Tweaks on the Horizontal Navigation

Let's move to the final details of our navigation. The alignment in our navigation should match the logo above. You may remember that was 40px from the left. We'll need to subtract the 12px of padding on the left of our links from the total amount needed. Grabbing a wandering fourth grader, we quickly figure out that 28px of left padding on the **ul** will be needed to hold the links away from the edge of our document 40px.

You'll also remember from the comp that we need two subtle lines on the bottom of the navigation bar. You can't put two borders on an element. However, we have two elements at our disposal—the **ul** and the **header** div it is within—so we'll get creative and use both.

1. The first border, the darker purple (#575691) will go on the inner element—the **ul**. The second border, the light purple (#9290BF) will be placed as a bottom border on the header.

2. Our adjusted code looks like this:

```
#header {
  background: #FFF url(images/logo_background.gif)
no-repeat right;
  border-bottom: #9290BF 1px solid;
}
#header ul {
  padding: 0 0 0 28px;
  background: #FFAD00 url(images/nav_bar_back.jpg)
repeat-x;
  overflow: auto;
  border-bottom: #575691 1px solid;
}
```

Preview your page in a browser this time (Firefox or Safari—don't go to IE yet). This will allow you to increase the size of the text to see the effect. No matter how large the text gets, as the horizontal navigation grows vertically, it's a seamless transition—from background graphic, to background color to the two borders. It's as if the artist's original vision was able to stretch. This is the beauty of CSS!

FIGURE 4.19 Even with giant text, the navigation doesn't fall apart!

PLEASANTVILLE REGIONAL CHAMBER
CAPITAL REGION ECONOMIC
DEVELOPMENT CORPORATION

Regional Living   Regional Business   Regional Chamber

Creating the Hover and Focus States

Now that our menu is all set, let's create a hover state for the links there. Since the navigation bar is orange with white text, a good hover indication color would be the deep blue we used for our page background. It's dark enough to give good contrast but still blend with the page.

Since we want to allow people who navigate in a variety of different ways the same visual indication of where their focus is, we'll use more than just the typical :hover pseudo-class. The :hover pseudo-class works for a user navigating with a mouse. But what about the person using keyboard navigation? For them to see the same change in color when a link has focus, we'll need to use the `:focus` pseudo-class. But wait, using those two would be too simple. For some reason, Microsoft decided to use the `:active` pseudo-class for keyboard navigation instead (most other browsers use `:active` as you're activating or clicking the link).

- Create a grouped list of selectors for this rule. It looks like this:

```
#header li a:hover, #header li a:active, #header li
a:focus {
  color: #1B1A52;
}
```

The above rule selects a link with focus that is a child of a **list** element that is within the header div. All three selectors are there, separated by commas, so the same color is applied and indicates focus with any method of surfing.

In Live Preview, hover over the links in the menu to be sure your hover state works.

N *In order to work properly, the* hover, active, focus *order must be honored. Be sure not to put a comma after the last selector in a list since that will cause the rule to fail.*

Regional Living   Regional Business   Regional Chamber

FIGURE 4.20 The middle button shows the hover/focus state for our button.

Current Page Indicator (or You Are Here)

A common way to show a user what page or section of a site he or she is on is by placing a class on the link you want to indicate. In that scenario, each XHTML page has a class on a different menu item. But what if we're using server-side includes or Dreamweaver templates where the navigation menu is in a locked region? We couldn't move the class to a different menu item on each page (unless we did it programmatically).

CSS saves us. (Of course!) With a unique ID on each list item, we can easily create a descendant selector that controls our page indicator and never touch the actual menu again. We'll add a class to the body element that matches the ID on the menu.

N *Using a class on the body element (instead of an ID) allows us to place multiple classes there if needed for various reasons. An element can only have one ID, so using an ID on the body would be limiting.*

We discussed earlier that it was a best practice *not* to use class and ID names that were specific to the placement or look of the element they're placed on. Well, rules are made to be broken. Since it will actually help us track the proper page later, now is the time to break this rule.

Using the same name for both the body class and the list item ID keeps us from getting confused later and makes it easy to write the selectors needed. For example if the Regional Living list item is given an ID of `living`—we'll add a class of the same name on the body element. There's no problem having a class and ID of the same name—as long as it doesn't confuse *you*. Lest you get completely confused now, let's just do it!

1. Choose Source Code on the Related Files toolbar. In the actual code, place your cursor into the first link of the menu— Regional Living.

   We're doing this in the code because, in Live View, if we click into the menu item, we see the hover state and can't actually select the link so that we can access it on the tag selector.

2. On the tag selector, right-click the `<li>` and select Quick Tag Editor.

   A dialog appears that lets you set the ID and name. (You could, of course, also type this directly in the code if you prefer.) The Quick Tag Editor works very much like Code view in that it uses code completion.

   Since all of the links here begin with the word Regional, we'll drop the word Regional on each and simply use the second word to identify the link.

3. In the ID field, type `living`.

4. Continue in the same way with the next two list items, naming them business and chamber respectively.

   ```
   <ul>
     <li id="living"><a href="#">Regional Living</a></li>
     <li id="business"><a href="#">Regional Business</a></li>
     <li id="chamber"><a href="#">Regional Chamber</a></li>
   </ul>
   ```

   Now, with the IDs placed on the list elements we can write a selector to target them.

5. Create a descendant selector to target any link descending from an item with an ID of **#living** that is a descendant of an element with a class of **.living**.

   ```
   .living #living a
   ```

6. In the Type category, set the color to #1B1A52 and set the font-weight to bold.

7. We'll also place the **.living** class on the body element.

   The current page indicator rule and the XHTML code for the body element look like this:

   ```
   .living #living a {
     color: #1B1A52;
     font-weight: bold;
   }
   <body class="living">
   ```

We'll create a grouped list of selectors for each page, or section, for which we'll need an indicator. In the case of our horizontal navigation, we'll create three. To activate these, we place the appropriate class on each page's body element.

```
.living #living a, .business #business a, .chamber
#chamber a {
  color: #1B1A52;
  font-weight: bold;
}
```

Regional Living   Regional Business   Regional Chamber

> **N** *This rule will select any link that descends from an element with an ID of* #living *(our list item) that is a descendant of an element with the class of living (our body element). It could also be written as* body. living li#living a, *if you think you might forget what the selector controls. Once you get used to the CSS, though, you probably don't need the extra code.*

> **N** *One of the pluses to having IDs on each list item is that we can now target only the first or last link in the ul. This can be useful when you have padding, margin, or a link separator background image that you'd like to change or remove for one of them.*

FIGURE 4.21 Users of the site will have a visual indication of which page or section they're in.

Clean Up One More Time

This would be a great time to do another round of CSS cleanup.

Switch the CSS Styles panel into All view again and organize your rules as we discussed earlier. When complete, go back to the Current view.

We moved all the rules beginning with **#header** to the **#header** section of the page. Though it's certainly a matter of preference, we placed the grouped selector for the current page indicator there—since it's related to the menu in that section. Finally, we moved the **a** element selector up under the **body** selector.

FIGURE 4.22 Our rules before and after their organization.

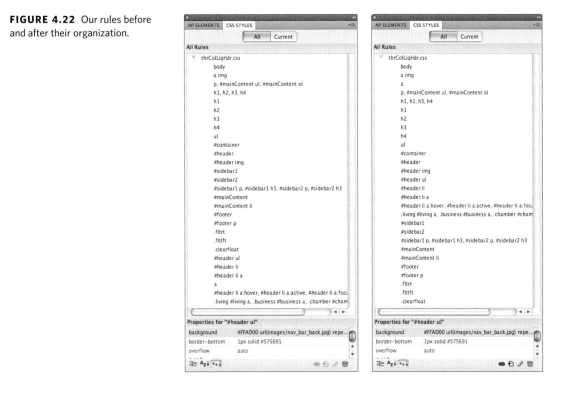

Using Design-time Style Sheets

It's starting to look pretty good in Live View, huh? You remember we had a little issue with the menu in Design view (the background doesn't show). Now that we've styled our links with the white color they'll need for the navigation bar, switching back to Design view (to work on the HTML) makes the links invisible. That's not very useful. We've got a tool in Dreamweaver we can use to make the links show again. The tool we'll use is a **Design-time Style Sheet**. It won't make the color on the navigation come back, but it will make the links visible.

For those unfamiliar with Design-time Style Sheets (DTSS), they're a separate CSS document, attached within Dreamweaver, and *only* rendered within Dreamweaver. They affect nothing on the server or in a browser. Though Dreamweaver's rendering has gotten substantially better with each release, it still occasionally has odd moments. Attaching a DTSS allows you to correct the rendering of your page, within the Dreamweaver design environment, without affecting your browser view. Let's do it:

1. Create a new CSS document using File > New > CSS or by right-clicking inside the files panel and choosing New File.

   We've named our document dtss.css so we don't forget what it is later. Inside this document, we simply need to give our anchor element a dark color to show up on the white background.

Alternatively, another property that will show the background color and fix Dreamweaver's Design view, is overflow:hidden; *Use that in the Design-time Style Sheet instead of the color and don't forget the* !important *declaration.*

2. Create a rule just like our menu's link rule, #header li a, and make it black (#000). Add the !important declaration.

   Here's what we placed in our dtss.css document:

```
#header li a {
color: #000 !important;
}
```

   The !important declaration tells DW to always render this rule within DW: otherwise, because the rule has the same specificity as the one in your regular style sheet, the styles will conflict.

The specs from the W3C say that an author's style sheet always overrides a user's style sheet. However, the !important *declaration takes precedence over a normal declaration. If both style sheets contain an* !important *declaration, then the user's declaration wins out. This is a change from CSS1 where the author's won.*

3. To attach this style sheet, click on the new Design-time icon on the Style Rendering toolbar or use the contextual menu in the top right-hand corner of the CSS Styles panel and choose Design-time.

   The Design-time Style Sheets dialog will open.

FIGURE 4.23 The new Design-time icon on the Style Rendering toolbar.

4. Select the + sign in the "Show only at design time" drop-down list and navigate to dtss.css.

   You'll notice that you can also hide an entire style sheet in this same dialog—though this is usually only necessary in the rare occasion of extremely complex pages that Dreamweaver just can't handle. (And we haven't seen those in a long while.)

5. Click OK.

The words are now visible in the links. This keeps your navigation area, within Dreamweaver, more like the final browser or Live View version.

FIGURE 4.24 Our modified navigation bar in Dreamweaver.

Laying Out the Main Content Area

It's time to get down to the real meat of our page—the content area. In your builds directory, there's a page you can check your work thus far with—index_3.html. We need to re-create the overall gradient and shadowed side columns. Let's begin with the gradient that runs across the main content and right sidebar area. This background gradient needs to begin where the horizontal navigation ends—no matter where on the vertical axis that happens. If we place it on the container that holds the entire page, we can't anticipate text size changes (which affect the vertical point the navigation ends). Since the overall sizing of the columns is fluid, we can't simply create one graphic that includes the imagery in the right column. We need a seamless, repeating background image across the top of the main page area. Then we can add the other page details. That means we need to add another wrapper div around the three columns to contain them all.

In your graphics editor, slice from, but not including, the light lavender single-pixel line—remember we placed that line on the header—to the area where the gradient ends and becomes a solid color. Once again, you're saving page weight by using CSS to place the overall background color and putting the gradient on as a background image. Since it's so subtle, how do we know where the gradient changes to a solid color? More super scientific methods!

Our method is to eyeball it. In our graphics program, we put a guide where we think the transition is, and sample the color on both sides of the guide. If the color number is the same, we move the guide up a bit to find the highest place we can place the guide where the color still matches on both sides. If the color number is different, we move it down a bit until it matches. The color we sampled, about 465 pixels down in our comp, was #403E8A. We'll slice down to that guide, and since it is a gradient, we'll export it as a jpg with the name main_back.jpg.

Modifying the Columns

1. In the CSS, delete the background colors from both `sidebar1` and `sidebar2` so that they are transparent. Also delete the background color from the overall `#container` since all the divs it contains now have their own background colors.

2. In Code view of the XHTML document, highlight both columns as well as the `mainContent` div and the clearing element.

3. On the Common pane of the Insert bar, choose Insert Div Tag.

4. In the dialog, choose "Wrap around selection" and give the ID the name of `outer_wrap`.

5. Click New CSS Style and choose to add the style to the three-ColLiqHdr.css style sheet. Click OK.

6. Go to the Background pane and navigate to the image we just created setting the Background-repeat to repeat on the x axis (horizontally).

7. Set the Background-color to the color the gradient ended on—#403e8a.

This lets us have any amount of content in the portion of our page containing the `mainContent` div and side columns. If the page is extremely short, it will end, still showing the image, before the background color starts. If the page is very long, it will continue on seamlessly with the solid background color. Users can't tell where the image ends and the color, created with CSS, begins.

> **N** Be sure the clearing element is included in the new div. That's what makes the new container aware of where the floats inside end.

> **N** If you create a new rule with your focus in the CSS document from the Related Files toolbar, you might come across a confusing drop-down list when choosing where to define your rule. The name of your style sheet (most likely where you want to place it) won't be included in the list. Instead, you'll have a choice of (This document only), (New style sheet file), and dtss.css. Choosing (This document only) will actually place the rule in your external file. Dreamweaver is giving you this confusing choice because your focus actually **is** in the page in which you want to place the rule.

FIGURE 4.25 With and without the background color. You can see how well our CSS background blends at the bottom—it looks like one graphic!

Dealing with Margins

In most browsers (IE is an exception), and as shown in Figure 4.25, there's an odd space where the overall body background color shows through right below the horizontal menu. This is a perfect example of one version of *margin collapse*.

When two vertical margins meet, and the margined elements have no padding or borders specified, the largest margin takes precedence over the smaller. When both margins are the same size, the space rendered is the size of one of the margins—not the two added together. This is why you can zero the top margin of an element, yet still have space between elements.

As we discussed in Chapter 2, margin collapse occurs when two margins touch. One margin, the smaller of the two, will disappear (or collapse), allowing the larger margin to take precedence. For example, when you have a heading followed by a paragraph element, the margin that is larger will be rendered—the margins are not added together. If a margin on the first or last element is not contained by its div, it can create a space between divs. It appears to push the div away from the adjacent div. Believe it or not, this is correct behavior—it's not a bug. But in this case, it's unsightly.

There are three basic ways to prevent margin collapse, and the page design determines the best method to use. Contain the margin using a border or padding on the parent div. Or simply remove that margin from the element altogether and create the space using padding on the div itself.

In our case, we're dealing with the top margin of the **h1** that is protruding above the **mainContent** div. We can either get rid of the top margin on the **h1**, leaving only the bottom margin; add the **padding-top** property to the **mainContent** div (or the **outer_wrap** container div); or add a border to either of those divs.

Our design doesn't lend itself to a border (though it's possible at times to use a border that is the same color as the background it sits on). Due to different defaults on headings, and the different way IE interacts with margins, we'll need to use an IECC to make them appear even if we choose to use padding (which is how the layouts come by default). Thus we're opting to zero the top margin of the **h1** in the main content area and the **h3** in the right sidebar. We're not worrying about the left sidebar as it will be a menu list shortly and all our list defaults have already been equalized with zero values. We'll create a simple class selector that removes the top margin of anything we place it on.

1. Create a new selector named .no_top

    You, of course, can name it anything you like. This name just helps us remember what it's for.

2. Give it the property of margin and a value of 0.

3. Place your cursor into the h1 element in the main content area. Either right click the **<h1>** on the tag selector or use the HTML area of the Property inspector to attach the .no_top class.

    The gap below the top navigation immediately closes. The h1 seems a little high. We'll place the padding on the **#mainContent** div that contains it.

FIGURE 4.26 The h1 is now sitting *right* under the menu bar.

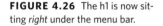

4. Select <mainContent> on the tag selector and in the Properties pane of the CSS Styles panel, add the padding-top property. Give it a value of 30px.

    Yes, you remember correctly. The padding alone would have gotten rid of the margin collapse. But we also have the issue of the way IE treats margins. We're leveling things here. That means we need to remove the top padding for the **#mainContent** in the IECC.

5. Go to Source Code in your related documents toolbar. In the head of your document (yes, in the code), remove the margin-top on the main content div.

   The area you're looking for looks like this. The highlighted portion is what you need to remove.

   ```
   #mainContent { zoom: 1; padding-top: 15px; }
   ```

6. Repeat the same process in the right side column. First, add the `.no_top` class to the h3.

7. Add the space back in by changing the padding on the `#sidebar2` div. Place 40px on the top and leave 15px on the bottom.

   We didn't want to give the bottom as much space as the top, but we still like to leave a little breathing room there in case it's the longest.

8. Again, remove the padding in the IECC in the head of your document. Go ahead and remove both the `#sidebar1` and `#sidebar2` selectors. We won't be using either.

Planning the Background Placement

If you'd like to create three equal length columns within a liquid, percentage-based layout, it's quite doable as well! Please refer to Zoe Gillenwater's free article at Community MX—Creating Liquid Faux Columns, http://www. communitymx.com/abstract. cfm?cid=AFC58.

*Remember, only one background per customer please— errr—per element, that is. At least till CSS3 is in full swing. Probably about the time we have grandchildren. (Okay, that's not **so** far away, but still!) For now, we have to come up with other creative methods to create the styling we need.*

In the fixed-width layout chapter, we looked at a simple method to use one graphic and create the effect of two or three full-length columns called faux columns. Of course, it's easy to create faux columns when you know the exact pixel dimensions. But in a liquid layout, you can't anticipate the screen size of your user, and guessing at the column width isn't going to work. We're just out of luck, aren't we? Think again. Not only is it possible, once you understand the principles, it's really not difficult.

Let's analyze the comp. We've got a full-length column on the left column and two background images to place: the triangles and the drop-shadowed column top on the right. We can't slice the drop-shadowed area and triangles as one image since the width of the column is flexible. We've already placed a background on the `outer_wrap` div. That leaves the `sidebar1`, `sidebar2`, and `mainContent` divs with no backgrounds yet declared. It's quite obvious that the triangles in the right corner can only go on the `sidebar2` div since the `mainContent` div is margined away from that area. That means the `mainContent` div gets the drop-shadowed column separator that creates the right column.

If you have an element (child) nested inside another element (parent), and they both have background images, the element that comes later in the flow (child) will cover the earlier (parent container). Children are contained in, and essentially sit on top of, their parents. Thus, the child's background image will cover the parent's.

That leaves the left column. It needs to appear to go the full-length of the page. When we created the fixed-width, full-length faux column, we found we can't use the actual side column div itself. That div quits displaying its background when the content within it ends. We can't force it to go down to the footer (and no, adding a whole lot of **
** elements doesn't count). We can't use the **#container** like we did with the fixed faux columns. That's not due to the technique (it will work flawlessly on the container); that's due to our design. If we placed the liquid faux column on the container, the gradient background we just placed in the main area would sit on top of it, covering it up.

The Illusion of a Column

We'll begin placing the backgrounds with the full-length left column. Since we've determined we can't place the background image on either the container or the left side column itself, what's left to use? Well, nothing. At least nothing we currently have. We'll have to create another hook to hang it on.

CREATING THE DIV

1. Place another div right inside the **#outer_wrap** div. Yes, in code view. Using code hinting. By now, you can do it! Name it **#inner_wrap**.

FIGURE 4.27 Dreamweaver makes it easy to type your element tags in Code view.

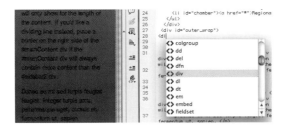

2. Move down toward the bottom of your page. Place your cursor between the close of the **#mainContent** and **#outer_wrap** divs. Type the **</** and Dreamweaver will automatically fill in the rest of the tag.

Notice the **#mainContent** closing tag is commented. This would be a good time to comment both the inner and outer wrap divs we've created. It's easy to lose track when you have a more complex page.

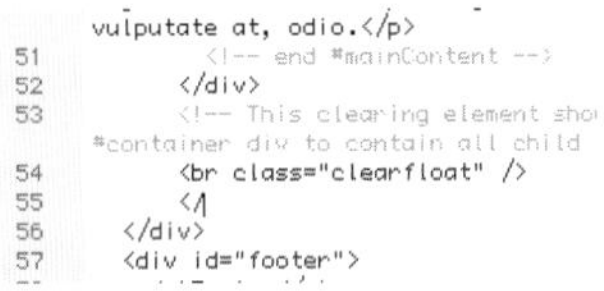

FIGURE 4.28 Place the close of the div between the two that exist already.

3. Place closing comments in the code for each of the closing divs. Ours looks like this:

FIGURE 4.29 Nicely commented closing div tags.

```
      augue conaimentaii aaipiscing. meneum  augitteis. Litam
      vulputate at, odio.</p>
51        <!-- end #mainContent -->
52        </div>
53        <!-- This clearing element should immediately fi
      #container div to contain all child floats -->
54        <br class="clearfloat" />
55        <!-- end #inner_wrap -->
56      </div>
57      <!-- end #outer_wrap -->
58    </div>
59    <div id="footer">
```

We now have a div directly inside the div that holds the three columns. Without any width, margin, or padding properties added to form it, it is 100% of the width of its parent.

We want to create the proper width for the **#sidebar1** div since that's crucial for the next steps.

4. Place your cursor into the **#sidebar1** div. Change the width value in the CSS Styles panel from 22% to 20%.

In some designs we'd also want to adjust the left margin of the main content area since the margining is what creates the space between them. In this case, we'll leave it as is—our designer envisioned a good bit of "white space."

CREATING THE GRAPHIC

We've created a column that is 20% of the width of the container it's in. Here's the first part of the technique that makes this effect work. The graphic used for it will not come from our designer's comp. It's much too small. We want to use a graphic as wide as we believe a browser viewport will be. For ease of demonstration, we'll use 2,000 pixels. Your mileage may vary. We will use a max-width later to constrain our design for usability/readability reasons, so we're safe with this number.

In the source directory for this chapter, open the liquid_left.psd. This file has the look of the left column of the main comp, but is created in the dimensions we need for our technique.

FIGURE 4.30 The column on this 2,000px wide graphic is 400px, or 20% of the overall width.

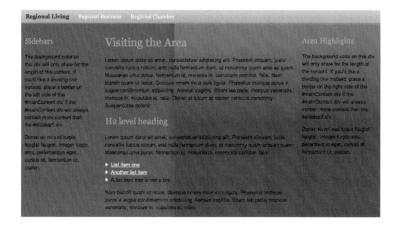

If the technique for your column is more complex, creating a nice, 200px tall graphic might be easier. Then crop or slice it to be only 10-15px tall.

Our overall graphic is 2,000 pixels wide. When creating your own column using this technique, just remember that it's simple math that decides the pixel width of the column area. Our column has a 20% width. Our column in the graphics program must be the same percentage width. So 2,000px x .2 = 400px. 400px is 20% of our 2,000px wide graphic. (Now you understand why an even number like 2,000 is so nice to work with!) We typically create a 10-15px tall graphic.

It's also possible to use a non-transparent graphic with the color of the column and the color of the remaining portion of the page all in one graphic. In our case, the gradient makes that impossible since it needs to repeat on the x axis (horizontally) and the column must repeat on the y axis (vertically). But if your design has no gradient, that's the best way to do it.

You probably noticed our graphic is transparent for the other 1600 pixels. As we mentioned earlier, since the div we'll place this graphic on is inside the div with the gradient, its background image will render on top of the gradient background. If we left a color on the rest of this graphic, it would completely cover the gradient. We exported the graphic as a gif to keep the transparency. It's called liquid_left.gif and is in the images directory of your site.

CREATING THE CSS

Now that we have our graphic, let's take a look at the CSS.

1. Create a CSS rule for the #inner_wrap div.

2. In the Background Category, navigate to the graphic for the left column—liquid_left.gif. Set the Background-repeat to repeat-y. Click Apply (not OK).

   Notice how the 400px wide column is, well, 400px wide. This is because by default, a background image is applied from the top, left of the element you're placing it on, unless otherwise positioned. Let's fix that now.

FIGURE 4.31 Oh my, this doesn't really have the look we wanted, does it?

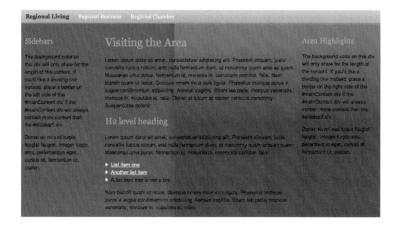

3. We still want our background graphic to start at the top of our element, so we'll set the value of the Background-position (Y) to 0. But here's the part to pay extra attention to—the Background-position (X). This is the final step that creates our special CSS effect. The setting for the Background-position (X) needs to equal the percentage of both our left column and the column on our graphic. As you probably recall, that was 20%. Set that position and click OK.

Due to Dreamweaver's limited workspace, this is one of those times where previewing in a browser is helpful. View your page in a standards-compliant browser. Make the window wider and then narrower.

If you completed this step successfully, your column is resizing automatically based on the width of your viewport. How cool is that? Think of the possibilities!

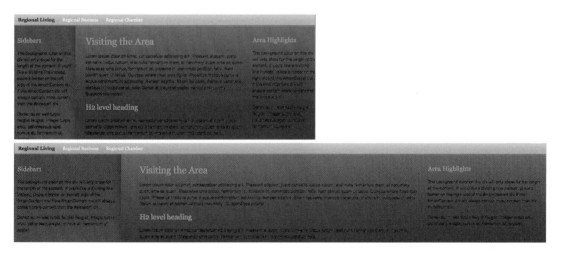

FIGURE 4.32 No matter the width of the page, the left side column is still 20% and extends to the bottom of the window.

The Right Column

Remember to turn off any layers with text sitting on top of a graphic you're slicing. You'll add the text within Dreamweaver.

Moving back into your image editor, slice each of the other two areas as tightly as you can. For the right side drop shadow, slice from the lighter column area to the other side of the shadowed area, staying as close as you can. Vertically, slice until the area where the color becomes solid and the shadow ends. Export the triangles as side2_back.jpg and the right column shadow as main-content_back.jpg. These are now named for the column they'll be attached to, which makes it easier if you have to come back to the site later.

FIGURE 4.33 Notice slices 16 and 17 in our Photoshop comp.

Back in Dreamweaver we'll add these to our page on the div for which they were just named. We'll position them properly and set a `min-height` on the right side column. This keeps the graphic from ending abruptly if there is too little content in the side column.

1. Select `<#sidebar2>` on the tag selector. Click the Edit Rule icon. In the Background Category, Background-image, navigate to the side2_back.jpg. Set it to Background-repeat **no-repeat**. Set the Background-position (X) to **right**. Set Background-repeat (Y) to **top**. Click OK.

   Remember that if we don't explicitly set the background's position, it would be positioned at the top left of the div. We'll move to the min-height now. You may have noticed that there is no way to add min-height using the CSS Rules dialog. We'll have to move to the CSS panel (or, dare we suggest, the code).

   There are properties like min- and max-width, and min- and max-height that are not available in the CSS rules dialog. Those properties are not supported in IE6. The dialog was updated in Dreamweaver CS4 so that the property names are written correctly, but no new properties were added.

2. In the Properties pane, and with the right sidebar still selected, type min-height into the property. Give it a value of 145px.

   145px is just slightly taller than our graphic, assuring us that it will show in its entirety.

3. Continue in the same way with the main content div. Add the background graphic called maincontent_back.jpg, set it to no-repeat and position it at the top, right of the element. Click OK.

The code should look like this:

```
#sidebar2 {
 float: right;
 width: 23%;
 padding: 40px 0 15px;
 background: url(images/side2_back.jpg) no-repeat right top;
 min-height: 145px;
}
#mainContent {
 margin: 0 24% 0 23.5%;
 padding-top: 30px;
 background: url(images/maincontent_back.jpg) no-repeat right
top;
}
```

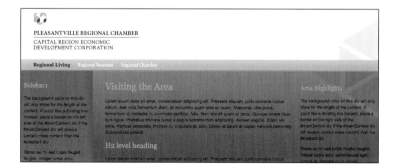

Refer to previous chapters for more information about Internet Explorer Conditional Comments.

Min-height works in all current browsers, including Internet Explorer 7. But it isn't supported in IE6 or below. In those browsers, we can imitate the same behavior using the **height** property. IE will expand a box to contain its content, so if the column has more content, it will simply grow longer. If it has less, it will remain at the height given. We only want to do this for IE6 and lower, though, so we'll need to use an Internet Explorer Conditional Comment within the head of our document:

```
<!--[if lte IE 6]>
<style type="text/css">
 #sidebar2 { height: 145px; }
</style>
<![endif]-->
```

FIGURE 4.34 Viewed in Live View, it's looking like columns—but their content spills out!

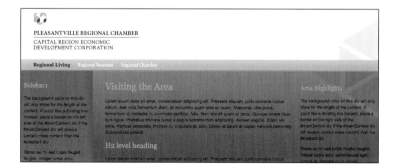

Tweaking the Right Column

Now is the time for all good designers to come to the aid of their columns. Though we graphically have our nice drop-shadowed, columned look, the measurements aren't exactly right. Viewing the designer's vision in Photoshop, we see that the alignment of the left column (`sidebar1`) is the same as the navigation and header above it—40 pixels from the left. The right column appears to have about 30 pixels on the right side.

 *If you choose to set actual pixel values for the side columns, instead of allowing them to be fluid like the center, you could place the padding on the columns themselves. It would be quite easy then to calculate the amount of margin needed on the `mainContent` div. Our designer has asked that the columns remain fluid like the rest of the design.*

With percentage-based layouts, we never want to add padding to the actual column itself. Instead, we want to use margin or padding on the elements within the columns. Remember, the actual width of an element is the width value *plus* the padding and border. If we add 40px of padding to the left column, currently set at 20%, our actual width would be 20% + 40px—a number we can't be sure of at all! Thus, margining the middle `mainContent` div away from the column is risky at best.

Let's start on the right column, since it's simpler, then we'll move over to left column, changing the paragraphs to a list and positioning them properly. We've already measured in Photoshop and seen that, in the right column, the approximate space we want from the right side is 30px.

In your style sheet, you'll find a grouped list of selectors:

```
#sidebar1 p, #sidebar1 h3, #sidebar2 p, #sidebar2 h3 {
  margin-left: 10px;
  margin-right: 10px;
}
```

Since we want differing margin values, we'll separate the right and left sidebar selectors into two rules and only make the change in the sidebar2 values.

1. Turn on the CSS Layout Outlines from the Visual Aids toolbar.

   Note that the shadow separating `mainContent` from `sidebar2` is actually contained in the `mainContent` div.

2. Place your cursor into the right sidebar. On the Rules pane of the CSS Styles panel, right-click the grouped rule and choose Go to Code.

FIGURE 4.35 Use the Visual Aids menu on the Documents toolbar to view CSS Layout Outlines.

The focus is now moved to the grouped rule in the CSS document. We'll separate it into two separate grouped rules: one with the two **#sidebar1** rules and the other with the two **#sidebar2** rules.

3. Copy the entire grouped rule. Paste it right below the first. On the first rule, remove the **#sidebar2 p, #sidebar2 h3**. **Do not forget** to delete the comma that follows the **#sidebar1 p** selector.

4. On the rule you pasted, do the opposite. Delete the **#sidebar1 p, #sidebar h3** selectors (along with that extra comma).

5. On the **#sidebar2** grouping, leave the left margin as it is, and give the right margin a 30px value.

```
#sidebar1 p, #sidebar1 h3 {
  margin-left: 10px;
  margin-right: 10px;
}
#sidebar2 p, #sidebar2 h3 {
  margin-left: 10px;
  margin-right: 30px;
}
```

When previewed, you'll see that we haven't changed the actual width of **sidebar2**. We've simply decreased the line length. The **mainContent** div's content is still too far to the right. We'll adjust that next.

FIGURE 4.36 The right column is in the right place but the main content area's spacing is still off.

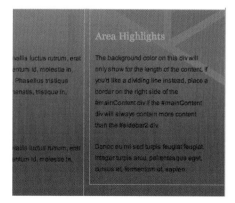

Styling the mainContent Area

Our columns will be looking perfect when we make a simple adjustment to the `mainContent` div. The shadow creating the right column is contained within the `mainContent` div so, unfortunately, using more right margin actually makes the right column itself appear wider. (Feel free to experiment with that to see how it looks.)

Instead we can use padding, which leaves our graphic where it is, and moves the content within the div away from the right edge. Since the designer has given a rather wide margin to the text in `mainContent`, we'll use about 100px of right padding and see if that achieves the desired result.

1. Place your focus into the `#mainContent` and in the Properties pane of the CSS Styles panel, add the padding-right property. Give it a value of 100px.

```css
#mainContent {
  margin: 0 24% 0 23.5%;
  background: url(images/content_back.jpg) no-repeat right
top;
  padding-top: 30px;
  padding-right: 100px;
}
```

While this is really starting to come together, it would be nice to see the dark text in the proper color, wouldn't it? Since all the paragraph text is white except the footer, an efficient way to handle this is to add it to the grouped selector we created for the `p. #mainContent ul, #mainContent ol`. When we move to the footer later, we'll simply assign a different color value there.

2. Place your cursor into the text. This will select the grouped rule. In the Properties pane of the CSS Styles panel, add the property color with the value #FFF (white).

Now that's more like it!

You may have thought that using padding would add to our overall box width, which could be dangerous. And if the main content div had been given a width, you'd be correct. In our case, the main content's width is created by carving out the margins on each side. Thus, the padding doesn't add anything to the width. The IECC in the head of the document shows a `zoom:1` declaration for the `#mainContent` div. That gives IE the `hasLayout` trigger it needs to render properly without any dimensions.

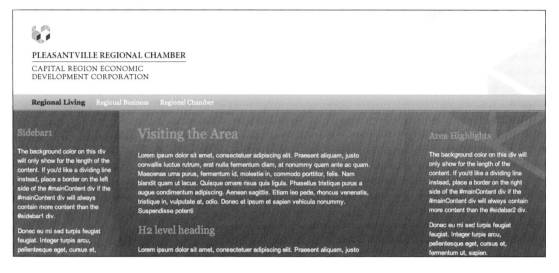

FIGURE 4.37 Our columns and text now match our comp nicely.

Creating the Left-hand Navigation

With our columns all set, it's time to work on the left column menu. If you need a fresh start, builds > index_4.html will help you see where you might have gotten off course. We have a challenge with this vertical menu in that the little marker by the menu item, that indicates which page the user is on, is all the way against the left side of the column. Let's first create the list itself (refer back to the horizontal list instructions if you don't remember how to create a list).

1. Remove all content in the `sidebar1` div and replace it with an unordered list of links using the link names given in the Photoshop comp.

   Remember that since we want to use the same current page indicator trick we used on the horizontal menu, each list item needs a unique ID:

   ```
   <ul>
    <li id="visiting"><a href="#">Visiting the Area</a></li>
    <li id="moving"><a href="#">Moving to the Area</a></li>
    <li id="maplocator"><a href="#">Interactive Maplocator</a>
   </li>
    <li id="directory"><a href="#">Business Directory</a></li>
    </ul>
   ```

Since we removed the heading and paragraph elements from `sidebar1`, we don't need the selectors for them.

2. Using the All pane of the CSS Styles panel, remove the `#sidebar1 p` and `#sidebar1 h3` selectors from the CSS document.

3. Create a descendant selector for the `ul` in the left side div and increase the text size slightly since the menu text in the comp is larger than a normal list:

```
#sidebar1 ul {
  font-size: 105%;
}
```

If we hadn't already zeroed the list defaults, we would do that here. Our `ul` element selector has already taken care of that for us.

Most of the time, we'd create the space on the left of the menu with a left margin on the `ul` itself. However, with this design, we want to be able to add the visual indicator all the way on the left side of the page, so we can't move the entire list over. We have two other elements to choose from, though. We can either move the list item itself, or the link within it. Before we give you the answer, think about which one you would put it on—and why…

If the list marker needs to change on hover, you'll be happy you put the list marker on the anchor. IE6 and earlier doesn't support the hover pseudo-class on anything but anchors.

Okay, time's up! If you chose to put the padding on the link within the list item, you made the same choice we did. If you chose the list item itself, you're not wrong: remember, there are many ways to do the same thing with CSS. But we chose the link because, when we add the CSS to create the page indicator, it will not only add the graphic on the left, it will also change the color of the link. Since we'd have to create a selector to change the link color, using it to add the graphic as well is more efficient than creating another set of rules. For this reason, we'll put the padding on the link element.

FIGURE 4.38 We've got the list sitting right up against the left side of our page.

Styling the Menu Links

Ready to style the links? You've got a pretty good idea by now how to set the properties needed. We'll give you the name of the selector and the declarations you need. If you have to poke around a bit to find them, that's okay. You'll remember them better that way.

We could have written our selector as #sidebar1 a (leaving out the li portion of the cascade). It would have selected the links within the list items. It would have also selected any other link that might be put in that column later, or in other pages in the site that use the same layout. So being specific here can be helpful down the road.

1. Create a descendant selector for the links: `#sidebar1 li a`. Set the display to block, the color to white, remove the underlines, and set the padding to 5px for the top and bottom and 40px on the left to match the alignment of the elements above.

```
#sidebar1 li a {
  display: block;
  padding: 5px 0 5px 40px;
  text-decoration: none;
}
```

We set the display to `block` just as we did in the horizontal navigation, since we want the entire link to be clickable. We've added a bit of padding for space around our button and placed the 40px of padding on the left for alignment with the other elements on the page.

If you look at Internet Explorer now, you'll see that there's a great deal of space between each menu item. Don't panic. IE will need some tweaking in this area due to hasLayout issues (discussed in Chapter 2 and related to dimension). Ignore it for now. We'll add the zoom:1 fix at the end of the chapter.

If you look in Live View, you'll see that the alignment of the top of the ul is a bit high. You'll probably remember we zeroed the first element on the other two columns and put the padding on the div itself to avoid margin collapse. We've already zeroed the top margin with the `ul` element selector. We'll add padding to the top of the div.

2. Give the `#sidebar1` a top padding of 30px to move the elements within down:

```
#sidebar1 {
  float: left;
  width: 20%;
  padding: 30px 0;
}
```

FIGURE 4.39 We're getting there. We've created space and removed underlines.

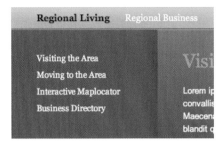

Placing the Page Indicator on the Vertical Menu

We'll indicate what page the user is on the same way we did before: by placing an ID on each link.

First we need the arrow graphic. We'll use the arrow.gif file we used for the unordered list in our main content area.

1. Create a descendant selector for the link as if the body class indicates we're on the page for the first link, Visiting the area:

    `.visiting #visiting a`

2. Put arrow.gif as the Background-image set not to repeat. Leave it positioned to the left and vertical center. Set the color to #FF9F00.

    ```
    .visiting #visiting a {
      background: url(images/arrow.gif) no-repeat left center;
      color: #FF9F00;
    }
    ```

If you place the graphical indicator on the vertical center of the list item's link, if the user's text is large and it wraps to the next line, the graphic will be centered on both lines. You can also align it to the top for your own designs.

3. Place the `.visiting` class for the vertical side menu on the body element by typing it into the code. We've already placed the `.living` class there for the horizontal menu. Add the new class, separated by a space.

    `<body class="living visiting">`

    You can put more than one class on an element if you separate them with a space. This can be very useful at times.

4. Create all the other descendant selectors for the vertical menu. Follow the same pattern we just used:

```
.visiting #visiting a, .moving #moving a, .maplocator
#maplocator a, .directory #directory a {
  background: url(images/arrow.gif) no-repeat left center;
  color: #FF9F00;
}
```

Notice how when viewing in Live View, you have an orange hover state in the left side bar and deep blue on the horizontal navigation. That's the beauty of descendent selectors.

5. Finally, use the same orange color for the vertical menu hover state as used on the headings and page indicator.

Remember again, whenever we define a hover state, we also want to define the active and focus so that users with alternative methods of navigating your site can also see where their focus is.

```
#sidebar1 li a:hover, #sidebar1 li a:active, #sidebar1 li
a:focus {
  color: #FF9F00;
}
```

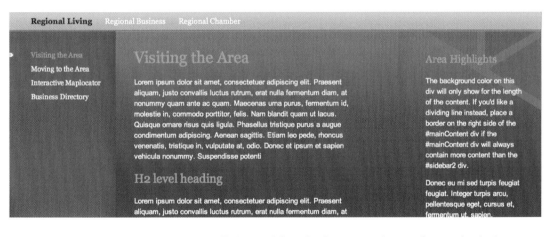

FIGURE 4.40 And there she is—our side bar menu!

We'll do a quick code cleanup and some formatting before we move to the badge image in the right column.

6. Since you've been typing in Code view a bit, you may want to be sure your (X)HTML source code is neat and easy to read. With your Source Code selected in the Related files toolbar, select Commands > Apply Source Formatting from the program menu.

Your (X)HTML code is now cleaned up and nicely indented.

N   *Dreamweaver lets you choose your CSS code formatting. Go to Preferences > Code Format > Advanced Formatting and click the CSS button. CSS Format Options are available for you to create the style you like to work with. If you receive a CSS page that is not using this format, use the same Apply Source Formatting command we just used on the (X)HTML to your CSS page. It will be placed in the format you've set in your preferences.*

7.   It's time for one more cleanup of our CSS document. You know what to do at this point. Start from the All pane of your CSS Styles panel.

We moved the **#outer_wrap** and **#inner_wrap** to just below the header styles. Our reasoning is that these divs wrap the area that holds the three columns. That comes after the header, thus we placed them there in the same order as the flow of the page.

We also moved all the new left side menu styles up to the sidebar1 section. If you have any confusion from this past portion, you may check your work in the builds directory using the index_5.html file.

Adding the Badge Image

The last element to place in the right column is the Walking Tour badge. Obviously, we could do as we have been doing and simply slice this image in an image editor and export it. But we're going to do something slightly different this time. (If you don't have access to Photoshop, please export the badge from the graphics editor of your choice.)

1.   Open the design in Photoshop, locate the Walking Tour layer group and open it in the Layers panel. Ctrl-click on the icon for Layer 1 in the layer group to select the area of the badge image. Select the Walking Tour layer group in the Layers panel and choose Edit > Copy Merged.

Photoshop creates a merged (flattened) image containing all of the elements within the layer group's active selection area and places it on the clipboard.

2.   In Dreamweaver, place the cursor at the end of the text in the last paragraph and tap the Enter key to create a new paragraph. Choose Edit > Paste.

Dreamweaver recognizes that the content on the Clipboard is not text, but rather an image and opens the built-in Fireworks optimization dialog. We can now set the optimization level for the image.

One advantage of optimizing images from Photoshop by pasting within Dreamweaver is that Dreamweaver uses the "headless Fireworks" optimization engine. Since Fireworks creates smaller file sizes, this makes our page weight even lighter.

3. Click the small window pane icon divided into four sections in the lower right of the dialog.

The 4-up view lets us compare different compression settings side-by-side. You'll notice that the GIF 256 has a smaller compression size, but the gradient background doesn't look as nice. Comparatively, the default JPG compression of 80% looks good.

4. Click on the page that has the 80% optimization to make it active, and click OK. Name the image walking_badge.jpg and place it in the images folder for the site.

Dreamweaver prompts you for alternative text for the image just as it did when we placed the logo earlier.

FIGURE 4.41 Fireworks optimization within Dreamweaver.

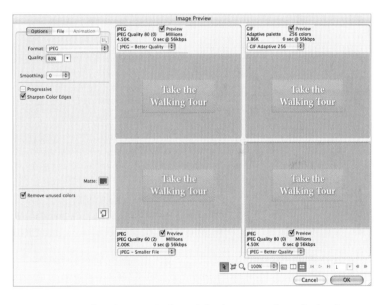

5. Enter text that is descriptive of the image such as "Take the walking tour" and click OK.

Of course anytime that we are dealing with a website, there is always the chance that the client will change their mind about an image or piece of text. Changing text is easy since it is part of the HTML, but with images, we're forced to go back to the original image file—whose name and location we hope we remember—and then make the requested change, re-exporting and potentially placing the file in the layout again.

N *If you have closed the original Photoshop or Fireworks image, Dreamweaver launches the application and opens the file. However, Dreamweaver has no way of indicating to the other application what the selection area or slice was that was used to create the image, so you'll need to manually reselect it. We're crossing our fingers that future versions of the applications might bring us this functionality.*

N *If you want to re-optimize the image, you can select the image and click the Optimize icon in the Edit section of the inspector. This reopens the optimization window, but the source image for the new optimization is the original Photoshop or Fireworks image in its entirety. You'll have to use the slice tool in the optimization dialog to re-slice the desired section of the graphic and this can be difficult. A better bet is to delete the image from the page and start over.*

N *If you're thinking to yourself that we could have used the copy/paste technique during the creation of the page logo or background images, you're right! But since this is a book about CSS and Dreamweaver, we didn't want too many of our exercises to require you to use Photoshop.*

With the new Photoshop integration, Dreamweaver takes the guesswork out of the process. Compare the badge image on the page to the Photoshop comp. Do you notice any difference? In the Photoshop comp the badge image has a drop shadow that is missing in the image on the page. Unfortunately when we used the automatic pixel selection for the layer in Photoshop, it did not select the pixels that make up the drop shadow effect.

Let's correct that now. Notice in the Property inspector that there are two Photoshop (or, if the image came from Fireworks, Fireworks) icons. The one in the bottom row of the inspector identifies the path to the original Photoshop file that was used to create the image.

6. Click the icon in the Edit section of the inspector.

   Dreamweaver opens the original file in either Photoshop or Fireworks, depending upon the original file type.

7. Back in Photoshop, click Layer 1 in the Layers panel in the walking tour layer group. Be sure nothing is selected in your Photoshop comp by choosing Select > Deselect. Choose Layer > New Layer Based Slice. Choose Edit > Copy.

8. Back in Dreamweaver, choose Edit > Paste again.

   This time Dreamweaver simply updates the graphic without taking us through the optimization dialog. In other words, Dreamweaver assumes that we would like to use the same optimization on the image that we applied before.

It's also possible to drag an entire PSD out of Bridge (choose File > Browse in Bridge) and drop it into a Dreamweaver layout. Just remember that you'll be placing a flattened version of the entire file into Dreamweaver. But this can be quite handy if the image is a photograph or simple image that you need in its entirety on your page.

Getting to the Bottom of It— Styling the Footer

We're very close to being done. But we need to get rid of the gray background in the footer so that the footer will use the background color from the page's body element.

We also still have the issue of the two 10px stripes of color between the main area and the footer to contend with. But that's fairly easy—and image-free! Just as in the header, all we need is a couple of borders.

1. Click into the footer on the page. Delete the gray background from the `#footer` selector using your method of choice.

2. Place a `#2d2d70` 10px solid border on the top of the footer.

3. Set the left padding to 40px (like the left column) and the right padding to 30px (like the right column). Remove the top and bottom padding.

   This will ensure that our alignment matches the upper areas. Since the padding of the `#footer p` element already has a 10px top and bottom margin, we'll leave the top and bottom `padding` zeroed here.

   Using shorthand, the code looks like this:

   ```
   #footer {
     padding: 0 30px 0 40px;
     border-top: 10px solid #2d2d70;
   }
   ```

   Now, remember our three columns are placed in a single div called `outer_wrap`. We'll use that div to place what appears to be the topmost border of the footer. However, it will actually be the bottom border of the `outer_wrap` div.

4. In the `outer_wrap` div, place a `#36357d` 10px solid bottom border on the bottom of the div.

This gives us the following code:

```css
#outer_wrap {
  background: #403e8a url(images/main_back.jpg) repeat-x;
  border-bottom: 10px solid #36357d;
}
```

We're really making progress—and with no images! We need to create a little bit of breathing room at the bottom of the main content area. If we place the bottom padding on our `outer_wrap`, it would push the `inner_wrap` up, and the faux column it contains won't appear to go all the way to the bottom any more (the background color of the `outer_wrap` would show in the space). Instead, we'll place it on the `inner_wrap` itself.

5. Select `#inner_wrap` on the tag selector. Place 20px of padding at the bottom.

```css
#inner_wrap {
  background: url(images/liquid_left.gif) repeat-y 20% 0px;
  padding-bottom: 20px;
}
```

Floating Left and Right

With the stripes created, let's turn our attention to the content within the footer itself. We have a copyright and an unordered list of links. One is on the right side and the other is on the left. It's not uncommon to want to align elements both left and right. There are several ways to accomplish this—from absolute positioning to floating one or more elements.

For our footer, it seems simplest to float the unordered list and leave the **p** element on the left. Let's put the XHTML code into our page first. Because a floated element must precede the element you want it to sit next to, place the **ul** before the **p** element in the source order.

1. Add the following code to the footer (removing the holder p element there now):

```
<ul>
 <li><a href="#">Home</a></li>
 <li><a href="#">Site Map</a></li>
 <li><a href="#">Contact Us</a></li>
</ul>
<p>Copyright 2005-2009 Pleasantville Regional Chamber.
All rights reserved</p>
```

Let's quickly look at the CSS code beginning with the footer's p element. We previously created a global element selector for the p element. It is controlling the color and **font-family** for all p elements on the page. The footer is the only area where the p elements differ. They're not white, nor are they Arial, so we must override those properties with this more specific selector— #footer p.

2. Select the **#footer** p rule and give it the color value of #5C5A99. Select the Font-family that begins with Georgia, just like our headings. We'll also give this p element a width of 59% so that it only covers a little more than half the page—even if the text size on the page is a good deal larger than we designed for.

```
#footer p {
 margin: 0;
 padding: 10px 0;
 width: 59%;
 color: #5c5a99;
 font-family: Georgia, "Times New Roman", Times, serif;
}
```

We'll turn our attention now to the unordered list. Since we've built two menus already, it should be pretty simple for you to create this one. We'll structure it like the top horizontal navigation, but style the links as in the vertical menu.

1. Since we globally zeroed the list defaults, we'll start by creating a descendant selector (**#footer ul**) and floating the list right.

2. In the Properties pane of the CSS Styles panel, give the new rule a **max-width** of 39%.

N *IE6 and older does not support max-width. In that browser, if the text size is larger or the window very narrow, the copyright text on the left (non-floated p element) will simply drop to the next line, getting out of the way of the floated ul. There are JavaScript solutions, but we find many times, it's fine to give IE5 and 6 access to the same content, but in a slightly different way. We're fine with the possibility that the p element might be one line below the links on the right.*

N *Dreamweaver wrongly stacks the links in the footer up when you float the ul one direction and the li the other. No, we don't know why, but we know it's been this way for a while. Just ignore it—Live View gives you the correct rendering.*

N *If, in your own designs, you need to give your horizontal ul a width, using ems instead of pixels or percentages will allow you to keep the lists floated left and in the proper order. If you can't do that for some reason, you'll likely have to float the lists to the right to keep them right aligned. But remember, the first list item floats right first— so if you float the list items right, your links will be in reverse order, with the first link the farthest to the right.*

Notice that the 59% width added with the 39% `max-width` gives us 98%. Staying below a full 100% width assures us that our p and ul elements will stay on the same line if the page is viewed with a larger text size.

```
#footer ul {
   float: right;
  max-width: 39%;
}
```

3. Float the list items themselves to the left by creating a `#footer li` selector.

```
#footer li {
  float: left;
}
```

Since we didn't give our ul a width, and it is floated, it has "shrink wrapped" its content and thus we can float our li to the left, keeping the links in the order we desire.

4. Create a selector for the links - `#footer li a`. Set them to `display: block` (to keep them clickable for the full width), and style them with the light blue color (`#5c5a99`) and 10px padding all the way around. Remove the underlines.

5. Finally, create a grouped selector to set the hover/active/focus color to #FF9F00.

```
#footer li a {
  display: block;
  padding: 10px;
  color: #5c5a99;
  text-decoration: none;
}
#footer li a:hover, #footer li a:active, #footer li
a:focus {
  color: #FF9F00;
}
```

Copyright 2005-2009 Pleasantville Regional Chamber. All rights reserved   Home   Site Map   Contact Us

FIGURE 4.42 With the footer complete, we're down to some simple styling.

Putting on the Final Touches

Our page is looking great and with just a little more styling, some bug busting and clean up, we're done!

The Plain Vanilla Links

We've already made our links white. In case there's a user agent that doesn't give them underlines by default, we'll add underlines. We'll set a pale gray to indicate a link that's been visited and for our hover style, we'll simply remove the underline.

1. Click into a link on the page, select the **a** element and add the underline value.

N *Remember to keep your links in proper order. LVHA(F) or LoVeHAte is another trick people use to recall the order.*

2. Create a grouped selector for the hover pseudo-class along with the active and focus pseudo-classes. Remove the underline.

```
a {
  color: #FFF;
  text-decoration: underline;
}
a:hover, a:active, a:focus {
  text-decoration: none;
}
```

Limiting the Page Width

Our very last chore in the main CSS page is to give our overall container a minimum width and maximum width. It's not imperative, but it is a good idea to limit the width, especially when you're dealing with a three-column layout. On the small size end of the spectrum, you want to be sure your columns remain readable and don't get everything squished and flowing out of bounds. On the large size end, you want to be sure your line length remains readable. Lines that run *too* long become very hard to read.

1. Select the container div. Add a min-width of 770px and a max-width of 1500px.

    The max-width value is arbitrary really. We opened the page really wide, looked at the length of the lines, moved it down to the point where it looked readable and measured. The max we felt was readable was 1500px. (Yes, there are more scientific ways to deal with line length issues and many studies have been done. Search the web to read more about the subject.)

If the viewport is wider than 1500px, the dark blue body background color (that shows from the footer down) will appear on the right side. It's not especially attractive in this case, so we'll center the container to give it a more balanced look.

2. Since the container already has a width, all we need to center it is auto left and right margins. (You might as well give the top and bottom zero as well.)

```
#container {
 width: 100%;
 text-align: left;
 font-size: 80%;
 min-width: 770px;
 max-width: 1500px;
 margin: 0 auto;
}
```

FIGURE 4.43 Our page shown with a really, *really* wide viewport.

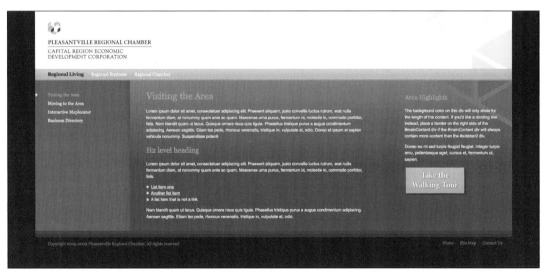

If IE Ain't Happy, Ain't Nobody Happy

We've now completed the page for browsers that render well to standards. Go ahead and preview it in a few browsers. If you're on a PC (or if you have IE available to you on the Mac), you'll probably see a lovely page until you view it in Internet Explorer. Well, IE6 or older. IE7 actually renders just fine.

FIGURE 4.44 IE6 is a real beauty!

As scary as it looks, the fix really isn't that tough. In fact, both things that need to be added are related to the one thing you should remember if you forget everything else—hasLayout. If hasLayout isn't triggered in some way, IE is a very unhappy camper.

Let's analyze our blown-up page. The first thing we see is that the horizontal navigation bar has no color. And furthermore, we have a sneaking suspicion that the fact that the vertical navigation is sitting to the right of the horizontal navigation bar (which comes next in the flow) further indicates the issue is related to the horizontal ul element. We'll do the first thing any good web developer should pull from their arsenal when working with IE issues: zoom:1.

The zoom property, as we explained in the CSS review chapter, is a proprietary Microsoft property. Setting it to 1 changes nothing. No harm, no foul. But it fixes many a hasLayout (dimensional) issue, so it's the first thing we'll try. Since it is proprietary and it won't validate, it should always go into an IECC. Since IE7 is not showing the same issues, we'll put this into our `<!--[if lte IE 6]>` IECC.

1. In the `<!--[if lte IE 6]>` IECC that already exists in the head, add the same rule we wrote in our style sheet for the horizontal navigation—`#header ul` and give it the declaration `zoom: 1;`.

    The fact that there's no width or height on the navigation, as well as any other properties that trigger `hasLayout`, was our clue that this is where we need to go first. Refresh the page if you have IE6. Things are looking better. The only problem we see left is the space in the left side vertical menu.

2. Again, our links don't have any dimension and they're set to `display:block`. This triggers a white space bug in IE. Guess what the fix is? Yup, you got it. The `hasLayout` trigger, `zoom:1`. Add the `#sidebar1 li a` rule, creating a grouped rule, to the rule we just created for the `zoom:1` fix.

    ```
    <!--[if lte IE 6]>
     <style type="text/css">
    #header ul, #sidebar1 li a { zoom: 1; }
    #sidebar2 { height: 145px; }
    </style>
    <![endif]-->
    ```

The bugs are squashed flat.

Take a moment to do a last tidy to your CSS. Move the rules around in the All pane of the CSS Styles panel to organize them as we've done before. The grouped selectors starting with `a:hover` should follow the `a` element selector. Move the new footer selectors into the footer section.

You've probably wondered about those comments Stephanie put into the CSS documents for the CSS layouts. They're a great learning tool if you need them as you build, but more often than not, you'll want to lighten up the page before you put it on the server. (After you get really comfortable, you may want to remove them from the beginning!) Dreamweaver doesn't come with a built-in way to remove them, but you can remove them with a regular expression in the Find and Replace dialog.

N   *Regular expressions are powerful tools you can use within Dreamweaver. To learn more about how to utilize them more fully, read "Introduction to Regular Expressions in Dreamweaver" at Adobe's Developer Center, http://www.adobe.com/devnet/ dreamweaver/articles/regular_ expressions_02.html.*

N *David Powers' "Stored Query to Remove CSS Comments" is available, free of charge, at his site: http://foundationphp.com/ tools/css_comments.php.*

If you haven't learned to write regular expressions yet, or really don't care to, David Powers has come to your rescue. He's provided a free extension (with instructions) that gives you a simple way to delete them all in one fell swoop. If you still need the comments but want to lighten up the page (or hide the training wheels from your client), make a copy of your page to keep. And strip the comments from the document that you're placing on the server.

When we strip the comments at the end of the project, we take a brief moment to comment the main sections of the CSS document to make it easier to find what we need later.

Your page is complete! Take a look at it in your browser and admire your work.

So what have you've accomplished in this chapter? You've learned how to deal with percentage-based layouts and to overcome the challenges that margin and padding give in these layouts. Additionally, you've learned how to effectively use background images within percentage-based columns as well as creating a liquid faux column; you can style lists, including both horizontal and vertical menus without the use of inline images; and create a current page indicator. Finally, we've explored the use of Photoshop CS3, together with Dreamweaver CS4 to optimize or streamline the production process.

CHAPTER 5

Creating a More Complex Design with Elastic Layouts

AS WEB DESIGNERS and developers, we generally have a lot of smart and professional reasons for building a site the way we do. We position and size page elements to direct the focus of users, making it easy for them to find what we want them to see and to do what we want them to do. We carefully design and develop what we plan to be an enjoyable, engaging experience for our audience—and a profitable one for our client.

But let's pause for a moment and consider the situation for some of our site visitors: in particular, those with low vision. We're not talking about blind people, but rather those with trouble viewing text comfortably at default font sizes. This includes a large percentage of people in their late thirties or older (your authors included!), as well as people with eyesight issues that aren't age-related.

Although not all of these users are savvy enough to know how to manipulate font sizes in their browser, many are—and those with exceptionally poor vision almost definitely are. But when increasing the font size in a browser, the width of the layout usually constrains the text. Text becomes big in comparison to everything else on the page, and line lengths can become ridiculously short, making online reading a difficult and frustrating exercise.

Checkpoint 3.4 of the W3C's Web Accessibility Initiative (WAI) Web Content Accessibility Guidelines (WCAG) 1.0 recommends the use of relative units. See http://www.w3.org/TR/WAI-WEBCONTENT/wai-pageauth.html#tech-relative-units.

Yes, it's pretty inconvenient, not to mention inconsiderate, of users to be less than perfect, grow older than their thirties, or for whatever reason have low vision. The spoilsports! But the good news is that we can design accessible web sites that will allow more design precision and scale—with text, layout and even images—while retaining the proportions of our intended design. These layouts are referred to as being "elastic" due to their overall stretchiness.

FIGURE 5.1 The comp for our fictional travel site.

In this project, we are building a web site for a fictional client, a travel agency specializing in land-based travel.

Create a folder called **TheRoadAhead**, and define the site, making the folder you just created the site root. Be sure to place the sliced images you download from the book's site in the images folder.

Let's roll!

What Is Accessibility and Why Should I Care?

An accessible web site is a site that doesn't exclude user groups from accessing the site's content. It is not merely about catering to blind people; an accessible web site embraces all aspects of making content available in as many formats, to as many people, in as many user agents and devices, as possible. Truly accessible content can be accessed and processed independently from its visual appearance in a browser.

Writing well-structured, semantic markup is the first and most important step in providing accessible web sites. Fortunately it's not hard to do, nor is it expensive to implement! It enables alternative devices, including mobile devices as well as screen readers, to render content appropriately and according to their own standards and specifications. It also assists people with all kinds of disabilities—the blind and deaf, quadriplegics, people with motor difficulties or arthritis or carpal tunnel or any other condition that makes using a mouse or keyboard challenging, and yes, even those who simply need glasses to see clearly. And the list goes on: web accessibility also includes internationalization and the arrangement and writing of content in such a way as to assist those with poor language skills or cognitive difficulties.

What web accessibility is:

Web accessibility is about making sure the content of a web site is accessible to as many people on as many devices and as many user agents as possible.

What web accessibility is not:

Web accessibility is not about duplicating experience.

Why should I care?

- **Humanistic principles:** caring that people with disabilities or using alternative devices have as much right and need to access the content of a web site as those who are totally fit and sitting at desktop computers with the most modern equipment.

- **Business principles:** people using alternative user agents are your customers, too! Why exclude them? In fact, when a web site is built accessibly, buying online can be much easier for a person with a disability than leaving the house.

- **Anti-discrimination laws:** these are becoming more widespread and more strictly enforced and litigation can be costly to a business in terms of time, money, reputation and goodwill.

The New Document

Let's begin with one of Dreamweaver's built-in elastic layouts and modify it for our client.

Open the New dialog and in the Blank Page section, select 3 column elastic, header and footer layout. Set the DocType to XHTML 1.0 Transitional and in the CSS Layout drop-down list, select Create

New File and save the file in your site under the default name of `thrColElsHdr.css` (or change it to whatever you desire). Save the (X)HTML page as `index.html`.

Title the open (X)HTML document "The Road Ahead :: Travel the Roads", either using the Title input in the Document toolbar or directly in the head section of the (X)HTML code.

Resetting the CSS Defaults

In this project we are only going to be working with a three-column layout, so we don't need the `thrColElsHdr` prefix on all our rules. If you've forgotten how to remove it, head back to Chapter 4 and apply the instructions in *Simplifying the CSS Selectors* to the `thrColElsHdr` prefix. Using the Find and Replace dialog, delete this class in both the CSS and (X)HTML document as well as from the body element.

In this chapter, we're going to use a new method of zeroing out the default settings in the different browsers to give us a solid starting point.

1. Open the `thrColElsHdr.css` file.

2. Add the following code to the top of the document:

```
/* v1.0 | 20080212 */
html, body, div, span, applet, object, iframe,
h1, h2, h3, h4, h5, h6, p, blockquote, pre,
a, abbr, acronym, address, big, cite, code,
del, dfn, em, font, img, ins, kbd, q, s, samp,
small, strike, strong, sub, sup, tt, var,
b, u, i, center,
dl, dt, dd, ol, ul, li,
fieldset, form, label, legend,
table, caption, tbody, tfoot, thead, tr, th, td {
    margin: 0;
    padding: 0;
    border: 0;
    outline: 0;
    font-size: 100%;
    vertical-align: baseline;
    background: transparent;
}
```

N *The title is the only required element in the head of the document. If this were a real client, we would be sure to use good keywords in the title of our page so that the search engine spiders would find them relevant and even delicious, and would come back often! It's always a good idea to feed the spiders well.*

N *Though we don't use a reset file ourselves, it's a common way for many to start their CSS documents and, as such, we felt you should be aware of it.*

N *Though many elements are included in this initial zeroing of values, you may notice that certain form elements are missing. These were left out since, due to the nature of form elements, zeroing them gives poor results in some browsers. This is also the reason we don't recommend using the universal selector (*) to zero everything at once.*

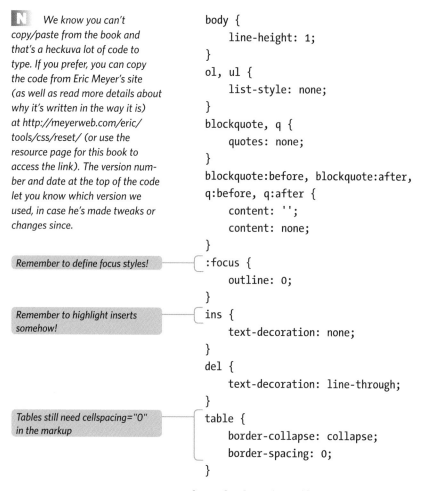

We know you can't copy/paste from the book and that's a heckuva lot of code to type. If you prefer, you can copy the code from Eric Meyer's site (as well as read more details about why it's written in the way it is) at http://meyerweb.com/eric/ tools/css/reset/ (or use the resource page for this book to access the link). The version number and date at the top of the code let you know which version we used, in case he's made tweaks or changes since.

```
body {
    line-height: 1;
}
ol, ul {
    list-style: none;
}
blockquote, q {
    quotes: none;
}
blockquote:before, blockquote:after,
q:before, q:after {
    content: '';
    content: none;
}
```

Remember to define focus styles!

```
:focus {
    outline: 0;
}
```

Remember to highlight inserts somehow!

```
ins {
    text-decoration: none;
}
del {
    text-decoration: line-through;
}
```

Tables still need cellspacing="0" in the markup

```
table {
    border-collapse: collapse;
    border-spacing: 0;
}
```

The code above is a nifty way to combat some potential cross-browser issues, as well as to simplify the CSS, in one hit. Our thanks to the inimitable Eric Meyer for this technique. If, as the design progresses, we want any of our elements to have something other than a zero value (and we will!), we will add the necessary value to the relevant rule in our style sheet.

In your own sites, you may not use all the selectors included in this block of code. But using this CSS reset technique means that if you add selectors at any point in the future, the groundwork is done to avoid unexpected surprises.

As you remember (you do remember, right?) from the CSS review chapter, specificity being equal, the last declaration on the page for any given selector overrides any previous declarations and will be applied by the browser. However, in the majority of cases, zeroing values in a block of code at the top of the style sheet means we don't have to zero the same values individually later. We simply allow our new values later in the cascade to override the zeroed values we don't desire.

Creating a Reset Snippet

> **N** *To reuse this snippet, simply place the cursor wherever you wish the snippet to be added, open the Snippets pane, and double-click on the snippet. It will be inserted at the cursor. And if you're really into time-saving aids in Dreamweaver, you can even add a keyboard shortcut to the snippet. To do this, choose Keyboard Shortcuts from the Edit menu (PC). You'll need to duplicate the default shortcut group by clicking the Duplicate set button. Give your new set a name, then choose Snippets from the Commands drop-down list. Locate your new snippet and assign a keyboard shortcut by pressing the plus "+" button. Press your desired shortcut keys and then click the Assign button. Voilà! Now you've always got the snippet at your finger tips!*

This reset is so handy, let's add it to our Dreamweaver Snippets for future reuse. To do so:

1. Highlight the reset code in the CSS document.

2. Select the Snippets tab in the Files panel.

3. In the interests of snippet organization, we'll create a new folder for CSS snippets (that is, if you're not so organized that you already have one!). Make sure none of the existing folders are selected. (If one is, click in the area at the bottom of the list of folders and the selection will clear.) Click the New Snippet Folder icon at the bottom of the Snippets pane. Name the new folder CSS.

4. Click the Add Snippet icon at the bottom of the Snippets pane or right-click the selected code and choose Create New Snippet from the contextual menu.

   In the dialog that appears, you will see that the CSS code you previously highlighted is already inserted in the text area.

5. Name the snippet CSS Reset, give it a description if you wish, and choose the Insert block radio button. Click OK.

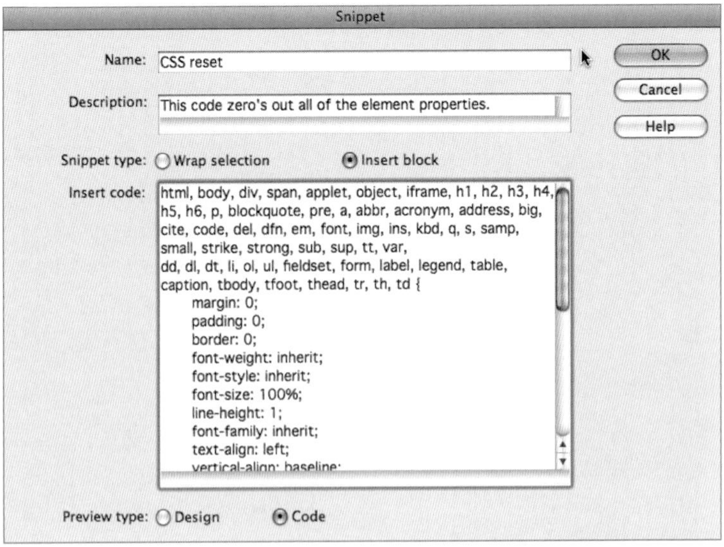

FIGURE 5.2 Our handy CSS reset code will always be available to us as a code snippet.

While we will further define many styles in our style sheet, some of the declarations in the CSS layout "out of the box" that zeroed margin and padding now become duplicated CSS. We'll clean these up as we come across them to avoid making the style sheet unnecessarily large. As always, when deleting anything, be sure to test each change, ready to Undo if required. Sometimes styles influence, or are influenced by, other styles in a way that is not obvious at first glance.

It's Just a Jump to the Left

N *The scrollbar area is what is referred to as part of the browser chrome. Approximately 15–20 pixels should be accounted for in your overall page width for browser chrome to avoid a horizontal scroll bar. So, for example, an 800px wide page should actually be designed at 780px wide.*

Centered pages can actually appear to jump depending on whether or not a scrollbar is present. It's not an actual movement, but it looks as if it is, because the layout is in a slightly different position in the browser window. This can be very disconcerting when it's not obvious to the user (and especially the designer) what is happening, and it may be perceived as a design flaw. But not to worry, there's a quick fix!

Since we don't want to remove the scrollbar from all pages (that would be silly), we're simply going to give every page a scrollbar. The code below will apply a height of 100% to the body and html elements—and then add a margin of 1 pixel. Add it to your page right below the reset:

```
html, body {
  height: 100%;
  margin-bottom: 1px;
}
```

The margin adds 1 pixel to the full height of the viewport, and thus creates a scrollbar. Even small pages with very little content are convinced they have just a pixel more than will fit. It's not ideal, but neither is the layout jump. We've decided to go with the lesser of two evils. Save and view the page.

Tweaking the Body

We want to be judicious about customizing the CSS reset: often, it doesn't make sense to do so. But within reason, it's made to be customized. Since our designer chose a blue for the headings and text, we'll set the color universally in the body element. But which body element selector should we use? Currently, the body selector is included in the first grouped rule in the set of reset rules, a single element selector in the reset, the rule we just added (grouped with the html element) and the body selector that is included in the CSS layout.

Logically, since our designer chose a blue for the headings and text, we could actually place it in the reset. However, to keep things simpler for following along in this chapter, we're going to adjust the body rule that came with the CSS layouts in Dreamweaver.

1. Click inside the (X)HTML document and choose **<body>** on the tag selector. In the CSS Styles panel (Current view) select the last single body rule in the Rules pane.

   Do not select the first rule of the CSS reset, which also includes the body element, since it also embraces many other elements.

2. In the Properties pane, change the color property to a value of #336.

3. Select both the margin and padding property and click the trashcan icon to delete (or right-click and choose Delete).

N *As described in Chapter 3, this is shorthand for the longer #333366. The color displayed will be exactly the same for both; however, it is easier and more efficient to use the shorter version.*

FIGURE 5.3 After applying the CSS reset, some of our styling has been lost.

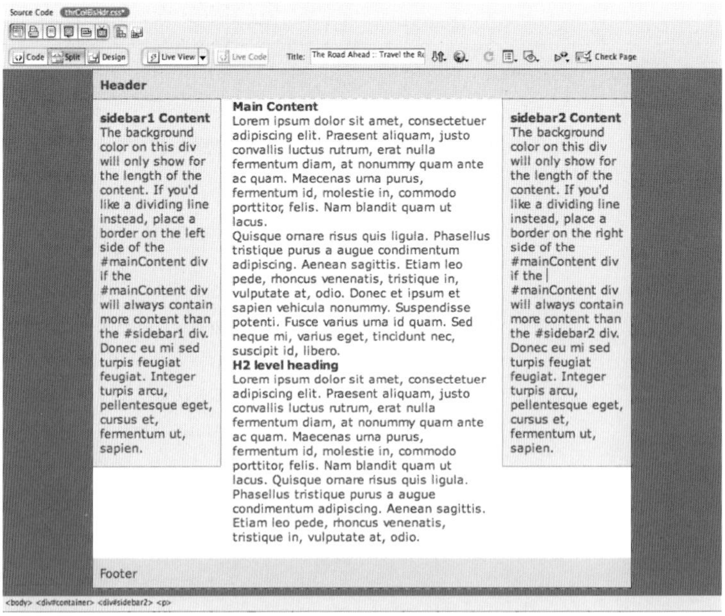

Now the text on our page is colored blue to match our comp and we've gotten rid of some redundant properties. Due to the reset rule, it looks a bit odd since none of the elements have their default margin or padding. Don't worry about that for the moment; we'll have everything peachy in a bit.

Before we go on, let's review the basic structure of the page. A container with a specified width is centered in the browser window. Within it is a header and footer and a three-column content area. The center column has no width specified and uses side margins to clear the two, narrower side columns. The side columns are floated and have set widths. This is exactly like the basic structure of the other CSS layouts we've used thus far: nothing new, here. Or is there?

The Significance of the Em Unit

This particular layout is special because the widths on the divs are set in em units, rather than in the more common pixels or percentages. In print, an em is a unit of measurement based on the width of the uppercase letter M, which varies for different fonts. Em unit measurements have been in use for typesetting since movable type was invented—and no, we're not talking about the blogging software! A browser interprets 1em to equal the default font size of the browser, which (unless it has been changed by the user) is 16px (regardless of the font-family specified).

The Em Is Relative

Unlike pixels, an em is a relative unit. Since an em unit is based on font size, the actual width of a div (or size of an em) changes if a font declaration is set directly on the div or if the overall font size is increased by the user. In contrast, divs sized using percentages, also a relative unit, calculate their size based on their parent element.

In other words, when using ems for layout, the dimensions of the layout expand or contract depending on the user's font size: the overall proportions of the page and its contents, including line length, remain the same. A person viewing your page with a default font size of 32px sees the same number of words per line as the person with a 12px, 16px, or 25px default.

Let's take a quick peek before this gets too confusing.

1. Head back to our `index.html` page and preview it in a standards-compliant browser (meaning not Internet Explorer—we never go there till the end of a project).

2. Using your browser of choice's method, increase the text size (Ctrl+ on Firefox and Safari). You can even decrease the text size.

    Notice how the entire layout resizes—not just the text? That's the beauty of the em. Unless you set a maximum width, your user has full control—and perfect line lengths!

TEXT SIZING

N *Remember: though 100% = 1em, this equality only applies to the font-size property. A block level element given a 20em width is not the same as one given a 20% width since the em unit is based on font size, and a percentage is based on a specific portion of the containing element.*

All the CSS layouts in Dreamweaver have a body rule with a font-size value of 100%, meaning 100% of the browser's default font size. Since 1em is also equivalent to the browser's default font size, for all practical purposes, a font-size value of 100% equals 1em. When we set font sizes elsewhere in our (X)HTML document in em units, the sizes are relative to this value.

DIV SIZING

Some developers set font-sizes directly on divs to size everything within them down by the same, relative amount. We won't enter the debate of whether that's best practice, but we will discuss when it's safe—or not—in elastic layouts. Since the container holds all other divs in the layout, setting a font-size on the container resizes everything within it the same relative amount. This gives us consistency.

However, if the side columns are given differing font sizes, their widths relative to each other will vary. In fact, doing this can completely break your layout. Let's look at this in Dreamweaver to make it crystal clear.

N *If you can't drag the guides out, go to View > Rulers and choose Show. Once the rulers are showing, you can click and drag the guides across the page.*

1. Select the `<div#sidebar1>` in the tag selector.

2. From the left edge of your document window, click, hold, and drag a guide out to the left edge of `sidebar1`. Do the same thing for the right side of the `sidebar1`.

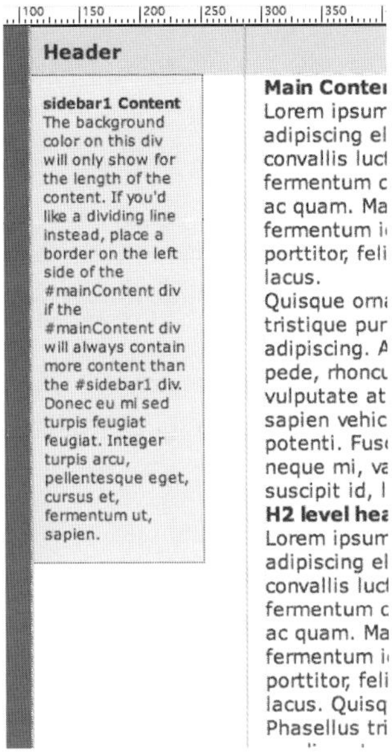

FIGURE 5.4 The overall width of sidebar1 has decreased, yet the rest of the page remains the same.

3. Place your mouse between the two guides (you don't have to click). Press the Ctrl key.

   Dreamweaver tells you the actual pixel width between the two guides. Ours measured 177px.

4. In the CSS Styles panel, add the `font-size` property to the `#sidebar1` selector and give it a value of `.8em`.

   You'll notice an instant shrinking of not just the fonts, but the overall div width as well. But the `mainContent`, whose width was not affected, retains a margin using the em unit sizing that descends to it from the container. So we have more white space between the `sidebar1` div and the `mainContent` div than we anticipated.

5. Move the guide, which should be sitting out in the margin of the `mainContent`, back to the `sidebar1`'s right side where it belongs.

6. Measure the actual pixel space using Ctrl again.

   Although both sidebars have an overall width of 11em units, the size of `sidebar1` has shrunk to 142px, while `sidebar2` remains at the original size. Imagine the problems you'd have if all the divs had their own font-sizing placed on the div itself—especially if they were all floated. Buyer beware!

7. Remove the `font-size` you just placed on `sidebar1` since, as you can see, this is definitely not a safe way to size our layout.

To avoid this scenario, the best practice is, if you're going to put the `font-size` on a div at all, only use the containing div. The `font-size` is then applied uniformly to all contents of the page. From there, you can change the `font-size` on block elements within the individual containers of the page, such as the **p** and **heading** elements themselves. This won't change the overall div size.

Limitations of Em-Based Layouts

Here are a couple more things to consider when designing with em-based layouts:

Images are generally assigned a fixed pixel width (even if no width property is set, the browser calculates the image's width in pixels). Though we can set the width of an image using em units, and thereby allow them to scale with the font size as well, most images will only scale nicely to a point. After that, they can start to look somewhat ugly and pixelated. We'll look at scaling images in more detail later in this chapter.

Due to the expansive nature of em widths, your design must allow for horizontal growth. As the layout resizes beyond the width of the viewport, a horizontal scrollbar appears. Workarounds have their own limitations and we'll consider these later in this chapter as well.

Even with a few things to keep in mind, the accessibility and flexibility of em-based layouts make them very attractive indeed.

Some Overall Type Adjustments

N *It is often quicker to simply type the unit of measure in the value field after typing the value rather than clicking and selecting the unit of measure from the adjacent drop-down list. Dreamweaver honors the value typed into the field even if another unit, for example pixels, is pre-selected in the drop-down list.*

Now that you understand how fonts are sized, and how em units are applied, let's style the container of our page.

Typically, the browser default font size, which we've left at 100%, is too large for most developers, clients, and users. We're going to scale the font-size down on the container.

1. Click to place the cursor anywhere in the (X)HTML document and select `<div#container>` from the tag selector.

2. In the `#container` rule, click the Add Property link in the Properties section and set the font-size to 0.8em.

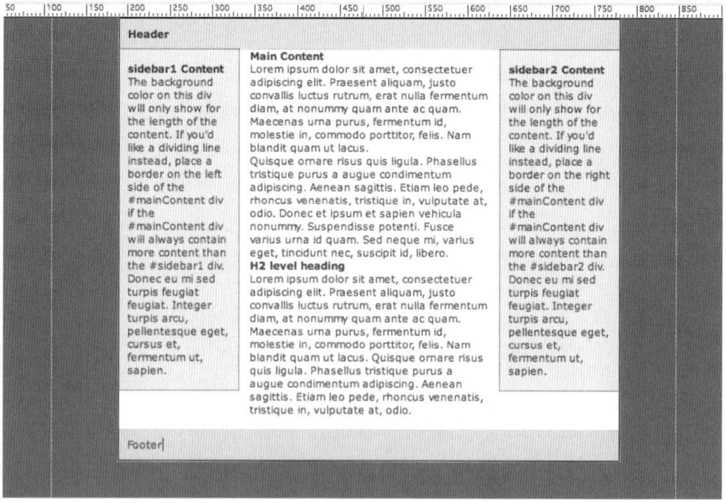

FIGURE 5.5 You can see by Dreamweaver's guides that the overall width of the container has decreased due to the change in font size.

Currently our style sheet has #container set to 46em, which under normal circumstances would be the approximate equivalent of 736 pixels, where 1em is the default browser font size of 16px. As soon as we reduced the font size on the container element, the page shrank in width. But according to our designer's comp, we want it to take up to 760 pixels (or its em equivalent) when the page loads, so that users with default font sizing set will see a page that fits nicely in a 800px wide screen resolution.

N *Wondering how we calculated that? Here's the math. By default, 1em = 16px. The font size on #container is 0.8em. To get the pixel equivalent for the actual font size used in the page, we multiply the default pixel size by the em unit we've given the div—16 x 0.8 = 12.8px. So 1em in the container is 12.8px. We want the overall width to be 760px. We simply divide our overall 760px by the size of our font. 760 ÷ 12.8 = 59.375em. Easy, right? You can see why it might be easier not to place any sizing on the container, and simply size the font on each element.*

1. Select the #container rule in the CSS Styles panel's Rules section again.

2. Set the width property to 59.375em. (A very odd number indeed!)

    You can see the changes reflected in the CSS file (with the comments removed here to avoid clutter):

    ```
    #container {
      width: 59.375em;
      background: #FFFFFF;
      margin: 0 auto;
      border: 1px solid #000000;
      text-align: left;
      font-size: 0.8em;
    }
    ```

DEFINING OUR MAJOR TYPE ELEMENTS

Now that we've got our overall font size and container scaled down, we'll turn our attention back to the compressed page we were left with after our CSS reset. Let's redefine our p element as a start.

N *We are going to reuse this font selection, so it makes sense to add it to the drop-down list. In the drop-down list, select Edit Font List to open a dialog box where individual fonts can be selected, grouped together, and placed in the list. (Specific instructions for this are included in Chapter 3.)*

1. In the CSS Styles panel, click the New CSS Rule icon. Choose Tag and type p into the Selector box (or choose p from the drop-down list). Click OK.

2. In the Type section, add the fonts "Lucida Grande", Arial, Helvetica, sans-serif.

3. Next to Size, type in 1em. Alternatively you can type 1 and select ems from the drop-down list. Either method works. For the line height, type 1.5. Line height defaults to pixels so select multiple from the drop-down list.

4. In the Box category, for Margin, uncheck the check box next to "Same for all" and add a `margin-top` of 0.4em and a `margin-bottom` of 0.7em. Click OK.

5. Switch to the open style sheet document and scroll to the bottom of the file. If your Dreamweaver preferences are set to display CSS shorthand, you'll see this rule added at the bottom:

```
p {
    font: 1em/1.5 "Lucida Grande", Arial, Helvetica, sans-serif;
    margin-top: 0.4em;
    margin-bottom: 0.7em;
}
```

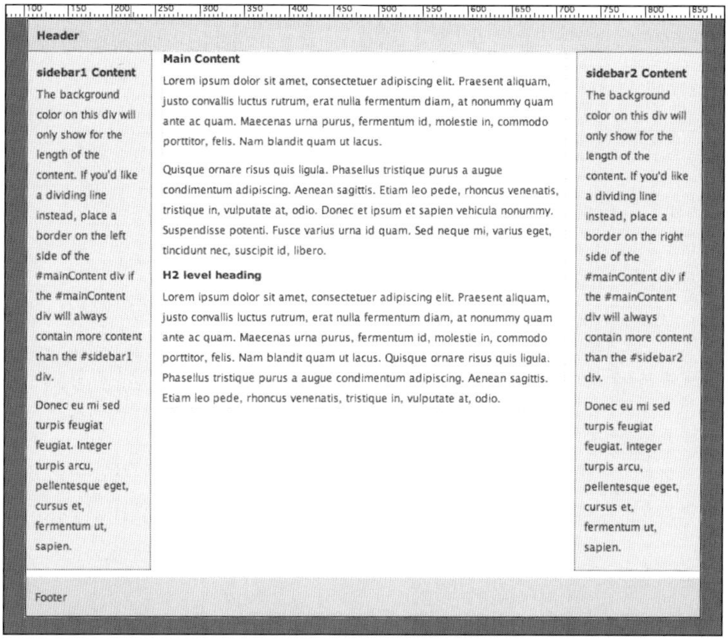

N *The 1em before the forward slash refers to the font size, and the 1.5 after the forward slash refers to the line height.*

FIGURE 5.6 We can see the increase in line height as well as the color applied to text on the page.

STYLING THE HEADINGS

Place your cursor into the heading with the text Main Content. In the tag selector, we can see this is an `<h1>` heading. But the rule shown for the h1 in the CSS Properties pane, and on the CSS area of the Property inspector, is the first grouped selector of the reset rule. h1 is listed as only one of many other selectors. We'll create a separate, specific h1 selector.

N *Dreamweaver gives you several different ways to create new CSS rules now. There's something to fit everyone's style!*

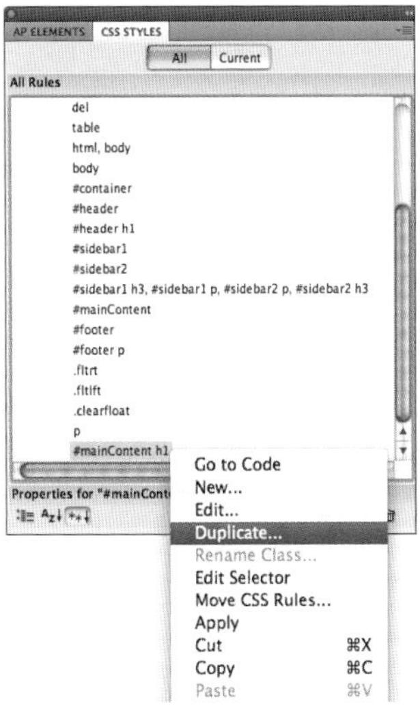

FIGURE 5.7 Duplicating a rule saves a lot of time.

1. With `<h1>` selected, select `<New CSS Rule>` on the Targeted Rule drop-down on the CSS area of the Property inspector. Click Edit Rule.

   The New CSS Rule dialog opens just as if we clicked the New CSS Rule icon at the bottom of the CSS Styles panel. Dreamweaver suggests a descendant selector of `#container #mainContent h1`, the full path to our element. All of our content is in `#container` so it's overly specific to include that as part of the selector.

2. Click the Less Specific button, leaving `#mainContent h1`, and click OK.

3. In the Type category, set the Font-family to `Helvetica, Arial, sans-serif` by adding these fonts to the font list via the Edit Font List dialog as we did previously. For Font-size, type in `1.8em`. For Font-weight, choose `normal`. Click OK.

   Our main heading is now much larger but not as bold as a typical `h1` because we overrode that behavior with the `weight:normal` declaration.

   The style for `h2` should be identical to that of `#mainContent h1`, except that the size should be set to 1.6em. We could go through the process of creating the rule using the methods we used so far, or we can do it even faster. Hmm… we vote fast!

4. Switch to All mode in the CSS Styles Panel, and select the `#mainContent h1` rule that we just created.

5. Right-click and choose Duplicate. Name the selector `#mainContent h2` and click OK.

   The rule is added at the bottom of the style sheet below the h1 rule.

6. With the new rule selected, change the value of the font-size property to `1.6em`. (Remember it's in shorthand.)

7. Let's also add a bit of padding to the top of the h2 elements by clicking the Add Property link and typing `padding-top` and assigning the value `0.7em`.

N *The distance created by this top padding, along with a zero bottom padding, creates a visual association between the heading and the content directly below it.*

The CSS layouts in Dreamweaver all have a **h1** and **h2** element in the **mainContent** area, while the sidebar areas use an **h3** for their headings. Of course, we might want to add a **h3** to the **mainContent** area as well. Therefore, we'll create a rule for all **h3** elements regardless of their source location.

8. Duplicate the **#mainContent h1** rule again. Rename it to make it a simple element selector—**h3**.

    Creating an element selector will allow the settings here to cascade to any **h3** on the page, including the sidebars.

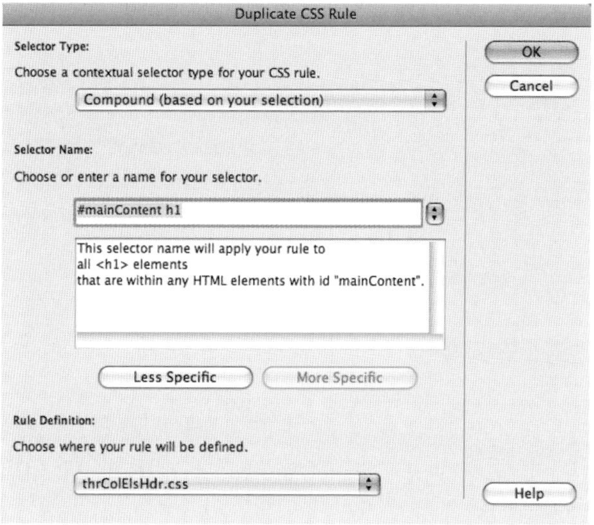

FIGURE 5.8 Duplicating a rule opens the Duplicate CSS Rule dialog, allowing you to create the proper name immediately.

9. Set the **font-size** of the new rule to **1.5em** in the Properties pane of the CSS panel.

    Now, we've created three simple rules to handle the **h1**, **h2**, and **h3** elements on the page.

```
#mainContent h1 {
  font: normal 1.8em Helvetica, Arial, sans-serif;
}
#mainContent h2 {
  font: normal 1.6em Helvetica, Arial, sans-serif;
  padding-top: 0.7em;
}
h3 {
  font: normal 1.5em Helvetica, Arial, sans-serif;
}
```

Though the headings are nicer, our page looks a bit gray and boring right now. Don't panic. Some small image files, and some smart CSS, and we'll have it looking as nice as our comp in no time.

The Visual Transformation

This is where the fun begins. Our framework for the page is established. All the basic CSS properties have been zeroed out and set to our liking. Now all that remains is to begin to add and style the actual page content. First up, let's get rid of all that ugly gray!

Styling the Header

We'll feel much better about our page when we have a nice logo in place. We're going to add the logo to the header, but as a background image so we can keep the nice gradient that extends down the page behind any text we later add to the page's content.

1. Click to place the cursor inside the header of the (X)HTML document, select `<div#header>` from the tag selector, and head back to the CSS Styles Panel. Click the Edit Style button to bring up the Edit dialog box.

2. In the Background section, remove the background color of `#DDDDDD`. We want the background to be transparent.

3. Click the browse button and navigate to the `logo.jpg` in the image directory of your site. Set Background-repeat to `no-repeat.`

4. Remove the values from the Padding section. Click OK.

    Naturally we don't want the existing heading text shouting Header at us, so we'll first change that to our company name.

5. In place of the word Header, type The Road Ahead—be sure not to delete the `<h1>` element while editing the text.

    Since we're using a background image that incorporates the logo, we want the company name accessible to those who won't see the logo. Let's use a trick to move the name off the screen but still keep it accessible to devices that read the text.

FIGURE 5.9 Well, at least we have a little slice of the header showing!

6. Make sure the cursor is placed inside the `<h1>` element in `<div#header>` and then click the Edit Style (pencil) icon in the CSS Styles Panel.

7. In the Box category, remove the padding and margin values.

Setting the width makes sure the name doesn't appear on the left side of the screen when a very large font size is used.

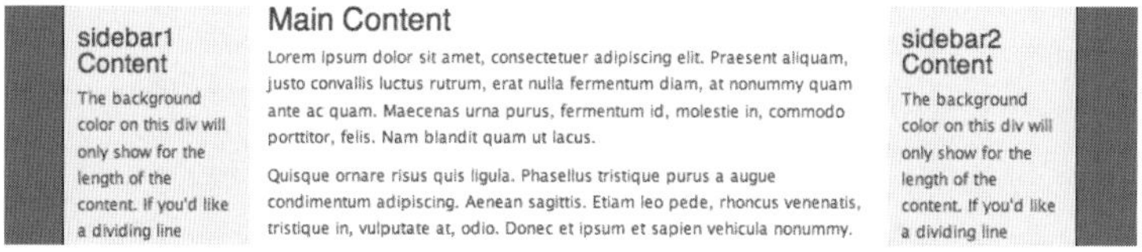

8. Go to the Positioning section of the CSS Rule Definition dialog box. From the Type drop-down list, set the position to **absolute** with a width of **80em** and set the left property in the Placement section to **-100em**. Click OK.

We now have the following rule in our style sheet:

```
#header h1 {
  width: 80em;
  left: -100em;
  position: absolute;
}
```

FIGURE 5.10 Egad! Now the whole thing has completely disappeared!

Warning! From here, we'll assume that you have gotten famil-iar with the way in which elements are selected in Dreamweaver, i.e., you click to place your cursor in an area of the page, then select X in the tag selector. You've only done it a thousand times at this point, so for brevity's sake, we'll begin to simply say "select X with the tag selector"—unless there is a real need for more explicit instructions.

But what just happened to our page?! Suddenly the sidebars have decided they want to be completely on top of the header!

As has happened in previous chapters, we've been slapped by the principles of positioning. We know that when an element is abso-lutely positioned, it moves out of the document flow and other elements around it no longer react to its presence and so attempt to move into its space. Before we positioned the **h1** element in the header, the header's space was reserved on the page (although, with the text so small, it wasn't much space). But the moment that the header's content, in this case the **h1** element, received posi-tioning information, the header collapsed because the elements that came next in the flow, namely the sidebars, no longer perceived it as needing or using any space.

The same effect would have occurred if we had floated the h1 element because, while a floated element is not completely taken out of the flow of the document, other floated elements attempt to move in around it.

In order to reserve the header's space on the page, and make it the height of the background image within it, we'll give it a height.

N *Don't worry about the fact that Dreamweaver is not respecting the height of the header yet; it will! All browsers show the project looking like Figure 5.11.*

1. Select `<div#header>` on the tag selector. (Since the header is completely collapsed, you may have to select the header from the source code of Code and Split view.)

2. Click Add Property in the CSS Styles panel. Type, or choose from the drop-down list, the property height. Give it a value of 110px (the height of the background image).

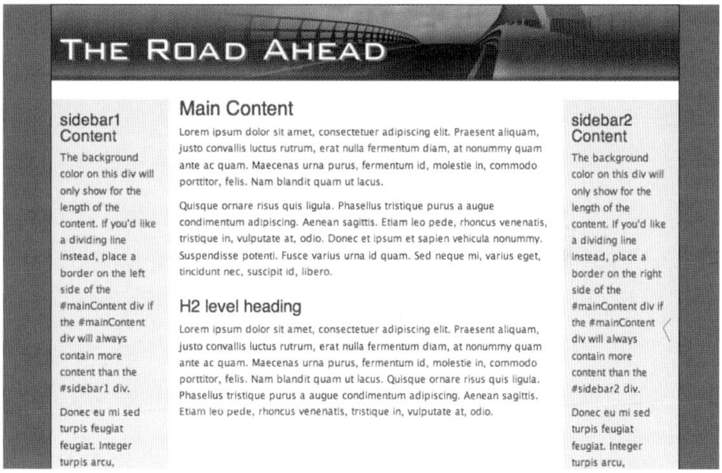

FIGURE 5.11 The height has forced the sidebars to begin 110px from the top of the container.

Our sidebars are beneath the header now, just where we want them. The logo is in the background of the header, the header text is gone, and our page is looking more like our comp all the time.

The Header Illusion

Our comp has the header color spanning the full screen, yet the header on our page is constrained by the #container and #header elements. This is easily remedied by applying a horizontally repeating background image (of the same gradient as our logo image) to the body element. The visual effect makes the header area appear seamless—as if it extends from the left to the right of the browser.

 *The background color on the container prevents the background on the body "behind" it (above it in the cascade) from showing through. We don't need to specifically set a background color on* container, sidebar1, *and* sidebar2 *because, as per the rules of CSS, they have a default transparent value, which is exactly what we want!*

1. Select <body> in the tag inspector. In the CSS Styles panel, click the Edit Style button to edit the body selector.

2. In the Background category, set the background color to #FFF.

3. Navigate to the tile.jpg background image in the images directory of the site.

4. Set the Backgound-repeat to repeat-x. Click OK.

   We have one more tweak to make before our header looks the way we want it to look.

FIGURE 5.12 Something's blocking the shadowed background image across our page!

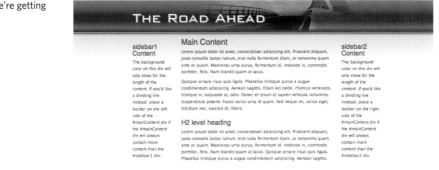

5. In the CSS Styles panel, open All mode and select #container.

6. In the properties for #container, select the background property. Right-click and choose Delete. Do the same for the border.

7. Repeat for #sidebar1 and #sidebar2. We don't need that ugly gray color anymore!

   Preview your page in Live View.

FIGURE 5.13 Now we're getting somewhere!

Adding the Horizontal Navigation

We're moving on to complete the header division of the page. If you've had any confusion or would like to check your work, this section starts with index_1.html in the builds directory of the site.

The last bit we need to complete the header division of the page is the two links on the right: Home and Contact. Most navigation is actually a list of choices (thus often called a menu) and this is no exception. Let's start with the markup, and then style it.

1. In order to place our code exactly where we want it, in the code portion of Code and Design view, place the cursor between the closing `</h1>` tag and the closing `</header>` tag.

    Make sure not to separate the comment noting the end of the header from its closing tag. `<!-- end #header -->`</div>`

2. In the HTML area of the Property inspector, click the unordered list icon.

    Viewing the code, you can see that an unordered list, including one set of list item tags, has been added on a new line under our `<h1>` element.

3. Place the cursor between the newly created `<li></li>` tags and type the name of our first list item, Home. Click in the Design view section, and the word Home appears in the header.

    It's not where we want it, or even the color we want yet, but we'll use CSS to sort that out shortly.

4. In Design view, place the cursor at the end of the word Home and press Enter or Return. We are now on not just a new line, but also in a new list item element. Type the second list item, Contact.

    In the Code view section, our header now contains the complete list.

```
<div id="header">
 <h1>The Road Ahead</h1>
 <ul>
 <li>Home</li>
 <li>Contact</li>
 </ul>
<!-- end #header --></div>
```

Now let's add the links.

N *If you would like more background on lists and navigation created from lists, you must have skipped Chapter 4! There's a wealth of information there—go check it out.*

 *Since we don't have a contact page yet, a placeholder hash mark (#) will give us the look of a link until we create the real one.*

5. In Design view, select Home. In the Property inspector, in the Link input field, type a placeholder hash mark (#).

6. Select Contact, and in the Link field, type #.

Our code is looking great, but the visual appearance of the list is far from ideal. It's time for some more CSS goodness!

FIGURE 5.14 We've got a list, but not a very pretty one—in fact, we can barely see it in Design view!

PLACING THE HORIZONTAL NAVIGATION

The CSS reset removed margins, padding, bullets, and all other styling that might apply to lists. We'll create a separate unordered list selector, unique to the header, in our style sheet and build the style up from this starting point.

1. Place your cursor into the unordered list. In the CSS Styles panel, click the New CSS Rule icon. Click Less Specific and create a rule for `#header ul`.

Once again, we'll place this in our external style sheet.

We've always said to be careful using absolute positioning with an element containing text that can grow in size. We still hold to that principle. But there are certain cases where it works. This list is positioned right above the bottom of the footer. Thus, as the text gets larger, it still remains at the bottom of the footer. It gets taller, but nothing within will grow and overlap.

2. In the Position category, select **absolute**. In Placement, give the right property the value of 0. Give the bottom property the value of 25px. Click OK.

The list is now positioned, but most certainly not in the header! What's gone wrong?

Remember an absolutely positioned element gets its position from its last positioned ancestor. Since the header has not been given position (and thus is static by default), the list goes up the document tree until it finds a parent to position within—in this case the body.

We are using pixels here because the height of the header is defined in pixels to allow for a background image defined in pixels. A pixel margin on the list provides consistency of positioning against the image background.

3. With `<header>` selected on the tag selector, add **position: relative** to the header rule.

If you glance at the document in Design view, you'll see that the list is now aligned to the right. That's a step in the right direction.

FIGURE 5.15 It's moving in the right direction.

Flattening the List to a Line

Though positioning our list took us in the right direction, we still need our list to be on a nice, even horizontal plane. We'll style the list item elements to take care of that.

1. Create another new CSS rule, this time naming the selector #header li.

In the last chapter, we created horizontal navigation by floating the list items. If you didn't do the last project and would like to understand when to float and when to create an inline list, head back to Chapter 4 and have a read.

2. In the CSS Rule Definition dialog, go to the Block category. For display, choose inline from the drop-down list.

   This setting causes the list items to display side-by-side.

3. Go to the Box category and uncheck the "Same for all" box for padding. Allocate a right padding of 0.3em and a left padding of 1.5em. This nicely spaces our inline list items, with a comfortable distance from the right side of the header. Click OK.

Styling the Horizontal Links

We've made progress on the positioning, but the font and colors leave something to be desired—in fact, they're downright unreadable! Thus far, we haven't needed to choose how to display the font in the header, because the **h1** element is positioned off the screen. But let's set a font family and a font size, and apply a color specifically for links in the **#header** div. We'll use the same font as in the paragraph text.

1. Duplicate the rule for the **p** selector. (You remember that trick, right? If not, go back and reread *Styling the Header*.) Name the new compound selector #header a:link. Click OK.

2. Select our new #header a:link rule. Delete the margin declarations that were applied to the paragraph by selecting each of them in the CSS Styles panel, Properties pane. Then right-click

and choose Delete (or simply press the trashcan icon while the declaration is selected).

We've gotten rid of what we don't want; now we'll add what we need.

3. Click the Add Property link. Set the color property to #FFF. Set text-decoration to none.

These styles will also apply to visited links for this navigation list. Instead of duplicating the rule, let's simply add #header a:visited to the #header a:link rule, creating a grouped selector.

4. Click into the list itself. The icon for the code navigator will appear (unless you've disabled it). If you disabled it, you can make it reappear by holding Ctrl+Alt and clicking.

FIGURE 5.16 The Code Navigator icon.

The Code Navigator appears, showing the full path through the CSS cascade to the element. Hovering over each rule shows you the declarations it contains. It does not, however, show you the declarations that apply or don't apply (with a strikethrough) to the element you've targeted. To see those handy strikethroughs, you have to use the CSS Styles panel. The Code Navigator is good for a quick jump to the code. Or for those who keep their CSS Styles panel minimized it can give you a quick look at the cascade.

FIGURE 5.17 The Code Navigator in its open state.

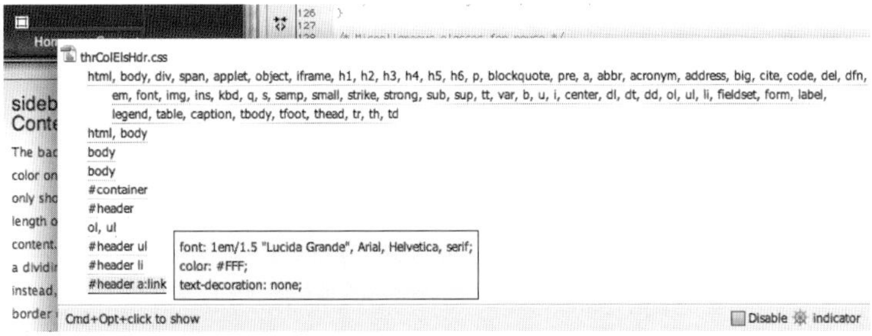

5. In the Code Navigator, click on the rule for #header a:link. This will place the cursor in the rule in our external style sheet. Place a comma directly after the selector name, then type in #header a:visited, leaving a space before the declaration block. We now have the following rule added to our style sheet:

```
#header a:link, #header a:visited {
  font: 1em/1.5 "Lucida Grande", Arial, Helvetica, sans-serif;
  color: #FFF;
```

```
text-decoration: none;
}
```

A common beginner's mistake when creating grouped selectors, especially for links, is to leave off the portion of the descendant selector that indicates the div you're doing the styling in—so for example, `#header a:link, a:visited`. The problem here is that the `a:visited` portion of our grouped rule is going to apply universally to all visited a elements. Remember that a group of selectors separated by commas is really a list of full selectors as they would be written if not grouped together. When the comma starts, a new selector starts, even though they're sharing the same declarations. So our group must show `#header a:link, #header a:visited` to apply to only the links in the `#header` div.

FIGURE 5.18 Now the list is looking more like a navigation bar.

We'll do something similar for the hover, active, and focus states of the links. We know in advance we're going to use a grouped selector, so we'll plan for that from the start.

6. Create a new rule by clicking on the New CSS Rule icon, create a Compound selector and name the selector: `#header a:hover, #header a:active, #header a:focus`

7. In the Type category, set the decoration to `underline` and the color to `#95B2E3`. Click OK.

There is just one more thing to attend to before our inline navigation is complete. Our designer placed a visual separator between the two links. We created a slice from it, but we won't (of course!) place it directly into the (X)HTML. To reproduce this look, we'll create a special style for the second (Contact) list item.

8. Create a new CSS rule for a class named .deco.

9. In the Background category, browse to the Background-image `dots.gif`. Set the Background-repeat to `no-repeat`, horizontal positioning (X) to `left`, and vertical positioning (Y) to `center`.

N *With a grouped selector, make sure you never leave a comma at the end of the comma delimited list. If you do, some browsers will ignore the entire rule and leave you scratching your head.*

N *We've found that leaving the Selector Type set to Compound at all times allows us to create any kind of selector we need. Dreamweaver won't gripe at you for creating a class in a Tag (element) selector or tell you your class or ID formatting isn't correct when you place it into the Tag category. As long as you're confident of your ability to create the proper syntax, choosing Compound lets you create everything from simple element selectors to the most complex sibling or descendant selectors. You're only limited by your knowledge!*

N   *If we had a horizontal navigation with several list items, we might place the background image on all of them by adding it to the #header li rule and then create a class to remove only the first or last one (based on which side we placed the separator on).*

10. Return to your (X)HTML document and place the cursor in the word Contact in the header navigation. Click its parent `<li>` element in the tag selector. From the Style drop-down list in the Property inspector, choose `deco`.

The visual separator has now been inserted between our two links—although because the elements are inline, Dreamweaver doesn't show this to us in Design view, but clicking Live View will show it to us.

Time to Tidy Up

Save the (X)HTML page and the CSS file and let's organize the rules a bit. It helps to keep our page in shape as we go. If you've followed the book's projects in order, you've done this. If not, place your CSS Styles panel into All mode and drag the selectors to move them. Place all element selectors up above the `#container` and place the `#header` and `#mainContent` selectors in their respective sections. Our list of selectors looks like the one in **Figure 5.19**.

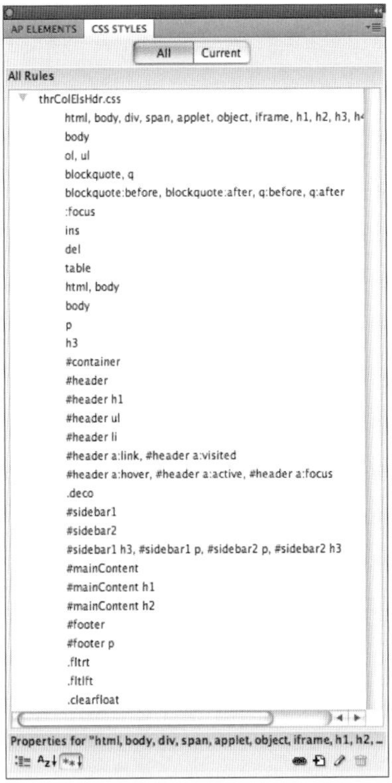

FIGURE 5.19 This is how we organize our rules. Your mileage may vary.

Great! Our simple navigation list is now in place and styled correctly using CSS.

FIGURE 5.20 The header navigation with dots to separate the navigation items.

The Main Content

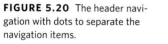 *Be sure you choose em units when you change margin and padding values that were previously set to zero. When a zero value has no unit set, opening it in the Edit CSS Style dialog will not automatically add a unit of measurement. Though zero can be written with no unit of measurement, any other value requires a unit to be specified. When initially adding a value, Dreamweaver will default to pixels. It's only in the case of a pre-existing number, with no unit of measurement (like zero) that Dreamweaver does not automatically add a unit of measure.*

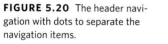 *Don't worry about the big space this leaves in each side; we'll be adjusting the side columns in a moment.*

The main content area of this web site is largely already in place, but we do want to adjust the margins and padding to retain our clean layout and avoid overlaps with the sidebars when we begin to edit them.

1. Select `<div#mainContent>` with the tag selector. Click the Edit Style icon and select the Box category. Under Padding, set the Top and Bottom fields to `1em`, and the Right and Left fields to `2em`. Under Margin, leave the top at `0`, and set the right to `16.5em`, the bottom to `1.5em`, and the left to `14em`.

2. In the Border category, apply a `1px solid #E6E6FF` border.

3. Move to the Background tab and browse for `box_top.jpg`. Select it and set repeat to `repeat-x`. Click OK.

In our code, the rule for `#mainContent` will now look like this:

```
#mainContent {
  margin: 0 16.5em 1.5em 14em;
  padding: 1em 2em;
  border: 1px solid #E6E6FF;
  background: url(../images/box_top.jpg) repeat-x;
}
```

FIGURE 5.21 With Dreamweaver in Live View, we can see the effects of our changes.

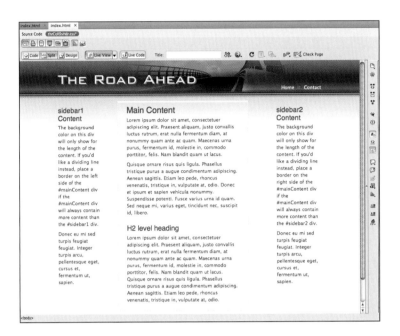

FORMATTING IMAGES

Many browsers now give users the ability to zoom a layout instead of only increasing the text size. When they do, they increase the entire layout, including the images, much like creating an em-based layout with image sizes set in em units. We usually turn that off since it can be unsightly and we usually set our image sizes, even in an em-based layout, in pixels for the same reason. But we thought you should know what's possible "just in case."

Almost no page today is devoid of images. Within our comp, our designer hasn't inserted any images, but we can assume by the layout that they are likely to occur in the `mainContent` area. We'll add one to give our client an idea of what it might look like.

Inserting an image is easy, but images in em-based layouts are special, and we must pander to them a little. Ideally, we want any images in the content to scale along with the text when the text is resized. But images on the web are made up of pixels and are fixed in size. Applying stretchiness to them via ems really only works to a point—after which, they can look too large and pixilated, or else too small and indistinct, depending on how they're scaled. In other words, we are not actually making the image larger and therefore clearer, as may be the case with scaling font size. We are scaling each pixel, which can degrade the overall quality of the displayed image.

Still, we can scale with relative success to a degree, so let's experiment with an image now.

N *If an image is placed into the document that is purely decorative and has no real meaning for a non-sighted user, it's best to leave the alt attribute empty. But empty doesn't mean we don't add it at all! It means we put the alt attribute into the image, but leave it with empty quotation marks (i. e.,: alt=""). This keeps assistive technology from annoying a blind reader by reading aloud the name of your image—especially if you're dealing with a dynamic site with long, meaningless names.*

N *If we had created a descendant selector called #mainContent img it would have styled all images placed in the mainContent area, which means the initial size and proportions of each image to be displayed in this area must be the same. If we want to size each image placed in the mainContent area individually, we need to use individual classes.*

N *We chose the value of 6.25em, not through any kind of rocket science, but through a simple mathematical calculation. 1 divided by the text size times the number of pixels for the width (or height) of the image equals the number of ems for the dimension. In our case, that gave us 6.25.*

1. Place the cursor at the beginning of the second paragraph in mainContent. Click the Insert Image button in the Insert panel and locate globe.jpg. When presented with a text insertion field for Alt text, type Globe of the world.

   The globe, a small image, is now at the beginning of our second paragraph. It doesn't look really good there, so it's time to set up a new style for our image. Note that Dreamweaver automatically inserts the image dimensions. But we're going to set the image size with CSS.

2. In the Property inspector, notice the size of the image, 80px by 80px, a 1 to 1 aspect ratio. We're going to strip these values out and apply the size via CSS. Remove the two instances of **80px**, leaving the size fields in the Property inspector blank.

3. In the CSS Styles panel, create a new selector called .mainImg.

4. In the CSS Rule Definition dialog box, from the Box category, set the height and width to 6.25em each.

   The new style is now at the bottom of our style sheet:

   ```
   .mainImg {
     height: 6.25em;
     width: 6.25em;
   }
   ```

5. With the image selected, use the class drop-down list on the image Property inspector to set the class to fltrt.

   That's it! Our image will now float right and have dimensions in scalable ems.

6. Save the page and the CSS file and test it in your browser. Increase and decrease the text size, and get a feel for the way the flow of the text around the image remains consistent—and also the level of image degradation that occurs.

FIGURE 5.22 The image has scaled with the text (as seen in Firefox). We've increased the font size three times.

sidebar2 Content

The background color on this div will only show for the length of the content. If you'd like a dividing line instead, place a border on the right side of the #mainContent div

Home :: Contact

:tuer adipiscing elit.
us rutrum, erat nulla
ante ac quam.
molestie in, commodo
acus.

sellus

1

pede,
tate at,
ula

Setting our image sizes in em units emulates a zoomed layout (already available in Opera, FireFox 3 and Internet Explorer 7 browsers). At the time of this printing however, Internet Explorer 6 (which still has 25-30% of the browser market) and Safari 3 do not offer zooming.

Belly Up to the Sidebars

We'll now tweak the sidebars to the width we want and set them up for the neat (we didn't just say "neat", did we?) display of the content they will contain.

1. Select the `<div#sidebar1>` in the tag selector. In the Properties pane of the CSS Styles panel, change the **11em** width to **13em**.

2. Still in the Properties pane, click on the values for padding and replace them with **0 0 1.5em**.

    Remember, this uses CSS shorthand: the first zero sets the top padding, the middle zero sets the left and right padding, and the **1.5em** sets the bottom padding.

3. Select the `<div#sidebar2>` on the tag selector. Click the Edit Style button and open the CSS Rule Definition dialog box. (We have more work to do on this div so this time it may be easier to use the dialog.)

4. In the Box category, change the width to 13em and set the padding to Top: **0.7em**, Right: **0.8em**, Bottom: **1em**, Left: **1.5em**.

Be careful to change the units here, as by default they are set in pixels, which won't give quite the effect we're after with the values we've chosen!

5. Switch to the Background category and browse for the background image, box_top.jpg. Set repeat to repeat-x.

6. Switch to the Border category. For style, select solid from the drop-down list. For width, type in 1, which will default to units of pixels, which are our desired units in this case. Set the color to #E6E6FF.

FIGURE 5.23 With the sidebars properly sized, we're ready for the content.

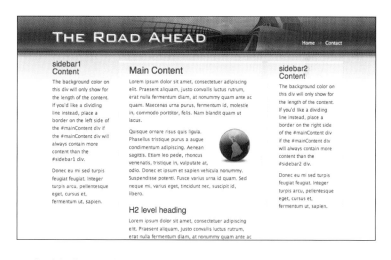

And with that, we've got the basic work done on our sidebars. If your page doesn't look like our image, check your work with the builds > index_2.html file to check for differences.

Time to start to adding content to the page. We'll start with the side navigation.

The Main Site Navigation

The main navigation of our web site also utilizes an unordered list. This list is located in sidebar1, the left column. Each list item looks like a button, and the color of the link text changes on hover.

As with the header navigation, we'll begin by coding the list markup, and apply all of the visual effects using CSS after the list code is complete.

1. Place an unordered list before the **h3** in the **sidebar1** div.

2. For the text for the first link, type Home. Placing the cursor to the right of the word Home in Design view, press Enter, and type the next menu item, About. Continue in this manner to create new list items for Services, Archives, Resources, and FAQ. The code should look like this:

```
<div id="sidebar1">
<ul>
<li>Home</li>
<li>About</li>
<li>Services</li>
<li>Archives</li>
<li>Resources</li>
<li>FAQ</li>
</ul>
```

3. Create links by highlighting each list item in Design view, one by one. Use the Property inspector to add hash marks (#) as placeholders so the list items look like links.

Adding a Background to the List Items

So far, the list looks plain—quite far from wonderful—so let's work some CSS magic.

1. Create a new rule and name the selector **#sidebar1 li**.

2. Switch to the Background category. Set the Background-color to **#FFF** and then browse for the **nav_back.jpg** image and select it. Apply a value of **repeat-x** to Background-repeat, and set the horizontal position to **left** and the vertical position to **bottom**.

This background image is going to create a shadow effect. When the layout is resized and the text increases, causing the **li** element to grow accordingly, we need the shadow to remained anchored at the base. The top of the image color is white. So making white the background color of the **li** will give us a seamless transition.

3. Switch to the Box category and insert a width of **100%**. This ensures the list item takes up the entire width of its containing block, **sidebar1**. In the same section, uncheck Margin's "Same for all" box and set the Bottom field to **0.2em**.

If you need to change your background image or color on hover, you'll want to place those properties on the a element instead of the li since li:hover is not widely supported yet.

FIGURE 5.24 The list elements have a background, but are still way too small.

Styling the Links Themselves

Our links still don't look right. They're too thin and the text needs some styling.

You could write the selector as #sidebar1 a:link *instead of including the* li *element if, and only if, there are no other links in the sidebar or you want them to inherit the same styles.*

1. Create a new rule with a compound selector of #sidebar1 li a, #sidebar1 li a:link, #sidebar1 li a:visited.

2. Set the font to the font set we created for the paragraphs: "Lucida Grande", Arial, Helvetica, sans-serif and the size to 0.95em. Set the color to #336 and decoration to none.

3. For the display property, select block.

    The a element is an inline element by default. When it's converted into a block element, it fills the width of its parent element (in this case, the li element), making the whole list item appear to be a clickable link.

Setting the vertical position to 50% keeps our image, indicating a rollover, in the center of the button. If the text on your button were to wrap to two lines, the image would be between them. You can decide how that works with your own design. If you don't like the way that looks, you can set the vertical position with enough em units to center it on the first line of text. As the text is scaled larger, the em unit setting will keep the image in the center of that first line.

4. Adjust the padding by setting the top to 0.5em, the right to 1em, the bottom to 0.3em, and the left to 1.5em.

5. Set a 1px wide, solid border with the color #E6E6FF. Click OK.

6. Add another new CSS rule and name the selector #sidebar1 li a:visited. For this rule, set the color to #55628B.

7. Add a final new CSS rule for our main navigation links, and name the compound selector #sidebar1 li a:hover, #sidebar1 li a:active, #sidebar1 li a:focus.

8. Set the color to #A23378. Add a Background-image of arrow.gif. Set the Background-repeat to no-repeat, the horizontal position (X) to 4px, and the vertical position (Y) to 50%. Click OK.

You won't see your rollover effect in the Design window, but go ahead and switch to Live View. Check it out now.

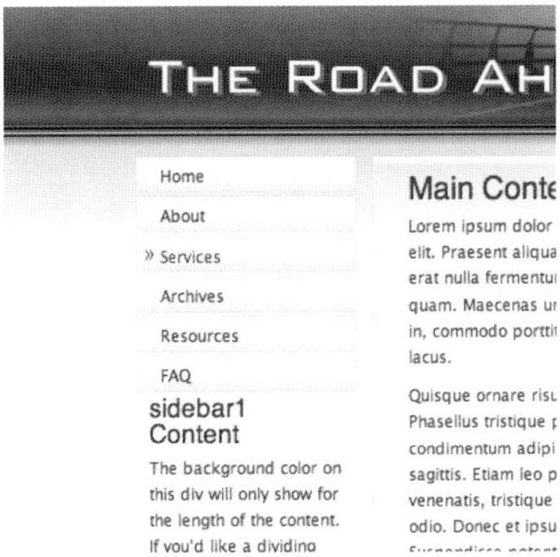

FIGURE 5.25 Wow! Look at those sexy rollovers!

Using the cite Element

Let's move further down the column and allow our client's satisfied customers to speak out. We are going to create a Testimonials section.

1. Click and drag to highlight the h3 heading and all the text in sidebar1. On the Insert bar, choose the Insert Div Tag tool. Choose "Wrap around selection." In the ID, type quotes. Click New CSS Rule. Leave everything set to the defaults and click OK to move to the dialog.

2. Set the padding, top 2em, right 1em, bottom 1.5em, and left 1.5em. Set a top margin of 15px.

   The top margin is set in pixels to prevent the gap between the main navigation and the quotes from becoming unpleasantly large if the font is resized.

   Reusing a graphic as we've done with box_top.jpg is a great way to save bandwidth.

3. Switch to the Background category, and again locate box_top.jpg and select it, and set repeat to repeat-x. In the Border category, set a 1px solid border with the color #E6E6FF. In the Type category, set the Font-size to 0.9em. Click OK in the CSS dialog and in the Insert Div Tag dialog.

 *The* cite *element should not be confused with the* cite *attribute. The* cite *attribute is applied inside the* blockquote *or other block level tag such as* p *to provide a URI reference to the source of the quote.*

Our testimonials will take the format of a quotation, followed by a new line containing the author's name. The name will be indented and italicized to make it obvious to visual users that it is not a part of the quote. For non-visual users or non-graphical user agents, we will use the (X)HTML `<blockquote>` tag to indicate quoted text and the `<cite>` tag to indicate a reference to another source. In this case the `<cite>` tags will enclose the author's name, but be aware that `<cite>` should also be applied to names of publications, including legal documents and legislation.

As always, let's start by writing the code, and style it later.

4. Click in the first paragraph of sample text in the sidebar. Select it on the tag selector.

5. Click the indent icon on the HTML area of the Property inspector.

In order to meet the W3C's specifications for `blockquote`, the `<p>` tags must be inside the `<blockquote>` tags. The specifications say that in a strict (X)HTML doctype, `blockquote` must contain another block element and the **p** element fits the bill perfectly. Conversely, the cite element must be contained *in* a block level element.

FIGURE 5.26 The indent icon on the HTML area of the Property inspector. *Not* to be used for indention!

6. Choose the blockquote on the tag selector and arrow once to the right. Create a new paragraph beneath our pretend testimonial by pressing Enter and typing in a name.

Thomas Quamley sounded good to us.

7. Select the name, right-click on the **p** that contains it on the tag selector, and choose Quick Tag Editor (Ctrl-T). Type `cite`, then hit Enter twice.

The `cite` element is now wrapped in the **p** element.

 *Don't be fooled. Clicking indent places a blockquote around the paragraph element. That said, indent should actually never be used just for presentational indention. That should be done with padding or margins. Blockquotes should semantically be used for marking up quotations.*

8. Repeat these steps for the second default paragraph in the sidebar, but choose a different name for the second testimonial. We chose `Sim Simley & Co.`

9. Change the text in the **h3** at the top to say They Said:

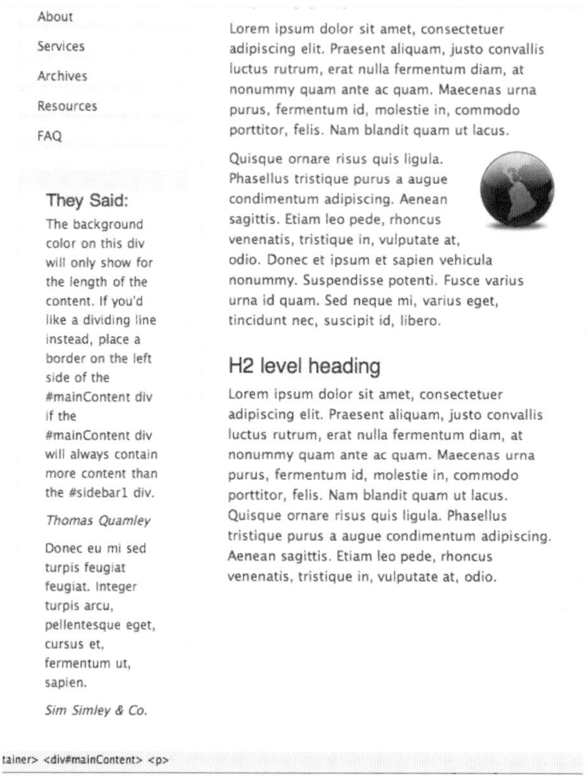

FIGURE 5.27 Our markup is complete—time for some more styling.

About

Services

Archives

Resources

FAQ

They Said:

The background color on this div will only show for the length of the content. If you'd like a dividing line instead, place a border on the left side of the #mainContent div if the #mainContent div will always contain more content than the #sidebar1 div.

Thomas Quamley

Donec eu mi sed turpis feugiat feugiat. Integer turpis arcu, pellentesque eget, cursus et, fermentum ut, sapien.

Sim Simley & Co.

Lorem ipsum dolor sit amet, consectetuer adipiscing elit. Praesent aliquam, justo convallis luctus rutrum, erat nulla fermentum diam, at nonummy quam ante ac quam. Maecenas urna purus, fermentum id, molestie in, commodo porttitor, felis. Nam blandit quam ut lacus.

Quisque ornare risus quis ligula. Phasellus tristique purus a augue condimentum adipiscing. Aenean sagittis. Etiam leo pede, rhoncus venenatis, tristique in, vulputate at, odio. Donec et ipsum et sapien vehicula nonummy. Suspendisse potenti. Fusce varius urna id quam. Sed neque mi, varius eget, tincidunt nec, suscipit id, libero.

H2 level heading

Lorem ipsum dolor sit amet, consectetuer adipiscing elit. Praesent aliquam, justo convallis luctus rutrum, erat nulla fermentum diam, at nonummy quam ante ac quam. Maecenas urna purus, fermentum id, molestie in, commodo porttitor, felis. Nam blandit quam ut lacus. Quisque ornare risus quis ligula. Phasellus tristique purus a augue condimentum adipiscing. Aenean sagittis. Etiam leo pede, rhoncus venenatis, tristique in, vulputate at, odio.

tainer> <div#mainContent> <p>

Our lovely, semantic (i.e., meaningful) code is now in place and alternative devices will know that there is a quote with a defined source (in our case, a customer), regardless of how the text is styled in the browser.

Speaking of styling, Dreamweaver has taken it upon itself to style the contents of the `<cite>` tags. Don't be concerned by this. When viewed in the browser, there is no styling. The browser is correct, because we reset the `cite` element in the CSS reset.

Styling the Blockquote and Cite

We'll style `<cite>` now, along with the `blockquote`.

1. Create a new CSS rule for `blockquote`. Set the top margin to `1.5em`. Click OK.

2. Create another CSS rule, this time for the element `cite`. In the Background category, browse to `arrow.gif`, setting Background-repeat to **no-repeat**, horizontal position to `left`, and vertical position to **center**. In the Type category, set Font-style to `italic`. Go to the Box category and add a left padding of **12px**. Click OK.

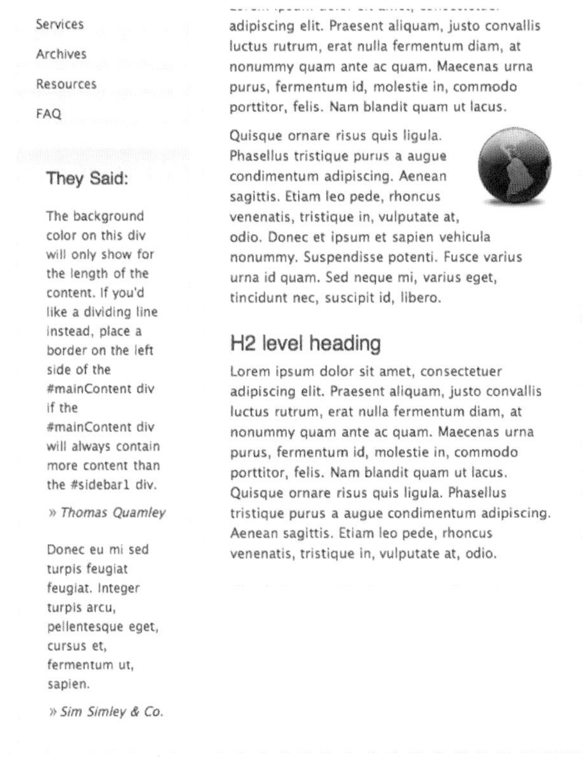

FIGURE 5.28 The styling is coming along as shown in Live View.

Services

Archives

Resources

FAQ

They Said:

The background color on this div will only show for the length of the content. If you'd like a dividing line instead, place a border on the left side of the #mainContent div if the #mainContent div will always contain more content than the #sidebar1 div.

» *Thomas Quamley*

Donec eu mi sed turpis feugiat feugiat. Integer turpis arcu, pellentesque eget, cursus et, fermentum ut, sapien.

» *Sim Simley & Co.*

adipiscing elit. Praesent aliquam, justo convallis luctus rutrum, erat nulla fermentum diam, at nonummy quam ante ac quam. Maecenas urna purus, fermentum id, molestie in, commodo porttitor, felis. Nam blandit quam ut lacus.

Quisque ornare risus quis ligula. Phasellus tristique purus a augue condimentum adipiscing. Aenean sagittis. Etiam leo pede, rhoncus venenatis, tristique in, vulputate at, odio. Donec et ipsum et sapien vehicula nonummy. Suspendisse potenti. Fusce varius urna id quam. Sed neque mi, varius eget, tincidunt nec, suscipit id, libero.

H2 level heading

Lorem ipsum dolor sit amet, consectetuer adipiscing elit. Praesent aliquam, justo convallis luctus rutrum, erat nulla fermentum diam, at nonummy quam ante ac quam. Maecenas urna purus, fermentum id, molestie in, commodo porttitor, felis. Nam blandit quam ut lacus. Quisque ornare risus quis ligula. Phasellus tristique purus a augue condimentum adipiscing. Aenean sagittis. Etiam leo pede, rhoncus venenatis, tristique in, vulputate at, odio.

3. Create a compound selector, naming it `#quotes p, #quotes p cite`.

We need to specifically include `cite` to override its properties in the CSS reset.

4. Set the color to `#A23378`. In the Box category, set all of the margins to 0.

Our sidebar alignment is a bit off, so we'll fix that before we leave this area.

5. Switch to the All mode in the CSS Styles panel and click on the compound selector `#sidebar1 h3, #sidebar1 p, #sidebar2 p, #sidebar2 h3`.

FIGURE 5.29 Sidebar1 is complete.

These items have margin, which is the cause of the weirdness in alignment.

6. With the compound selector highlighted, right-click and choose Delete or click the trashcan icon at the bottom right of the CSS Styles panel.

   The entire offending rule is deleted.

And Then a Step to the Right, uh... Sidebar

Before you move on, if you had any trouble with the left sidebar, check your work with the index_3.html file in the builds directory. In the right sidebar, the client has requested that we list the most recent entries on the web site. The column will have two headings, News and Events.

1. Change the default h3 text in sidebar2 to say News.

   Each item will consist of a date and a short extract, with paragraph formatting.

2. Before the first paragraph in the right sidebar, type a date.

   We typed November 22.

3. Press Enter to create another paragraph below it. Midway through the paragraph, press Enter to break the paragraph into smaller chunks.

4. As before, type in a date. Press Enter to create another new paragraph underneath this date.

5. Press Enter again, and in the Property inspector change the formatting to h3. Type the name of the second section, Events.

6. In the Events section, create the same two paragraphs. Either create them in the same way or copy and paste them in.

Our second sidebar now contains our semantic content, but needs to be styled.

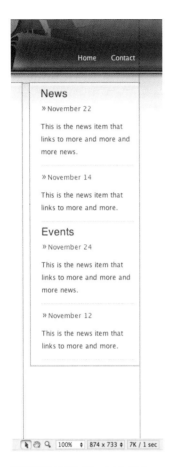

FIGURE 5.30 The right sidebar is looking great!

ADD A LITTLE STYLE

1. Right-click the date in Design view and select CSS Style > New from the contextual menu. Create a class called **date**.

2. In the CSS Rule Definition dialog box, go to the Type category and enter the color **#A23378**. Switch to the Background category and browse for and select **arrow.gif**. Set the repeat to **no-repeat**, the horizontal position to **left**, and the vertical position to **center**. Move to the Box category and set the left padding to **12px** and the bottom margin to **0.2em**. Click OK.

   The padding keeps the text away from our arrow graphic. The bottom margin overrides the larger bottom margin from the **p** element selector.

3. In Design view, select each of the dates in turn and in the Property inspector, use the Style drop-down list in the HTML area to apply the **date** class to each date.

4. Create another CSS class called **info**. In the CSS Rule Definition dialog box, go to the Box category and add a bottom margin of **1em** and a bottom padding of **1em**. Switch to the Border category and create a bottom border only, with a **1px solid** line of the color **#D6B0D9**.

5. In **sidebar2**, highlight each of our information paragraphs and use the Property inspector to apply the **info** class to these paragraphs.

Our design is really taking shape now. The only basic section of the page we have yet to style is the footer.

Last but Not Least, the Footer

We've reached the final piece of our page puzzle—the footer. At the moment, the width of the footer is constrained by the width of the container. This creates a visual imbalance because the header stretches across the screen. We already have a background image on the body, so we can't use the same element for the footer—one background image per customer, errr, element, please! Instead, let's move the footer outside of the **container** so that the footer fills the width of the body element.

When your code appears to be correct and you just can't figure out why the CSS does not render correctly, it is usually a specificity issue! Check to see what other rules are influencing the rule with the problem. The Rules pane in Dreamweaver can help: with the problem tag selected and displayed in Current mode, the CSS rules affecting that tag will be listed in Rules view under the Rules pane. Hover over them to see the specificity of each rule. View the Summary for Selection at the top to see what properties and values are taking effect. Hover over those for information on where that declaration comes from. For more detailed information about the rules of specificity, read our CSS review chapter or Andrew Tetlaw's article on Sitepoint: The Great Specificity Swindle.

At the bottom of the (X)HTML document, you'll see this code:

```
<br class="clearfloat" />
<div id="footer">
  <p>Footer</p>
<!-- end #footer --></div>
<!-- end #container --></div>
</body>
</html>
```

1. In Code view, select the footer div tags and their contents and drag them below the closing div for `container`.

    ```
    <br class="clearfloat" />
    <!-- end #container --></div>
    <div id="footer">
      <p>Footer</p>
    <!-- end #footer --></div>
    </body>
    </html>
    ```

    The footer now spans the width of the screen. Now *that* was easy!

    Let's change the footer text to something more appropriate, such as something more common, like a copyright.

Notice the text, once the footer leaves the protection of the container, is now centered. This is due to the `text-align` center in the body that was overridden by `text-align` left in the container. In this case we wanted a centered footer, so we'll leave it as is.

2. Highlight the word Footer and type © 2008–2009 The Road Ahead. All rights reserved. If you don't know how to insert the copyright symbol, go to Insert > HTML > Special Characters > Copyright.

    We can now apply an attractive background that will match that of our header.

3. Select `<div#footer>` in the tag selector. Open the CSS Rule Definition dialog to make changes. Set the Font-family to `Helvetica, Arial, sans-serif`, the Size to `0.7em,` and the color to `#CCC`.

4. Move to the Background category and browse for `foot.jpg`. Set repeat to `repeat-x`. Set the background color to #272E42.

5. Move to the Box category and under Padding, set top to `0.75em` and right, bottom, and left all to `0.5em`.

The CSS should look something like this:

```
#footer {
  padding: 0.75em 0.5em 0.5em;
  background:#272E42 url(../images/foot.jpg) repeat-x;
  color: #CCC;
  font: 0.7em Helvetica, Arial, sans-serif;
}
```

6. Save the page and the CSS file and preview it in a browser. Experiment with increasing and decreasing the size of the browser font and notice that everything scales beautifully.

FIGURE 5.31 And with that, it's done!

Quick IECC Tweaks

Remember at the end of Chapter 2, we discussed the Internet Explorer Conditional Comments (IECC) that add a fix to our page to correct the inconsistent rendering of margins between browsers? Since we used Eric Meyer's CSS reset in this layout, all our browsers are rendering the same zero values. Thus, we don't need the padding-top on any of the rules in the IECC. We'll remove them now, leaving only the `#mainContent { zoom: 1; }`.

We also need to add a fix for the extra space between the menu items in IE. It's the same fix we added to the menu in Chapter 4—the hasLayout trigger—`zoom:1`. Since there's no dimension declared for the `a` element creating the menu, this is the result. Since there's already a zoom selector for the `#mainContent` div, we'll group our `#sidebar1 li a` selector in with that.

```
<!--[if IE]>

<style type="text/css">
#mainContent, #sidebar1 li a { zoom: 1; }
</style>

<![endif]-->
```

Our basic page construction is done! The hard part is over. Move your styles around using the All pane of the CSS Styles panel to keep them organized. Now it's just a matter of adding the additional site content. Let's move on and build a simple contact form, linking to it from the header navigation.

FIGURE 5.32 The spacey left menu in Internet Explorer. A very common issue—zoom it!

Creating and Styling an Em-Based Form

We're going to use our basic layout for all of the other pages in the site, but one of those pages needs to contain a contact form. If you had any trouble in the last section, you may check your work (or start this section) with the index_4.html document in the builds directory. Customers and potential customers can use the form to contact our client (using a form helps avoid some spam, though even that seems to require greater measures these days), but the form needs to scale with the rest of the page layout.

Even within our em-based page layout, using the em unit to layout forms allows an extra degree of flexibility and accessibility. The form field expands and contracts when the font size is adjusted, so the user can still fit the same number of characters into the field and it will look the way it's meant to look, whatever the size of the font.

A Brief Form Refresher

A **fieldset** groups related form fields together. The fieldset defines a form control group, grouping associated form controls together in a logical way. Fieldsets may be nested.

A **legend** supplies a heading for the form as a whole. The legend should be short, concise, and relevant. The legend will be read by a screen reader (in verbosity mode) before *each* label, (for example, "Your Details: Name. Your Details: Address") so the legend should be brief and make sense when read in the context of the label.

The tag **label** with the **"for="** attribute associates a form field's label with the field itself. (You can also wrap the input with the label tag.)

Used properly, these elements increase a form's usefulness and accessibility.

Coding the Form

Submitting a form generally requires back-end programming, which is beyond the scope of this book. Imagine, if you will, that we're just building and styling a basic form, using XHTML and CSS, and then handing it off to a back-end developer to implement the form submission process.

1. Using index.html as our basic structure, choose File > Save As and save the file as contact.html.

2. Change the heading Main Content to Contact Us. In the paragraph below Main Content, type: We will never share your details with anyone else (except where required by law).

    Where a full privacy policy is unavailable, it helps to add a line or two in summary on the Contact page.

3. Delete the subsequent paragraphs and headings in the `mainContent` area.

Each form field must have a correctly marked-up label so that user agents can make the connection between the form control and its label, even when the connection is not visually obvious. This makes the difference between a form making sense—or not —to users relying on screen readers or other alternative devices.

We'll establish this connection between our labels and form controls by assigning both the label and the form control an ID of the same name.

4. If necessary, select the empty **p** element that remains on the tag selector, right click, and choose Remove tag. (Whether this is necessary or not depends on how you deleted the text in the `maincontent` area.)

N   *If you don't see the red outline, go to View > Visual Aids > Invisible Elements and make sure it's turned on (or use the Visual Aids drop-down list on the Document toolbar).*

5. Using the Forms section of the Insert bar, click the Form icon which inserts the basic tags for the **form** element.

A red-dotted rectangular outline appears around the cursor and in the code.

6. Leave the cursor in place and locate and click the fieldset button in the toolbar.

A dialog box appears asking for the form's legend.

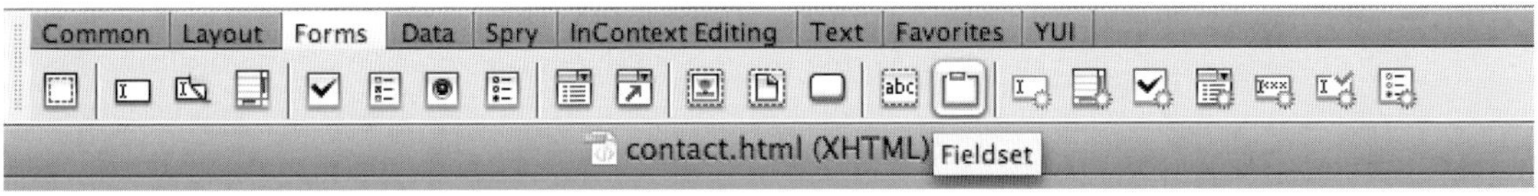

FIGURE 5.33 The fieldset tool in the Forms section of the Insert panel.

N   *A form may contain many fieldsets that group specific types of form information to make them more logical. Access keys can be used to target specific fieldsets in a long and complicated form, although these are probably best avoided until cross-browser support improves.*

7. Type Your Details.

We also want to let the user know which form fields are mandatory. Making the minimum information needed mandatory assures our client of at least getting basic contact information.

8. With the form legend text still selected, press the right arrow key. This moves the insertion point after the `</legend>` tag. Create a new paragraph by pressing the Enter key and type the following: `Fields marked with * are mandatory.`

   Now we'll turn our attention to inserting the input fields and their labels.

9. Select the paragraph you just typed in the tag selector and arrow once to the right.

   We are using Design view because the dialog box to add elements is slightly different in Design view from the dialog box to add elements in Code view.

10. Click the Text Field button in the Insert toolbar. Or choose Insert > Form > Text Field. In the Tag Editor dialog box, assign an ID of **name**, a label of **Name:**, and make sure the radio button "Attach label tag using "for" attribute" is selected. Leave the other settings at their defaults. Click OK.

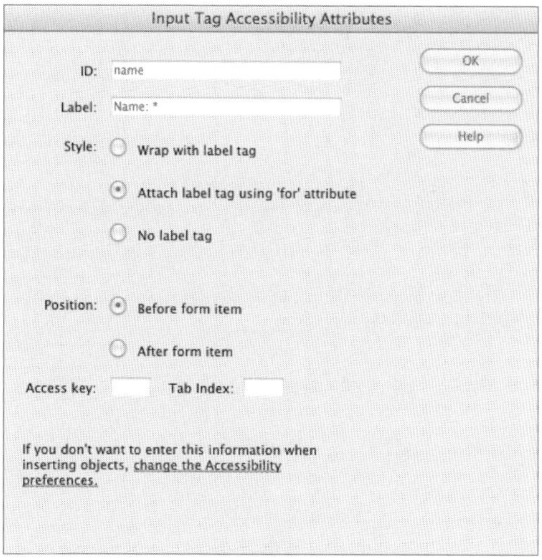

FIGURE 5.34 Input tag dialog when inserted from Design view.

11. Continue to build and modify the form in this way, adding text fields and associated labels for address, phone number, and email.

12. Add a text area with an ID message and the associated label
Your Message:

```
<form action="" method="post" enctype="multipart/form-data"
name="form1" id="form1">
 <fieldset>
 <legend>Your Details</legend>
 <p>Fields marked with an * are mandatory.</p>
 <label for="name">Name:</label>
 <input name="name" type="text" id="name" />
 <label for="address">Address:</label>
 <input name="address" type="text" id="address" />
 <label for="phone">Phone:</label>
 <input name="phone" type="text" id="phone" />
 <label for="email">Email:</label>
 <input name="email" type="text" id="email" />
 <label for="message">Your Message:</label>
 <textarea name="message" id="message" cols="45"
rows="5"></textarea>
 </fieldset>
</form>
```

Adding a submit button will complete our form.

13. In Design view, place the cursor to the right of the Your
Message text area. Select `<fieldset>` on the tag selector. Click
your right arrow to exit the fieldset.

If you look at Code view, your cursor will be between the closing fieldset tag and the closing form tag.

N *If using a Strict doctype,
the Submit button must be placed
within a fieldset in order for the
page to validate.*

14. Click the button icon on the form panel of the Insert bar. In
the Edit Tag dialog box that appears, apply an ID of `submit`
and leave the Label field blank. Select the radio button that is
labeled No Label Tag. Click OK.

The button is added to the end of the form as a `submit` type
of input.

N *It makes no functional difference whether or not the name
and ID are given identical values,
but making them identical can help
to avoid confusion.*

You can use the Tag inspector (Window > Tag Inspector) to add
to and edit all of the form tags. Look at our actual `<form>` tag.
By default, it has a name and an ID of `form1`.

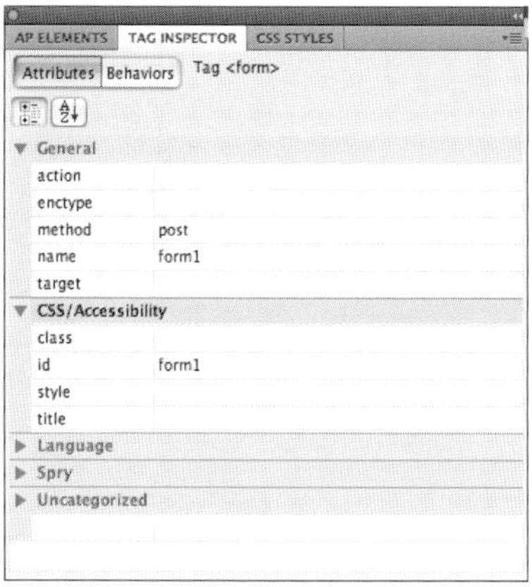

FIGURE 5.35 Dreamweaver's Tag inspector gives us yet another way to edit the attributes of our form elements.

When an element, including a form element, is selected, its attributes are visible in the Tag inspector and also in the Property inspector. Use whichever is easiest for you, but be aware that the Tag inspector offers a greater range of options that may be required in more complex forms or web pages.

Creating Accessible Required Fields

We want our three required fields, name, email, and message, to be accessible to people with assistive technology (AT). If we use an asterisk, many times AT reads it as "star," which really doesn't have much meaning, so we created an asterisk (you can create any graphic you desire) in a graphics program and we'll insert it before each required field.

Yes, we're inserting a graphic. Into the page. Uh-huh.

There's an excellent reason for using a graphic when simple text could look exactly the same. The alt attribute. By filling the alt attribute with the text "required" we can add meaning for many non-traditional viewers of our page.

1. Place your cursor before the word Name: and insert an image (star.gif) with the Insert bar. In the alternate text field, type required.

2. Continue in the same fashion with both the Email and Message fields.

   Placing the image into the Label assures that it will read by AT when in forms mode.

3. Finally, in the text at the top (Fields marked with * are mandatory.), replace the asterisk with the same graphic and alt attribute.

Our code is just right at this stage, but the visual result when viewed in Design view (or a browser) is less than perfect. Let's fix it with some more CSS goodness.

FIGURE 5.36 Our form in its default condition.

Styling the Form

We need to create five new form-related rules to cater to the elements we have just added to our (X)HTML.

1. Create a new CSS rule for the `fieldset` element. Apply a `1px` `solid` border with the color `#336`. Apply a padding of `0.8em` to all sides except the right, which should have a value of zero. Click OK.

   The padding is simply to keep the contents of the fieldset away from the edges and border.

   There's nothing wrong with having some right side padding—in fact, it's desirable. But because IE7 renders the border on the fieldset outside the padding (making it so the top and right borders don't meet up properly), we're leaving it at zero. Another option would be to include the padding for other browsers in the regular CSS document and then override the right padding using an IECC for IE7.

2. Create a CSS rule for the `legend` element. Set the font size to `1.5em`.

N *We are applying all font sizes, margins, and paddings in ems so they will expand and contract relative to the font size, maintaining the proportions of the page and of the form. The form itself is a block element and as such will fill the width of its parent unless otherwise specified.*

N *The label element is usually an inline element, but changing it to a block display forces the text field to a separate line below the label.*

3. Create a selector for the **label** element. Set the display property to **block**. Set the top margin to **0.5em**.

   You'll notice that setting **display: block** on the **label** element makes each element start on the subsequent line—as if a break element had been added.

4. Create a compound selector **input, textarea**. Set the top and left borders to **1px solid #336**, and the right and bottom borders to **#978EBA**. Set the background color to **#D9DEE8**, the width to **21em**, and give it .2em of padding. Click OK.

   The background color makes it visually intuitive to put the cursor in an input field. The padding simply gives the form a bit of breathing room.

5. Create another CSS rule for **textarea**, and set a height of **8em**.

   The Submit button has taken on the same width as the rest of the inputs. It looks really weird! Plus, since the button is outside the fieldset, it needs some margin to move it down a bit. We'll need to create a CSS rule for this single input element, and since the Submit button already has an **id** assigned, we'll use this **id** in our selector.

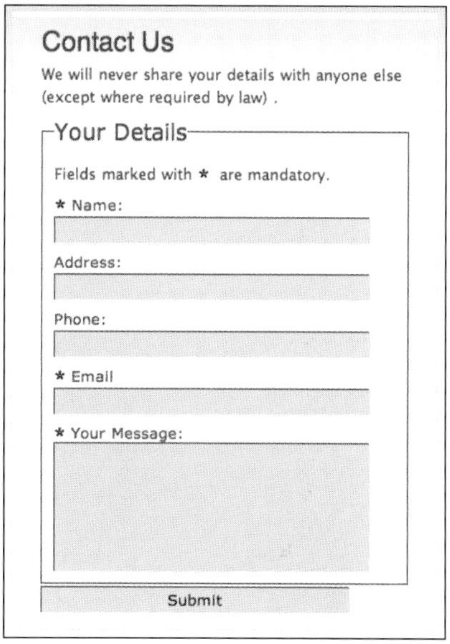

FIGURE 5.37 The wildly wide Submit button.

N *If your submit button has more words than ours, simply adjust your width. Since the button is created with em units, it'll get larger as the text size is larger. With em units, you need have no worries about cutting off some text!*

N *Since a radio button and check box are also form inputs, our general styling for an input will be adopted by those elements as well. It's likely that style won't translate well (especially background colors and borders), so we find it useful to create a class to counteract those properties and values that are unsightly. We apply the class to our radio buttons or check boxes and they change back to a more attractive rendering.*

6. Create a new CSS rule for the **submit** selector. Give it a width of 8em, and a top and left margin of .8em.

This will give the Submit button the same alignment from the left side of the fieldset and also a little breathing room at the top. The Submit button now has its own unique size, differentiating it from the rest of the inputs.

Be aware that the default styling for form elements varies wildly from browser to browser. Even though we've zeroed some of our defaults, giving us a more level playing field, what can be done with various elements still varies. Safari is the most different, locking us down to its inherent OS look. (Yes, we'd *love* to see this change!) Other browsers vary in the way they apply certain properties and values, so unless you stick with the basics, you'll rarely achieve the same look from browser to browser.

7. Create a new compound rule for `input:focus, textarea:focus` and give it a background of #E5EBF4.

```
input:focus, textarea:focus {
  background: #E5EBF4;
}
```

This lighter background color shows when the text area has focus, making the field appear to the visual user to "light up" a little. Unfortunately, Internet Explorer does not show `:focus` pseudo classes on anything except links so the IE user won't see the change. But it doesn't hurt anything and the other browsers will have a nice enhancement.

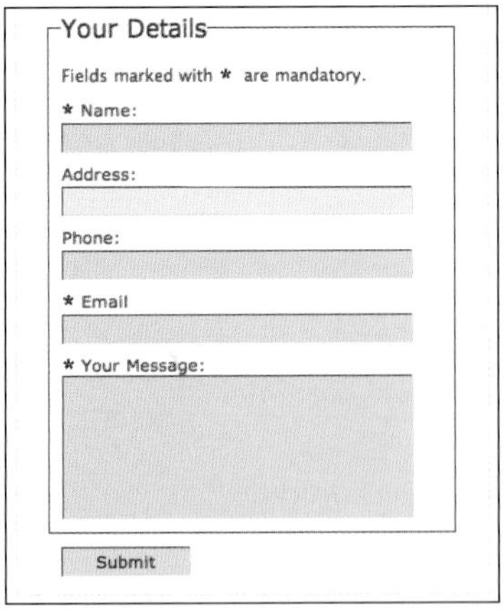

FIGURE 5.38 The address field lights up when the cursor is placed inside.

With that, our form styling is complete! You'll see differences between Dreamweaver and the various browsers, so be sure to test in each browser.

```
fieldset {
 border: 1px solid #336;
 padding: .8em 0 .8em .8em;
}
legend {
 font-size: 1.5em;
}
label {
 display: block;
 margin-top: .5em;
}
input, textarea {
 width: 21em;
 background: #D9DEE8;
 border-top: 1px solid #336;
 border-right: 1px solid #978EBA;
 border-bottom: 1px solid #978EBA;
 border-left: 1px solid #336;
 padding: .2em;
}
textarea {
 height: 8em;
}
input#submit {
 width: 8em;
 margin-top: .8em;
 margin-left: .8em;
}
input:focus, textarea:focus {
 background: #E5EBF4;
}
```

Adding Form Validation

At this point, we have a nice working form—well, it will be working after our co-worker puts the dynamic code in! However, we have one last enhancement to add to the form using Dreamweaver's built-in Spry form validation—a timesaver to be sure.

You'll remember that we set several fields as required fields but we need to enforce that. And we asked visitors to provide their phone number, but we need to make sure that they provide it in a properly formatted, 10-digit North American format of (XXX) XXX-XXXX. While we could rely on our back-end programmer to provide this functionality, we can also build it directly into the form using a feature of Dreamweaver CS4, the Spry framework for Ajax.

N *Spry has new password validation and radio button validation features in Dreamweaver CS4. Well worth checking out!*

We'll talk more about the Spry framework for Ajax in Chapter 6, but for now, let's use a bit of its functionality to enhance our form.

The Name field has been designated as a required field. In other words, we don't want to allow someone to submit the form if they have not provided this information.

1. Select the textfield **name**.

2. Switch the Insert panel to the Spry category and click the Spry Validation Text Field icon.

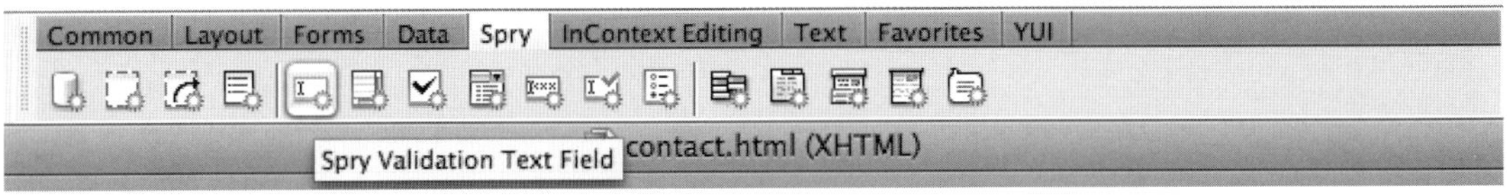

FIGURE 5.39 The Spry Validation Text Field icon.

The Spry Validation Text Field tool creates a `<span>` around the input field. This `<span>` provides the functionality, via JavaScript, to validate that the user enters text into the field. The Required check box is checked by default, so we don't have to do anything further.

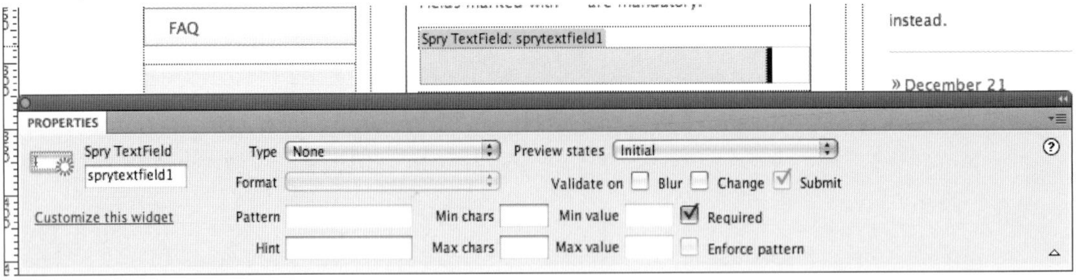

FIGURE 5.40 The Spry Validation Text Field tool provides advanced functionality for ensuring that a visitor enters the proper information.

Let's next ensure that the visitor provides the properly formatted telephone number.

3. Select the **phone** textfield.

4. Once again, click to select the Spry Validation Text Field from the Insert panel.

The phone number is not required, but we want to make sure that if the visitor enters their phone number, it is properly formatted.

5. In the Type drop-down list, select Phone Number.

6. From the Format drop-down list, select US/Canada.

We also want to let the visitor know exactly what we are expecting from them.

7. In the Hint field, enter (123) 456-7890.

This value gives the visitor a visual indication of what is expected, but disappears as soon as they tab or click into the field.

8. Check the Enforce pattern check box.

Using this check box causes the browser to automatically enter the parentheses and dashes without the visitor needing to do so by hand.

9. Uncheck the Required check box.

Finally, we need to establish when the validation will occur.

10. In the Validate on section, place a check mark in the Blur check box.

The Blur option tells the browser to validate the field if the visitor either clicks or tabs out of the field.

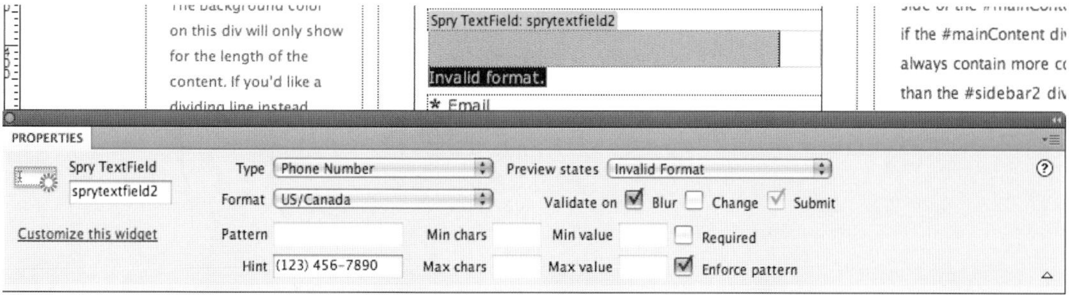

FIGURE 5.41 We'll provide a hint for the visitor and validate the field when they click or tab away from it.

11. Insert the Spry Validation Text Field for the email field, select Type email address, validate on Blur, and leave the Required box checked.

12. Create a Spry Validation Text area for the Comment field, just as we did for the Name field, and simply leave the Required check box checked.

13. Save the file and click OK to copy the required JavaScript files into your site.

By default, Dreamweaver places the Spry CSS and JavaScript files into the root of your site.

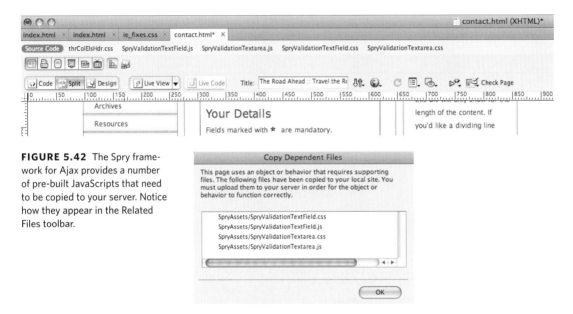

FIGURE 5.42 The Spry framework for Ajax provides a number of pre-built JavaScripts that need to be copied to your server. Notice how they appear in the Related Files toolbar.

14. Preview in a browser and experiment with an empty name field or a mis-formatted email, or by incorrectly entering a phone number.

FIGURE 5.43 Live View gives us an actual working test environment.

Creating and Styling Accessible Data Tables

Pure CSS layouts have become so commonplace in the last two or three years that it can be difficult to remember how to design tables at all, let alone how to style them to display data in a meaningful way. Fortunately, Dreamweaver CS4 makes creating standards-compliant and accessible data tables really easy.

N *This table can easily be adapted for other uses: for example, timetables, catalogs, employee directories, and so on.*

For businesses servicing customers from physical premises, it's always a good idea to have the business's opening or office hours clearly visible on the web site. These details are frequently placed on contact pages. We're going to go a step further than simply listing the office hours. We're going to provide a nicely formatted table so customers can see opening times at a glance.

For our fictional client, the office opening times are varied. The office is open on Monday and Friday mornings and afternoons, Tuesday and Thursday afternoons and evenings, and Wednesday and Saturday mornings only. The office is closed on Sundays.

We need a grid displaying the days of the week as headings on one axis, and morning, afternoon, and evening headings on the other axis. The time of day will be in the horizontal headers, so we'll need three columns for those. The days of the week will be in the vertical headers, so we'll need seven of those.

We'll also shade the opening times for fast and easy visual identification.

Let Dreamweaver Do the Heavy Lifting

Make sure that both the Layout tab of the Insert toolbar and the Tag inspector are open. We're going to rely on these to make our table building fuss-free.

1. With `contact.html` open in Code and Design view, either place the cursor in the Code view pane just after the form we created, but before the closing `</div>` tag of `mainContent`, or select the form on the tag selector and arrow right one time.

   This is where we'll place our Opening Hours table.

2. Click the Insert Table button in the Insert toolbar.

| Common | Layout | Forms | Data | Spry | InContext Editing | Text | Favorites | YUI |

| Standard | Expanded |

contac Table (XHTML)

FIGURE 5.44 The Insert Table icon can be accessed on both the Common and Layout panes of the Insert bar.

If you forget to allow for the headers, you can always use Dreamweaver to add an extra row or column. Place the cursor in a cell that will be adjacent to the new row or column. Right-click and select Table > Insert Rows or Columns from the contextual menu. Alternatively, simply change the number of rows/columns using the Property inspector.

A dialog box pops up immediately offering us all kinds of options for our new table. We choose the options, and Dreamweaver CS4 builds the table. That seems like a good deal to us!

We need to define the numbers of rows and columns our table will contain. We've already established that we need three columns for the time of day, and seven rows for the days of the week. These numbers don't take into account the header row and the header column, so we need to add one to each number.

3. In the first section of the Table dialog box, Table size, insert the values of **8 rows** and **4 columns**.

4. Remove the border of 1 pixel that Dreamweaver inserted by default, and leave the other options in the Table size section blank.

5. In the Header section, select the fourth option of Both, since we need headers on both axes of the table.

6. In the Accessibility section, give the caption a value of **Office Hours** and type in the summary:

   Office opening hours categorized as morning, afternoon and evening for each day of the week. There is a single header row and a single header column.

FIGURE 5.45 Dreamweaver's table dialog with accessibility prompts.

Table

Table size

Rows: 8   Columns: 4

Table width: percent

Border thickness: pixels

Cell padding:

Cell spacing:

Header

None   Left   Top   Both

Accessibility

Caption: Office Hours

Summary: Office opening hours categorized as morning, afternoon and evening for each day of the week. There is a single header row and a single header column.

Help   Cancel   OK

Accessibility and the Anatomy of a Data Table

A correctly marked-up data table has basic components that should *always* be present for the benefit of screen readers and other devices. These components are the caption and th elements, and the summary attribute.

From an accessibility viewpoint, the most important thing to remember when building data tables is to ensure that data is associated with the appropriate header in the table. This is easy to achieve visually for sighted users. But for users of screen readers, except in the simplest of data tables, the association must be explicitly indicated in the code in order for a screen reader to speak the header/data relationship to the user.

This is done using a combination of the table header element, th, by setting ids on the header, and by adding these ids to the headers attribute in the related data cells. Sometimes using scope together with col and/or row works, but using a combination of id and headers is a more reliable method.

All tables have an opening <table> tag and an associated closing tag. This in itself isn't enough to determine whether the table is being used for data or for layout. The most useful ways to let screen reader users know that the content of the table is data is through the use of the caption element and the summary attribute.

The caption element is placed directly after the table element and encloses the table's title. The summary attribute is applied to the <table> tag and provides helpful information for the screen reader user about how to understand the table. For example, as well as a brief description of what correlating data the table contains, the summary tag might also be used to warn the screen reader user when there are two or more rows or columns of header data. Tips like this can make the user's path to acquiring the required information much smoother.

Even so, tables with single rows or columns of headers are far easier for screen readers and their users to decipher than those with multiple levels, so it's a good idea to avoid complexity in data tables wherever possible. We'll keep our table very simple for that reason.

With a more complex table, however, it is necessary to explicitly make a connection between data cells and the relevant header. To do this, give each th element an id, and for each td (table data) element that relates to that header, apply a headers attribute containing the value of that id.

Be aware that the headers attribute can contain multiple values. It should contain a value for each th associated with it.

Giving the Table Dimensions

We'll start on the CSS now, because the table is too narrow for comfort. Let's set a width on the table.

FIGURE 5.46 Without dimensions, this table is a tad smaller than we'd like!

On some web sites, two or more tables of different styles and purposes could be located in different sections of the page. If that were the case here, we would use appropriate Advanced selectors and/or CSS classes. In our case, all we need is a simple table *selector because we know we won't be using tables on our site except for data and that they will always be in the* mainContent *area.*

Take a moment to hover your mouse over different areas of the table, including the edges. You'll quickly discover that hovering over the leftmost edge of a row highlights all the cells in the row, and that hovering over the topmost edge of a column highlights all the cells in the column. If you take it a step further and click, the entire row or column is selected.

Use the Tab key to move the selection to the cell on the right of the current cell, instead of continually reaching for the mouse to re-position the cursor.

1. Create a new CSS element (tag) selector for the `table`.

2. Set a width of **100%** for the table. Apply a **1px** solid border with the color **#336 collapse**.

   We applied the collapse value to the borders using our original reset, so that's not necessary here. border-collapse causes the borders to render as a single border—not a double.

   Click inside the top left table cell in the Design view pane. Look at the Code view pane and locate the cursor. It is inside the first `<th></th>` tag pair. We know this is the horizontal row of headers across the top of the table, because the attribute `scope` has been applied, with a value of `col`. This tells us that the table header cell heads a column.

3. Leave the top left cell blank, and type the following into the top row of cells: `Morning`, `Afternoon`, and `Evening`.

4. Again skipping the top left cell, fill in the days of the week down the left column of the table.

   There are some spacing issues, but ignore them for now. We'll fix them shortly when we style the table using CSS.

Office Hours			

» January 30

Lorem ipsum dolor sit amet, consectetuer adipiscing elit. Praesent aliquam, justo convallis luctus rutrum, erat nulla fermentum

```
 95    <tr>
 96        <th scope="col"> </th>
 97        <th scope="col"> </th>
 98        <th scope="col"> </th>
 99        <th scope="col"> </th>
100    </tr>
101    <tr>
102        <th scope="row"> </th>
```

FIGURE 5.47 The scope attribute is identifying the table cell as a header for a column of data.

N *When space is tight, abbreviate the table headers and mark them up accordingly with the ‹abbr› tag. Screen readers will read out the title attribute of ‹abbr› tags. There is also an abbr attribute specifically for use in th tags that has its own special use. When the header text is long and repetition would be tedious, an abbreviation of the long header text can be defined in the abbr attribute. On the first occasion the th is encountered, some screen readers will read it out in full but subsequently will read out only the abbreviated text in the abbr attribute.*

FIGURE 5.48 Our table with the opening times for each day.

We need a way to indicate when the office is open. As blocks of time are going to be selected, an indicator that visually fills each cell would be ideal. To achieve this, we can highlight the cell with a background color, using CSS.

But wait a second—what about the users of screen readers? After all, they won't benefit from the display of a background color.

For non-sighted users we'll put the words Open or Closed in the appropriate cells so a screen reader user will know the office is open at the day and time corresponding with that particular cell. This also means that a key to explain the highlighting is unnecessary for sighted users.

5. In Design view, type into each cell of the table its status of either Open or Closed. For Sunday, insert a single Closed for the morning period. We'll work more with Sunday shortly.

Office Hours			
	Morning	**Afternoon**	**Evening**
Monday	Open	Open	Closed
Tuesday	Closed	Open	Open
Wednesday	Open	Closed	Closed
Thursday	Closed	Open	Open
Friday	Open	Open	Closed
Saturday	Open	Closed	Closed
Sunday	Closed		

Providing Additional Feedback for Accessibility

The table structure is deliberately simple, but let's still apply the markup that allows screen reader users to discover the relationship between table cells and their headers.

We'll give each th an **id**, and each table cell a **headers** attribute containing a value identical to that of the **id** of the associated **th**. We will do this using the Tag inspector, so make sure it is open and in Attributes mode.

1. In the (X)HTML document, click in the **th** cell containing the word Monday. Select **th** in the tag selector. In the Tag inspector, expand the CSS/Accessibility section. Set the **id** attribute by clicking in the field to the right of **id** and typing the word mon. Press Enter to apply the new **id**.

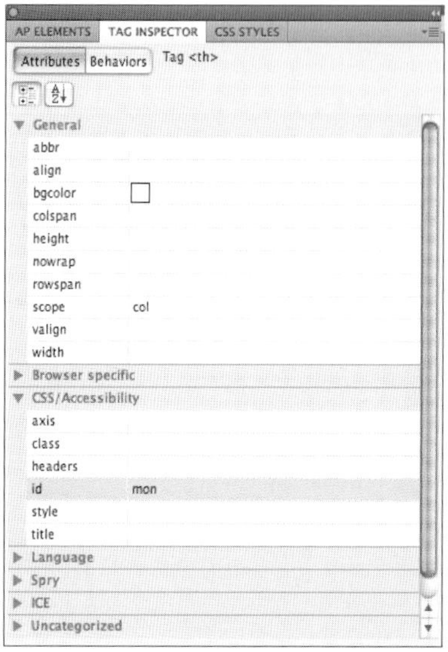

FIGURE 5.49 The Tag inspector showing the CSS/Accessibility pane expanded.

2. Do the same for the other days in the header column, obviously using the appropriate day name as the value for each **id**.

3. Assign an **id** to each of Morning, Afternoon, and Evening in the header row across the top of the table. For example, Morning would have an **id** of morning. Continue until each header cell in the table has an **id**.

    In the same way, we will now assign the values we just set for each **id** as the values of the **headers** attribute in each table cell. Each table cell has two corresponding headers and will therefore have two values for the **headers** attribute. When a screen reader selects the table cell, it will use the values for the **id**s and **headers** attributes to establish the relationship between that cell and its two headers.

4. Click inside the first **td** cell, which is the one to the right of the **Monday th** and beneath the **Morning th**. Select the **<td>** in the tag selector if it is not already selected, and look over at the Tag Inspector.

    You will see that **headers** is listed under the Attribute tab.

5. Type in two values for **headers**—mon morning—and make sure the values are separated by a space. These values are identical to the values of the **id**s on the corresponding **th** elements.

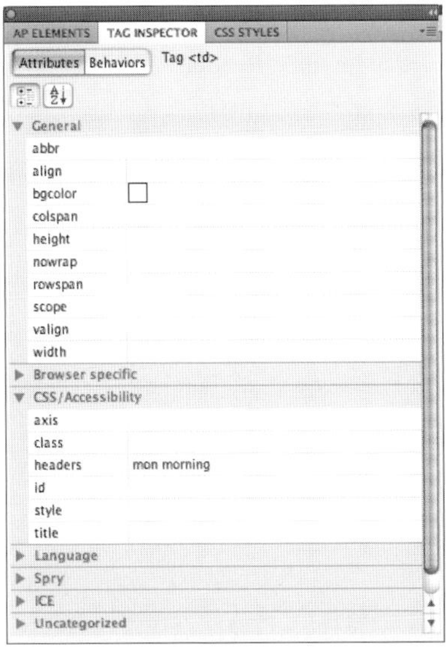

FIGURE 5.50 The Attributes tab
of the Tag inspector

FIGURE 5.50 The Attributes tab
of the Tag inspector

6. Follow this procedure to give all cells containing data a `headers` attribute.

   Before we move on to styling the table with CSS, we'll perform one little act of housekeeping to make our table easier to understand. On Sunday, the office is closed all day. We currently have the word Closed once, which keeps things nice and clean, but it is only in the Morning cell and the Afternoon and Evening cells are empty. Those cells actually do represent either an Open or Closed status so it's not an ideal situation.

   ```
   <tr>
    <th id="sun" scope="row">Sunday</th>
    <td>Closed</td>
    <td> </td>
    <td> </td>
   </tr>
   ```

   Instead of repeating the word Closed three times for that day, we will combine the Morning, Afternoon, and Evening cells to indicate that the Closed status spans all three.

7. In Design view, place the cursor in the cell that represents Sunday Morning and that contains the word Closed. Drag the mouse from this cell over to the right side of the table.

   You will see that the cells it passes through are selected.

8. With these cells selected, right-click and choose Table > Merge Cells or simply press the M key.

   Now, there is a single cell for Sunday.

9. Change the text to read `Closed All Day`.

A look at our code shows the changes.

```
<tr>
 <th id="sun" scope="row">Sunday</th>
 <td colspan="3">Closed All Day</td>
</tr>
```

Dreamweaver has applied a `colspan` of 3 to a `td`, creating a single cell combining the original 3 `td`s instead of using three separate `td`s.

Styling the Data Table

Let's start right at the top of the table and style the `caption` element. Captions can be problematic to style consistently across browsers so we'll keep our styling very basic. We already reset its properties in our CSS but a space above the caption would visually separate it from the form, and we also want the text to be larger.

1. Add a new CSS rule for the element `caption`.

2. Set the font-face to `"Lucida Grande", Arial, Helvetica, sans-serif`, and set the size to `1.5em`. For padding, set top to `1em` and bottom to `0.2em`. Set the text-align to `left`.

   The caption now displays on the left, and has a spatial association with the table below it.

   We need to move the `th` and `td` cell contents away from the edges of their cells and spread them out a little more. We'll also apply borders, thus creating a visual grid and making it easier for sighted users to identify the required information.

3. Add a new CSS rule with a compound selector of `th, td`.

4. For padding, set top and bottom to `0.1em` and left and right to `0.4em`.

   Add a border in order to display the rows and columns as a grid.

5. Switch to the Border category and add a **1px** solid border with a color of **#336**.

We also need to create a style for **th** alone, to clearly and visually differentiate between the header cells and the table data cells.

> By default the **th** element is bold and centered. This can be changed with CSS. In this case, we'll use the defaults.

6. Add a new CSS rule for the **th** element.

7. Set the font-size to **.85em**. Set the font-weight to **bold**, and the color to **#D9DEE8**.

In Design view, we can see that Dreamweaver has applied some cell spacing of its own, but when viewed in Live View, the table displays as intended. Dreamweaver maintains this additional space in order to help us more easily select elements of the table—while disconcerting perhaps, it does serve a purpose.

> If you need even more space, on the Layout tab of the Insert bar, you can choose Expanded Tables mode (F6).

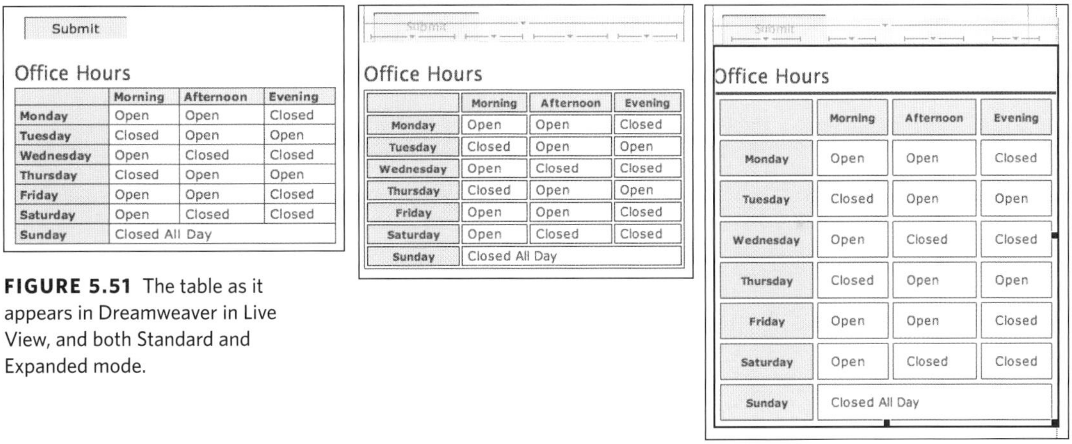

FIGURE 5.51 The table as it appears in Dreamweaver in Live View, and both Standard and Expanded mode.

Finally, in order to highlight the table cells that signify that the office is open, we can create a class that we'll apply just to the relevant **td** cells.

8. Add a new CSS class called **open**. Set the background color to **#EFE5EB**.

9. In Design view, place the cursor inside the first **td** that contains the word Open. This is the cell to the right of the header Monday and below the header Morning. Drag the mouse to select that cell and the one immediately on its right, which also contains the word Open. Holding down the Ctrl key, continue to select all the cells containing the word Open.

10. In the Property inspector, click on the Styles drop-down list and choose the class **open**. Alternatively, right-click on the group of cells that are selected and choose CSS Styles > open from the contextual menu.

A pale pink background has now been applied to all of the office opening times, drawing the eye to the most important data for sighted users, and our table is complete.

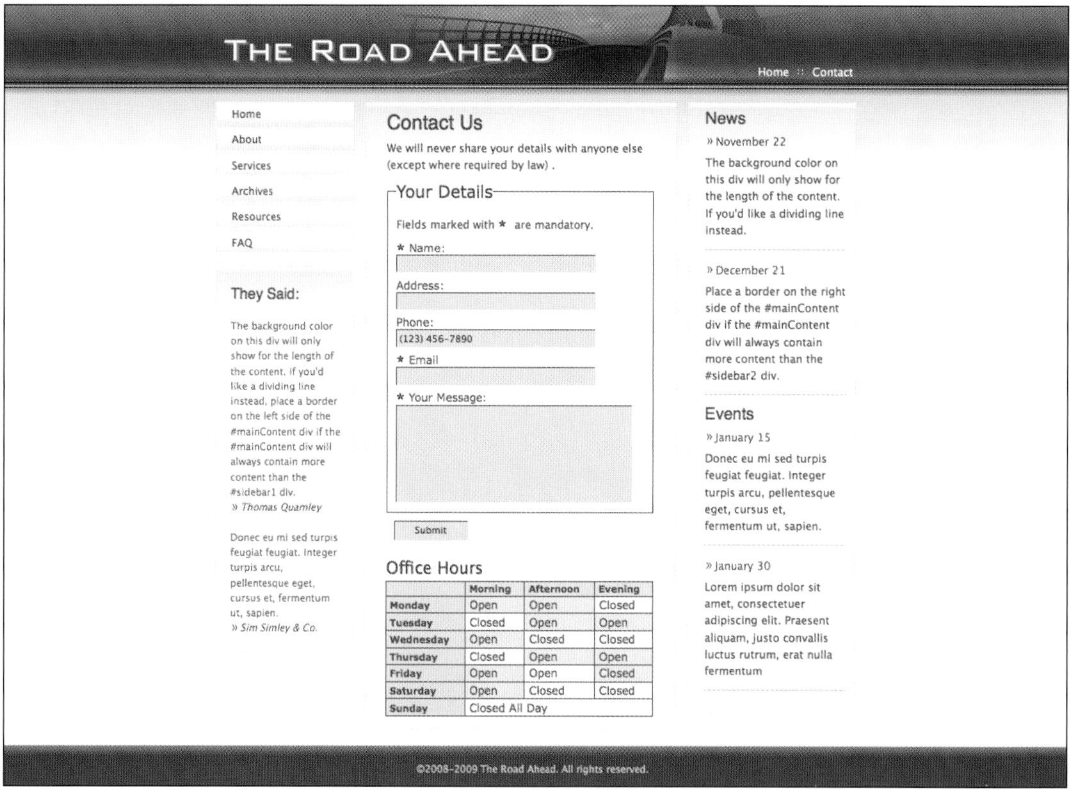

FIGURE 5.52 Our completed page as viewed in Firefox.

Do You Feel Accomplished?

In this chapter, you've used one of Dreamweaver's default elastic layouts to create and style a generic page and a contact page with data table and form. You've learned that containers with em widths will expand and contract according to font size, maintaining the intended page layout and proportions. You've also learned how to save and use snippets. You have created an accessible form with Spry validation and an accessible data table, both of which will expand or contract with the layout.

Give yourself a gold star for a job well done!

Building a Gallery Site with CSS and Spry

IN THIS CHAPTER, we'll create a site for a fictitious client, Rive Gauche Galleries. Along the way, we'll use and combine different CSS layouts in a single site, as well as explore the world of progressive enhancements using the Spry framework for Ajax.

As an art gallery, one requirement for Rive Gauche is that the site display a large number of graphics without a lot of scrolling, and at the same time offer a larger detail image without opening additional browser windows or linking to other HTML pages. Because of the amount of information to display, the client would like the content area of the pages to expand as the browser's viewport is widened. While we're at it, the owner would like us to ensure that the site's layout integrity is maintained when the browser agent's text size is increased or decreased—like many of us, he finds the small text on many web pages uncomfortably hard to read. Finally, the client also wants a form that potential customers can use to contact them.

Our client's site was originally built in the late '90's, and looks its age. Yep, we've got our work cut out for us.

FIGURE 6.1 The client's old site—did the web really look this bad in the 90s?!

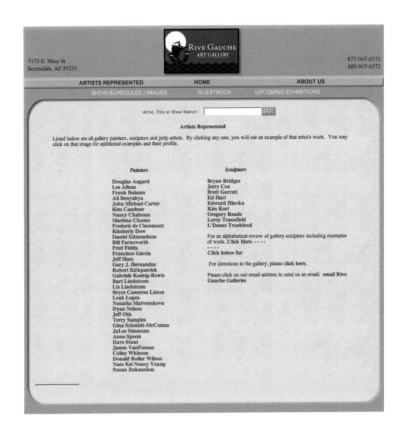

Selecting the Proper Starter Layout

Since the page needs to both expand with the browser agent's viewport width and expand or contract with the change of text size in the browser agent, there's only one type of starter layout to use—the hybrid layout. We simply need to decide on the number of columns and we'll be ready to go.

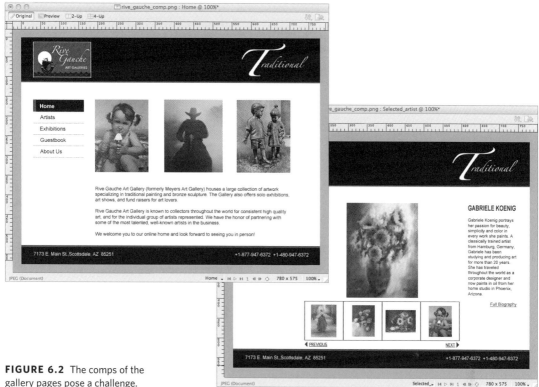

FIGURE 6.2 The comps of the gallery pages pose a challenge.

But should we use a two-column or three-column layout? For the home page, it's fairly easy to see two columns. The navigation could be in the left column and we could then divide the main content section to accommodate the thumbnail images and text. But the artists' page has a column of text on the right. No need, though, to reinvent the code equivalent of the wheel: we can simply use two separate CSS layouts and combine their rules.

1. Create a Dreamweaver site called Chapter_6 and copy the tutorial files into it, or use your own images.

2. Create a new document using the New Document dialog. Select the 2 column hybrid, left sidebar, header and footer layout. Ensure that XHTML 1.0 Transitional is selected as the DocType.

3. Choose to create a new style sheet file for the layout. Change the name of the style sheet from the default of twoColHyb-LtHdr.css to mainStyles.css and save it in your new site.

4. Save the HTML page as index.html.

5. As we've mentioned before, one of the great features of Dreamweaver CS4 is the ability to set the Code and Design views side-by-side. Go ahead and do this (if you haven't created your own workspace like this already), and select the CSS file from the Related Files toolbar.

FIGURE 6.3 The hybrid layout allows the page design to adapt both to a browser agent's window width and to changes in the browser agent's text size.

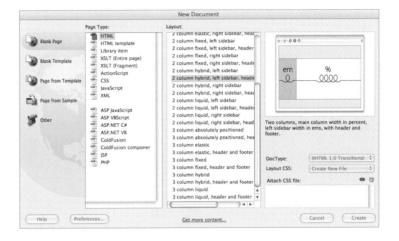

Building the Initial Framework

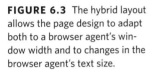 *Since we're giving the body a black background, even though the #container will have a white background, we want to change the text to a contrasting color on the body element. If any user agent has trouble displaying any of our values, we want to be sure we have contrasting colors on the divs that are displayed. Thus, the text on the body is changed to white (since it's on a black background) and the text on the #container is defined as black (since it's on a white background).*

The initial framework of all the pages within the site is relatively simple and by this point, you should feel comfortable creating it. Therefore, we'll do a quick review.

1. Remove the background color from the sidebar. Apply black (#000) as the background color to the body of the page and set the text color to white (#FFF). Change the padding on `sidebar1` to 0px.

2. Change the background color of the header and footer to black (#000) and the text to white (#FFF).

3. Remove the border from the container. Change the width of the container to 100% and the text color to black (#000).

4. Create a new rule for all h1, h2, and h3, elements as follows:

```
h1, h2, h3 {
    font-weight: normal;
    letter-spacing: -.05em;
    line-height: 1.1;
}
```

5. Remove Verdana from the font-family of the body rule. Add the line-height property set to 1.5 to give the text on the page an airier feel.

```
body {
    font: 100%/1.5 Arial, Helvetica, sans-serif;
    background: #000;
    margin: 0;
    padding: 0;
    text-align: center;
    color: #FFF;
}
```

6. Place the cursor in the header and use the tag selector to remove the **h1**. Go ahead and delete the word "header" from here as well.

7. Because we've deleted the **h1** and will not be using it in this site, it's probably a good idea to switch to the All view of the CSS panel now and delete the `.twoColHybLtHdr #header h1` rule. You can do this by selecting the name from the list, right-clicking, and choosing Delete.

8. Place the logo.gif in `<div#header>`. Apply 30 pixels of left and right padding and 10 pixels of top and bottom padding to the header rule.

9. Assign `"/index.html"` as the image's link in the Property inspector.

   Remember that visitors to a site generally expect the logo to be a link taking them back to the home page of the site. This link takes the user back to the index page at the root level of the site.

   You'll notice that (although it's really hard to see on the black background) the image now has a blue line all the way around it, indicating that it is a link. So we'll need to remove this— unless you just really like your images outlined in blue!

10. Create a new rule for images within a link element, `a img`, and set the border to **none**. Your code should look like this: `a img {border:none;}`

11. Add `logo_traditional.gif` as a background image to the header rule. Set it to **no-repeat**, with a right horizontal position and center vertical position.

One of the fastest ways to wrap an element in a tag, like the example of the ‹span›, is to select the text or element that you want to wrap in the Design area and then press Ctrl+T. This brings up the Quick Tag Editor. If you have simply placed your cursor into an element, the Quick Tag Editor will be set to Insert Tag. If you have selected an element, it will either contain the code for the element, or be set to Wrap Tag—based upon whether you have the entire element selected or not. Regardless, a second press of Ctrl+T will result in the Wrap Tag option. You can now simply type the name of the tag you wish to wrap the element or selection in. After typing the tag name, hit the spacebar to bring up a list of available attributes for the tag. When you're satisfied, hit the Enter key twice. If you love your code, but don't want to give up your Design area, the Quick Tag Editor is the best!

Another look at the comps (it's always a good idea to refer back to your comp now and then) reveals that we need to create a bit of separation between the header/footer and the content area by adding a red line and a bit of air.

12. Add a bottom border to the header rule. Make it **solid**, **6px** and **#AD2027**. To hold the content away from the bottom of the header, add **margin-bottom:50px**.

13. For the footer, we'll want the same padding as in the header, so set padding to **10px 30px** and then add a **border-top** using the same properties as we used for the header.

14. Last but not least, we'll add the gallery address and phone numbers to the footer. Add the following text to the footer:

    +1-800-123-4567 +1-800-987-6543 12345 Main St. Scottsdale, AZ 85251

    From the comp, we can see that the text appears to be two text blocks, one on the left and one on the right. It's very easy to achieve this effect using a float. Since we want the telephone numbers to appear on the right, they are ahead of the address in the source code order.

15. Wrap the telephone numbers in a **‹span›** element. Assign a class of **fltrt** to the span.

16. Add the font-size property to the **footer p** rule and set it to **0.7em**.

FIGURE 6.4 With the initial framework for the index page in place, we're ready to rock!

Lights, Camera, Content...

N *If you simply drag the cursor in Design view from the h2 to the end of the text to select it and then press Delete, the h2 element may be left on the page. We don't want that, so make sure it's completely removed.*

Before we begin to tackle the navigation, let's get the simple main content area out of the way. Based on our comp, the content area is nothing more than some text and three images. If you need to save, go ahead, or simply open index_1.html from the builds folder for this chapter.

1. Delete the h1 and h2 placeholder text in the mainContent area. Don't forget to remove the tags themselves.

   As we look at the page, something is not quite right. With the exception of the text in the footer, the text on our page is much larger than it is in our comp. But, as always when working with the CSS layouts, the best practice is to change the font-size on individual elements, rather than changing it globally using the body element.

2. Using the CSS panel or your preferred method, create a new rule for the paragraph elements of the mainContent area: #mainContent p

3. Set the font-size to 0.8em. So that the layout more closely resembles the comp, either break the remaining dummy text into several paragraphs, or copy/paste the text from the finished index page.

4. Save the page (and remember, if the CSS file is open, you'll need to save it as well) and preview it in the browser so that we can see how our page looks at different widths.

Because this is a hybrid layout, it should fill the viewport, as well as adjust to the browser's default text size. Experiment with this by changing the width of the browser window. Notice that the mainContent text adjusts accordingly. Try increasing and decreasing the size of the browser's font. Notice that the width of the sidebar adjusts as well.

Hmmm...did you see that? Do it again—open the browser to the full width of the screen. Whoa! That's not good! Look how long those lines of text are in the mainContent area. Text is less readable when the line exceeds 80 characters. Combine that with our smaller text size and you have to admit that this is not good.

FIGURE 6.5 Even without going full screen, the line length of the content area is waaaay too long!

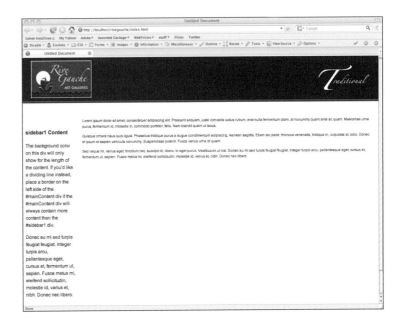

To limit this behavior, we'll use the `max-width` property. The problem with this approach is that a certain browser (that'd be Internet Explorer for those of you who've been sleeping through the book) only began to support this property in version 7. So, we're going to need a dual approach—one for standards-compliant browsers and one for the other guy.

Using max-width and min-width

Let's get our standards-compliant browsers happy first. In addition to keeping the length of the line from becoming too short, we'll also use `min-width` to make sure that the window can't be collapsed so far that we get a really short line.

1. Place the cursor in the `mainContent` element and click to select the `.twoColHybLtHdr #mainContent` rule in the Rules section of the CSS panel's Current view.

2. Click the Add Property link in the Properties section of the CSS panel. Type `max-width` and give it a value of 62em.

3. Select the container rule in the CSS panel, click Add Property again, and enter `min-width` as the property with a value of 60em.

> **N** *We picked this value by experimenting with how wide we personally felt the lines could still be easily read. We also didn't want too much white space to the right of the text, so a narrower (but probably more readable) width wouldn't work. We chose to constrain the width using ems instead of pixels to allow for changes in the font size by the viewer.*

4. Save your pages and preview in Firefox or Safari (or your standards-compliant browser of choice). Expand and contract the browser window and you'll notice our maximum and minimum widths kicking into play.

So now that we've solved the line width issue for our favorite browsers, we need to solve the problem presented by Internet Explorer 5.5 and 6.

Getting IE's Attention—min/max width Enforcement

Unfortunately, Internet Explorer has no simple way to solve our issue—or, perhaps more accurately stated, no standards-compliant way. But there is a workaround, known as an expression. An expression is an IE-only property that uses JavaScript within your CSS file. It needs to be placed in an IECC and actually allows us to get close to the max-width and min-width standard.

Since it gets us where we need to go for IE 6... what the heck. Let's do it.

1. Switch to Code view, or select the Source Code from the Related Files toolbar if you are in Split view, and scroll toward the top of the document until you locate the IECC (Internet Explorer Conditional Comment). The code block begins with:

   ```
   <!--[if IE]>
   ```

2. Add the following code above the closing `</style>` tag of the IECC:

   ```
   .twoColHybLtHdr #container { width: expression(Math.
   max((document.documentElement ? document.documentElement.
   clientWidth : document.body.clientWidth)/16,
   960/16)+'em'); }
   ```

What in the world is all that? Well, it's actually not as scary as it looks. Let's walk through it, piece by piece, remembering that because we've placed the code in the IECC, only Internet Explorer will read it.

First, we're telling IE to locate the element defined by the descendant selector `.twoColHybLtHdr #container` and then get ready to set its width property. Next, we use IE's proprietary `expression();` statement, which basically says "we're about to give you some JavaScript to execute."

The core of the expression uses the JavaScript `Math` class. `Math.max()` takes two comma-delimited arguments and determines which argument is bigger. As arguments we're giving it `(document.documentElement ? document.documentElement.clientWidth : document.body.clientWidth)/16` and `960/16`.

If expressions make your head spin and you want some of the other advantages IE7 has over IE6 and earlier, you may want to try out Dean Edwards's IE7 script. This script is basically a JavaScript framework that forces the earlier browsers to render like IE7 currently does (min/max width/height, alpha transparency on pngs, fixed positioning, more advanced compound selectors and more). http://dean.edwards.name/weblog/2008/01/ie7-2/

The first argument is a basic true/false statement that asks whether the viewer's browser is running in Standards mode or Quirks mode. The statement `document.documentElement` is asking, "is this true?"; in other words, does this browser know what we're talking about when asking about the document's DOM? The question mark ends the question or condition. This is then followed by the true and false options, separated by a colon (:).

In our case, the true statement `document.documentElement.clientWidth` states that we are interested in the width of the document, or in this case, the browser viewport in a browser running in Standards mode. The false statement is exactly the same, just running in Quirks mode. Finally, note that the true/false statement is enclosed in parentheses, indicating that we want to determine this outcome before we continue.

Remember, 1em is equal to 16px based on the default base font size used by modern browsers.

After we've determined the width of the viewport through either the Standards mode or Quirks mode, we then divide the resulting pixel value by 16. Now, did you hear that? The width value is delivered in pixels—this is our only choice—but we're dealing with a hybrid/liquid layout and want to measure our value in ems. That's why we're dividing the result by 16. Dividing the pixel value by 16 gives us the equivalent value in em spaces.

Our second argument is `960/16`. You'll recall that for standards-compliant browsers we limited the min-width to 60em. Grab your calculator and do the math... 960 divided by 16 is 60.

Are you wondering if there is a `Math.min` function? Yes, there is. It would limit the maximum value (in our case the width) that could be applied to an element. So... `Math.max` gives us a minimum whereas `Math.min` gives us a maximum. Now that makes perfect sense!

So basically, we've told the `Math.max` function to determine which is larger: the current width of the viewport (in pixels, but divided by 16 to give us the em equivalent) or 60.

Once we've determined which value is greater, we're adding "em" to the total to let the browser know that the value is using this unit of measure.

With that, we've now assigned the width value to the container element, telling Internet Explorer to respect the same min-width value of 60em that we assigned to our standards-compliant browsers. If the viewport is larger than 60em, the page content will continue to fill the viewport. Once the viewport shrinks to less than 60em, the content will not shrink beyond its defined 60em width.

Not Too Far... Constraining the Content Area for IE

With the overall width of the page container constrained, we need to ensure that the line length of our `mainContent` area doesn't become too long if the window is opened wide.

Create a new line in the IECC after the rule that we just created and add the following code:

```
.twoColHybLtHdr #mainContent {width: expression(container.
clientWidth > 1220 ? "62em" : "auto"); }
```

We're asking Internet Explorer to find the `.twoColHybLtHdr` `#mainContent` element and assign a width to it based on the result of an expression. Our expression uses syntax that's similar to the previous expression: if this is true, do this, otherwise do something else.

Stepping through the code, `container.clientWidth > 1220 ?` asks IE if the width of the element identified as container is greater than 1220 pixels. If this is true, it sets the width of `mainContent` to 62em. Otherwise—when the container's width is less than 1220—it sets the width of `mainContent` to `auto`. This means that as the viewport decreases below 1220, the content of `mainContent` will continue to reflow to fill that remaining space.

Of course, since we set a min-width (or its IE equivalent) on the overall container, it only reflows until the overall width of the container element reaches its minimum value.

We've now conquered Internet Explorer 6. So what about version 5.5 or earlier? Well, that's where it gets a little... um... less successful. For Internet Explorer 5.5 and below, our solution has a serious side effect: the page is no longer a hybrid/liquid layout. IE 5.5 and below can't understand the first argument value in the rule for

---

N *Remember that* `.clientWidth` *delivers its results in pixels.*

N *In researching this particular step in our workflow, we initially wanted to use the second syntax (without all that* `Math.max` *stuff) for the overall width of our container. That would have looked like this:*

```
.twoColHybLtHdr #container
{width: expression(document.
documentElement.clientWidth
< 960 ? "60em" : "auto"); }
```

Unfortunately, however, this won't work for our example. It would have worked if we'd only wanted to constrain the value of the container element, but we also needed to determine how to size the mainContent element. Using the value auto would have resulted in the browser reporting a value of 0 and that wouldn't have worked.

the container element. Therefore, those browsers select the second argument as the value. In this example, our page width would be 960px regardless of the viewport width. If the viewport is wider than 960px, black margins will appear on the left and right of our layout.

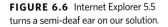
FIGURE 6.6 Internet Explorer 5.5 turns a semi-deaf ear on our solution.

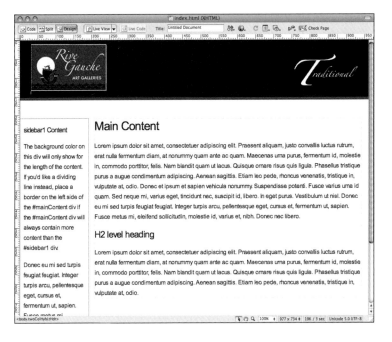

Spread Out the Pictures

With the overall framework of the content area set, our comp indicates that we have three images that need to be added to the index page above the main text. You'll also notice that the images seem to be evenly spaced across the defined area. But wait... that same relationship needs to be maintained even as the `mainContent` area is resized according to our min-width and max-width values. No worries—a little bit of floating magic will do the trick.

1. Place your cursor at the beginning of the text in `mainContent` inside the p element.

2. Either click the Insert Image icon from the Insert panel or drag front_1.jpg, front_3.jpg, and front_2.jpg in order onto the page. (Don't forget to add the title of the picture as the image's alt attribute.)

Notice that the images are not in numerical order. We'll explain this later.

3. Place your cursor after the third image and immediately in front of the first letter in the dummy text. Press Enter to force a new <p> tag to wrap the three images.

4. Create a new class, .centered, in mainStyles.css to use for the <p> element wrapping the images. Assign it the text-align: center attribute, and add a bit of padding to the left and right: padding: 0 5%. Add a bottom margin: margin: 0 0 30px 0.

5. Place the cursor within the <p> element wrapping the images (on the tag selector, be sure you've selected the p element and not one of the images). Use the Property inspector to assign the newly created .centered rule to the <p> element.

According to our comp, we'll need to make our images stand out a bit with a red border.

6. Create a descendant selector for images within the <p.centered> element: p.centered img. Give the rule a 1 pixel solid border: 1px solid #AD2027, and in order to move the border off the image, add 4 pixels of padding: padding: 4px.

FIGURE 6.7 Our images need some space.

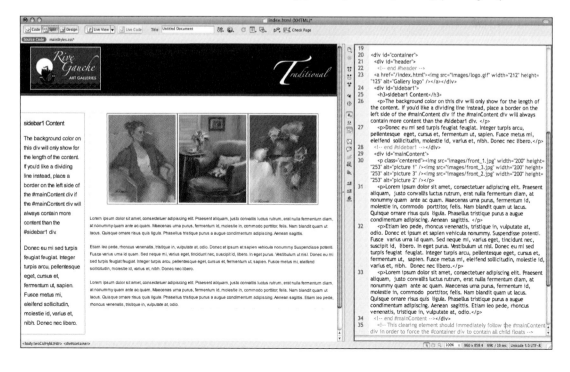

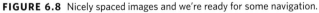 *You'll remember that we mentioned earlier that we were not placing the images on the page in numerical order—at least not by their names. Front_2.jpg is a non-floated element (and is aligned to the center of the page using the* text-align: center *value we gave the* p.centered *class that contains it. We want the front_3.jpg to move to the right and the front_1.jpg to move to the left of the front_2.jpg image. Both of these images must come before front_2.jpg in the source order since it's a non-floated element.*

Our images are looking good, but they're still sitting right next to each other; a little floating and we'll be in business.

7. Click to select the image on the left, and with the image selected, use the Property inspector to assign the .fltlft rule to the image.

8. Click to select the middle image, front_3.jpg and using the Property inspector, assign the .fltrt rule to the image.

   Okay! Things are looking good. We have one last page element to create—the navigation.

9. Save the page and CSS—or open index_2.html from the builds folder to continue.

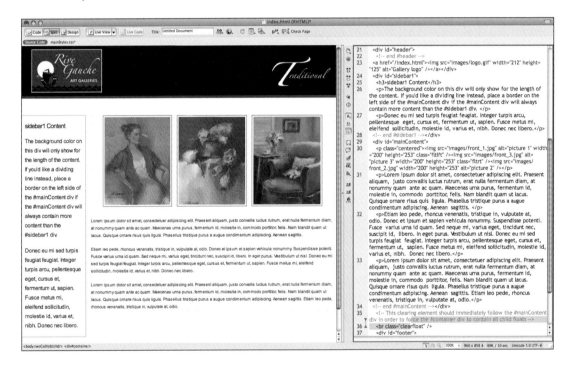

FIGURE 6.8 Nicely spaced images and we're ready for some navigation.

Directions, Please…

For the navigation on the site, our designer has specified a vertical navigation bar. No problem… except that at least one section of the site, the gallery section, needs sub-navigation to distinguish between the different types of art available. The client has asked for two sub-sections initially. In order to keep things as clean as possible, we decided upon a fly-out sub-menu.

Fly-out menus pose some inherent challenges. The biggest is making the information in them reachable for all users, even when JavaScript has been turned off or is simply not supported.

Enter the Spry framework for Ajax.

What Is the Spry Framework?

Ajax (short for Asynchronous JavaScript and XML) is really just a fancy way to describe the action when a page requests information (mostly from an external source, but also from within the page) and updates a specific area of the page without causing the traditional page refresh. If you'd like to learn more about it, there's tons of information in books and on the web, but the inner workings of Ajax are beyond the scope of this book. We're just going to use the tools provided within Dreamweaver CS4, specifically the Spry framework.

So what is the Spry framework? In order to implement Ajax within a page, designers have had two choices—write the JavaScript by hand or use a framework. A framework is basically a collection of scripts, but most frameworks are written by and for programmers, and unless you're a JavaScript guru and dream at night of manipulating the DOM, it can be excruciatingly painful to implement them. In contrast, the Spry framework was developed with designers in mind and with the CS4 release, there are a number of Spry objects built into Dreamweaver. A section of the Insert panel entitled Spry gives us direct access to these Spry objects that we can add to the page without coding.

Adobe is continuing to develop the Spry framework independently of Dreamweaver. The web doesn't hold still and the traditional 18-24 month cycle of Dreamweaver updates isn't fast enough for

If you've already used some of the Spry widgets in your site, Dreamweaver will not overwrite the older files without permission when you add the widget again. You must go to Site > Spry Updater and choose which widgets to update. Dreamweaver will make a copy of the old files and add the new ones.

FIGURE 6.9 The Spry page on labs.adobe.com is where you'll find the full Spry framework for Ajax, as well as any future updates.

the enhancements that are possible with Spry. In fact, there are even some Spry widgets, effects, and objects that are not part of the visual interface of Dreamweaver CS4. So before doing anything else, let's make sure that you have the latest version of the framework by visiting labs.adobe.com and looking for the Spry framework in the Technologies section. You'll want to download the entire framework, which includes one of the widgets that we'll be using later but also contains the full documentation for Spry should you want to continue your exploration after we finish our project.

Creating a Spry-based Navigation

A quick look back at our comp tells us that we're going to need the navigation in the `sidebar1` area.

1. Click to place the cursor in the `sidebar1` element. Select All and delete the contents of the element. Switch to the Spry section of the Insert panel.

The Spry section has three parts. The first contains tools for adding data to a page. This data can be provided by XML, as a JavaScript object (JSON), or from a web page as HTML. The second section contains some tools for working with forms, such as form field validators. The third section contains the Spry widgets, or interface elements.

One of the Spry widgets is called the Spry Menu Bar. That's the one that we want.

2. With the cursor still in the `sidebar1` element, click the Spry Menu Bar tool. Dreamweaver asks if you want a horizontal or vertical menu. Choose the vertical option and click OK.

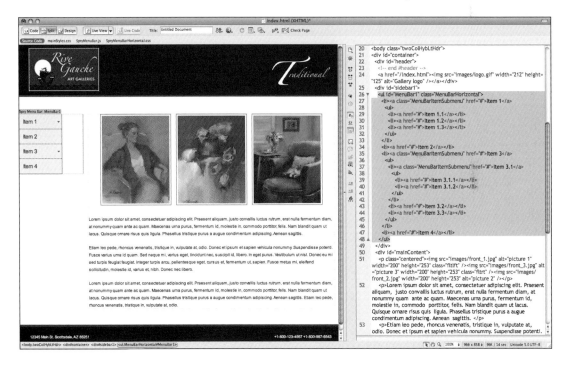

FIGURE 6.10 Our default Spry menu on the page.

We now have a default Spry menu on the page. The four items in the menu are the default menu entries. Two of the items have small triangles to the right of the text, indicating that the entry has a fly-out, or submenu.

Notice also the blue tab above the menu. This doesn't actually appear in the page, but is Dreamweaver's way of indicating the presence of a Spry widget.

PROPERTIES

Menu Bar
MenuBar1

Customize this widget

Turn Styles Off

Item 1
Item 2
Item 3
Item 4

Item 1.1
Item 1.2
Item 1.3

Text Item 1
Link #
Title   Target

FIGURE 6.11 The Spry Menu Bar can be modified using the Property inspector.

Spry Menu Bar: MenuBar1

- Item 1
  - Item 1.1
  - Item 1.2
  - Item 1.3
- Item 2
- Item 3
  - Item 3.1
    - Item 3.1.1
    - Item 3.1.2
  - Item 3.2
  - Item 3.3
- Item 4

FIGURE 6.12 Without the CSS applied, we can see the menu is a list of links.

FIGURE 6.13 In order for Spry widgets to be used in the site, the corresponding JavaScript and CSS files need to be copied into the site structure.

With the `<ul.MenuBarVertical#MenuBar1>` selected, in the Property inspector, you can see that we can modify the entries. We can add entries, delete entries or reorder the entries, as well as add submenus up to two levels deep. You'll also notice a button entitled Turn Styles Off. Click this button to see its effect. Wow—what just happened?

The menu is now made up of nothing more than an unordered list! This is the real beauty of these Spry widgets—they are nothing more than standard HTML elements, in this case, a list. Each Spry element is styled by CSS to give it its look. (Go ahead and say "cool"—it's okay, we did it too when we saw this the first time!) Turn the styles back on by clicking the button again (now titled "Turn Styles On").

3. Save your page… just in case. As you do so, you'll notice that Dreamweaver needs to inform you of something—specifically that it's going to need to add some files to your site.

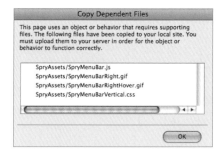

Copy Dependent Files

This page uses an object or behavior that requires supporting files. The following files have been copied to your local site. You must upload them to your server in order for the object or behavior to function correctly.

SpryAssets/SpryMenuBar.js
SpryAssets/SpryMenuBarRight.gif
SpryAssets/SpryMenuBarRightHover.gif
SpryAssets/SpryMenuBarVertical.css

OK

Each Spry widget is made up of HTML elements as we mentioned before. These HTML elements are then styled via CSS. JavaScript provides the interactivity or functionality of the elements. Therefore, Dreamweaver is offering to copy the necessary files into your site structure.

N *When you upload your site later, you'll want to be sure you upload the SpryAssets folder to your server.*

4. Click OK to allow Dreamweaver to copy the files.

   Notice in the root of your site structure a new folder has appeared entitled SpryAssets. This folder now contains the four files that Dreamweaver offered to copy.

   Now all we need to do is modify the menu entries and the associated CSS in order to enhance our page. Let's start with the menu entries.

5. Make sure that the Spry Menu Bar is selected—if it's not, click the blue tab for the Spry Menu Bar and check the Property inspector to see if it reflects that the menu bar is selected.

6. In the first column click Item 1 and change the entry in the Text field to Home. In the Link field, type index.html.

7. In the second column of the Home item, click to select each submenu item and click the minus "-" button to delete them.

8. Change the second menu item to Artists with a link to artists.html.

   The client has requested that this menu entry give the visitor the option of viewing either Painters or Sculptors.

9. With the Artist entry selected in the Property inspector, click the plus button "+" twice in the second column to add two submenu entries. Change the new submenu entries to Painters and Sculptors with links to painters.html and sculptors.html respectively.

10. Select the third menu item in the first column and change it to Exhibitions with a link to exhibitions.html. Delete the submenu items from this entry as we did for the Home item.

    Dreamweaver informs you that the first submenu item also has a submenu that will be deleted.

11. Click OK. Change the fourth menu item in the first column to Contact with a link to contact.html.

12. Add a final menu item in the first column by clicking the plus "+" button above that column. Change this entry to About Us with a link to about.html.

FIGURE 6.14 The modified
Spry Menu Bar with the submenu
showing.

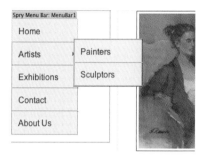

FIGURE 6.14 The modified
Spry Menu Bar with the submenu
showing.

Styling the Spry Menu Bar with CSS

With the menu entries now set, it's time to style them to match our comp.

In our comp, the menu is aligned with the left side of the logo in the header. The header itself has 30px of padding on the left and right. So it stands to reason that we need to move the menu 30px to the right.

1. Select the entire menu bar by clicking on the blue tab.

    In the Current view of the CSS panel, notice in the Rules section that there are two entries for `ul.MenuBarVertical`. The CSS for Spry Menu Bar widget is divided into two sections within the style sheet. One entry describes the layout properties for the widget, while the next entry describes additional attributes. We're going to need to modify a couple of the attributes in the first entry.

2. Select the first `ul.MenuBarVertical` entry in the Rules section of the CSS panel. Change the width in the Properties section to 12em. To push the menu over from the left edge of the window, modify the margin property (currently 0px) to: `margin: 0 0 0 30px;`

3. Finally, the text size is much too large, so set the font-size property to `0.8em`.

    Even though we gave the `<ul>` a width of `12em`, our menu items don't seem to have changed. This is because the individual `<li>` elements have also been assigned a default width in the Spry CSS sheet.

4. Click to place the cursor into one of the menu items and then select the `ul.MenuBarVertical li` entry in the Rules section of the CSS panel. Change the width property to `12em`.

We still need to change the background color and text color of the menu items, as well as position the text further to the right and modify the padding within the box. Notice that the next selector in the cascade (in the Rules section of the CSS panel) is the `ul.MenuBarVertical a` rule. This is where we'll find the last bit of basic styling for the menu items.

N   The easiest way to save your page and its corresponding CSS files is to right-click on the document tab and choose Save All.

5. Select the `ul.MenuBarVertical a` rule in the Rules section of the CSS panel. Change the properties of the rule to the following:

```css
ul.MenuBarVertical a {
    display: block;
    cursor: pointer;
    padding: 0.5em 0 0.5em 30px;
    color: #000;
    text-decoration: none;
    background-color:#FFF; }
```

6. Turn on Live View to see the menu in action. If you're happy (as we are), go ahead and save all of your files.

Notice when you mouse over the Artists entry, the submenu appears and it disappears after you mouse off. This is triggered by the SpryMenuBar.js JavaScript file that Dreamweaver added to the site.

N   While it is beyond the scope of this book, you can modify each of the JavaScript files included in the Spry framework. The files are heavily commented so that you know what each section of code does and any precautions you should take when modifying the file. But what kind of things can you do, you ask... Well, one simple modification that we might want to change on our current project is the time it takes for the submenu items to appear/disappear. These values can be found on lines 102 and 103 of the SpryMenuBar.js file:
`this.showDelay = 250;`
`this.hideDelay = 600;`
The values are in milliseconds, so if we wanted a one-second delay, we could change either of the values to 1000. Feel free to open the individual JavaScripts for the Spry framework. Just remember—if you're going to make adjustments or modifications to the files, make a backup first.

But our submenu is not appearing exactly where we want it. It's sitting a bit too high and the left edge of the submenu is overlapping the main menu. To understand how to modify this, you need to know "where" the menu actually resides when it is not visible.

Remember, when we turned the styles off for the menu, it was nothing more than an unordered list? The submenu items are actually in the source of the page, and in fact, are an unordered list within a parent list item. So, why can't we see the submenu all the time? The answer lies in the CSS—bet you didn't see that coming!

Within the SpryMenuBarVertical.css file, a selector hides the submenus from view until mousing over their parent list item (or menu item) triggers them to show.

Let's take a closer look using a tool that's new to Dreamweaver CS4 and designed with exactly this situation in mind, namely Live Code.

Hey, Code! Wake Up!

As we mentioned in the first chapter, Live Code was created to allow us to see the code exactly the way that the browser has processed it. In our situation, there's really no other way (without wading through lines and lines of CSS and JavaScript) to figure out exactly what's happening when the menu items are triggered and hidden.

1. Click the Live Code button next to the Live View drop-down menu. If you chose to preview the page in the browser rather than turn on Live View in the previous step, shame on you! Turn on Live View in order to catch up.

2. Click on any of the entries in the menu and watch your cursor move to the selected item in code. You might want to scroll down a bit in the Code area so that you can see the code for the menu easily.

3. Mouse over the Artists entry in the menu, and notice that a class of `MenuBarItemSubmenuHover` is being dynamically added to the element.

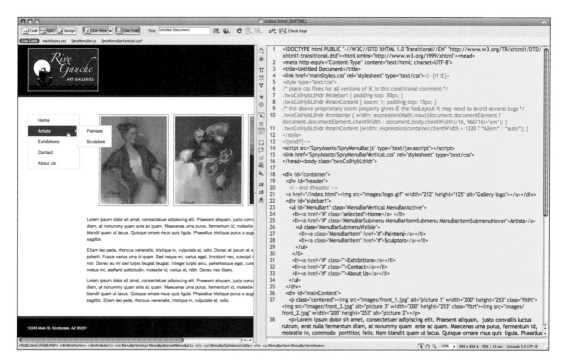

FIGURE 6.15 With Live Code enabled, we can see the inner workings of the Spry Menu Bar.

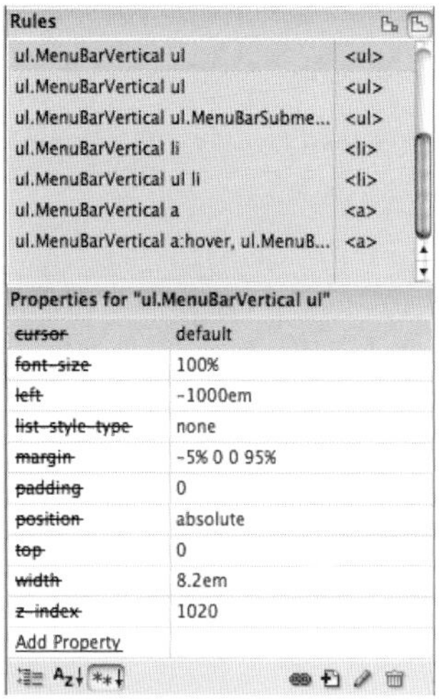

FIGURE 6.16 The magic behind the submenu is actually a left position of -1000em!

4. Click to select one of the entries from the submenu. Even though we are in both Live View and Live Code mode, the CSS panel continues to function.

5. In the CSS panel, locate the first `ul.MenuBarVertical ul` rule in the cascade of the Rules section in the CSS panel, and select it. Again notice that there are two of these rules in the cascade.

Many designers and developers attempt to use the `display:none` attribute to hide elements of the page from the viewer and then use JavaScript to modify the property to show the element. While this is not "wrong"—because there are always multiple ways to solve problems through CSS—it does present a problem for accessibility (and sometimes search engine optimization). An element set not to display is not read by assistive technology. In order to better accommodate these important technologies, the Spry framework for Ajax takes another approach: hiding the element by positioning it offscreen. This is done via two properties: `position:absolute;` and `left: -1000em;`.

Okay... then how does the submenu appear and, of equal importance, where does it appear? Once again, this is a function of the CSS, but this time CSS gets some help from JavaScript. When the JavaScript is triggered, it dynamically assigns a class of `MenuBarSubmenuVisible` to the nested `<ul>` that is the submenu.

6. Move your mouse on and off the Artists menu item. Watch the nested `<ul>` closely. It changes dynamically to:

```
<li><a href="#" class="MenuBarSubmenu MenuBarItemSubmenu
MenuBarItemSubmenuHover">Artists</a>
<ul class="MenuBarSubmenuVisible">
<li><a class="MenuBarItem" href="#">Painters</a></li>
<li><a class="MenuBarItem" href="#">Sculptors</a></li>
</ul>
</li>
```

Once the JavaScript has attached the class designator to the element, the browser rechecks the CSS and applies the rule. In this case, it's really simple: `ul.MenuBarVertical ul.MenuBarSubmenuVisible { left: 0; }`. The rule simply changes the left property for the absolutely positioned element from `-1000em` to `0`, thereby moving it back into view.

Since the left property is the only thing that is modified, all of the other properties remain constant from the earlier `ul.MenuBarVertical ul` rule in the cascade. That means `ul.MenuBarVertical ul.MenuBarSubmenuVisible` is responsible for the positioning.

7. Reselect the `ul.MenuBarVertical ul` rule in the Rules section and take a closer look at the properties and values. Notice the margin property has a value of `-5%` for the top margin. This moves the element up or "above" its normal position, which is exactly what we are seeing with the submenu.

   The left margin property is set to `95%`, which seems a bit strange. 95% from where? If you remember that this element has been absolutely positioned, then you should also remember that an element that is assigned an absolute position looks for the last positioned parent container to get its point of origin. This element's parent container is the `<li>` defined by the descendant selector `ul.MenuBarVertical li`. Viewing that rule, we see its been given a relative position. Thus, the nested `<ul>` is getting its point of origin from the parent `<li>` and positioning itself 95% from its left edge. We'll change the position and move the submenu flush with the item that calls it.

8. Modify the margin of the `ul.MenuBarVertical ul` rule to `margin: 0 0 0 99%`.

   If you've still got Live View and Live Code turned on, you should have seen a brief reload of the page, as Dreamweaver updated the rendering of the page based on the change to the CSS.

9. Place your mouse back over the Artists item to trigger the submenu.

   Now the submenu appears horizontally aligned with the Artists button. The 99% gives only a slight hint of an overlap to help visually tie the two elements together.

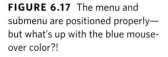

FIGURE 6.17 The menu and submenu are positioned properly— but what's up with the blue mouse-over color?!

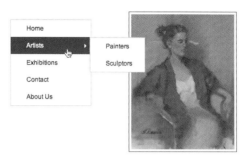

10. Save your files—or, if you prefer, open index_3.html from the builds folder.

Putting the Final Touches on the Menu Bar

Now that you understand that the Spry Menu Bar is being completely styled via descendant selectors of the `<ul.MenuBarVertical>` element, you can quickly finish off the styling to match the comp using a tool in Dreamweaver CS4 known as the Code Navigator.

1. Make sure that both Live View and Live Code are still enabled, then place your mouse over one of the Artists items' submenu items.

   You'll notice the lovely blue color that we've already seen throughout the rest of the menu upon rollover.

   In order to figure out exactly which rule is triggering the blue color, we could again wade through the CSS and JavaScript. Of course, you'll need to spot the change in the HTML using Live Code in order to see exactly which class you'll need to change. But even then it might be difficult to see, since every time we move the mouse off of the submenu item, the class disappears.

   For this very reason, Dreamweaver CS4 gives us the ability to stop the action.

2. With the submenu triggered and your mouse over one of its items, right-click and select Freeze JavaScript (or use the keyboard shortcut F6).

FIGURE 6.18 Putting the freeze on the page.

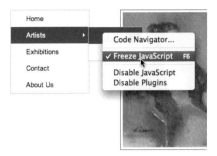

When we choose to freeze the JavaScript, Dreamweaver actually freezes the HTML code as it appears at that moment. That, of course, means that you are free to move your mouse.

3. Either right-click on the submenu element and choose Code Navigator from the contextual menu, or Ctrl+Option+Click (Cmd+Option+Click) on the submenu element to bring up the Code Navigator.

    The Code Navigator shows a complete cascade of all of the CSS rules that affect the selected element, very much like the Rules section of the CSS panel.

    Mouse over each of the entries and you'll notice a list of their respective property/value pairs. We're looking for a rule with a background-color declaration. There are three such rules in the SpryMenuBarVertical.css section that we can see.

FIGURE 6.19 Taking a peek behind the scenes with the Code Navigator.

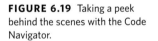

4. Click on the `ul.MenuBarVertical a:hover, ul.MenuBarVertical a:focus` which is the next to last rule in the cascade from the SpryMenuBarVertical.css sheet. This instructs the Code Navigator to take us directly to that rule in its corresponding style sheet.

5. Change the background-color to `#AD2027`, which is the same red tone that we've used several times.

6. Click back in the Design area again and either right-click again and deselect the Freeze JavaScript option, or use the F6 keyboard shortcut. Then mouse back over the menu.

    Notice anything? Like, uh, it didn't change anything! As you know, classes are applied dynamically, and that's causing some issues. The pseudo hover class in our Rules cascade is being overridden by the dynamically assigned class. We'll fix this by hand.

7. Move back into the SpryMenuBarVertical.css file.

    Immediately below this rule in the style sheet file, you'll see another rule, with the same attributes. These are the selectors that will be used by the dynamically assigned class.

8. In order to consolidate our CSS, copy the selectors `ul.MenuBarVertical a.MenuBarItemHover, ul.MenuBarVertical a.MenuBarItemSubmenuHover, ul.MenuBarVertical a.MenuBarSubmenuVisible` and paste them in the list of selectors for the rule above. Remember to add a comma at the end of the list *before* you paste. Then delete the duplicate rule you just copied.

    The consolidated rule looks like this:

    ```
    ul.MenuBarVertical a:hover, ul.MenuBarVertical a:focus,
    ul.MenuBarVertical a.MenuBarItemHover, ul.MenuBarVertical
    a.MenuBarItemSubmenuHover, ul.MenuBarVertical
    a.MenuBarSubmenuVisible {
       background-color: #AD2027;
       color: #FFF; }
    ```

9. With Live View still enabled, click back into the Design area to allow it to refresh, and mouse over the menu to see the changes applied.

FIGURE 6.20 Now that color looks good on you, Mr. Menu Bar!

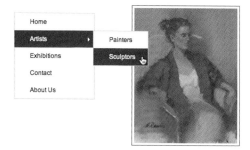

Where Am I? Giving Feedback via the Menu Bar

The visual indicator that lets the visitor know which section of the site they're in is the final bit of polish needed for the menu bar. Our designer has indicated that we need a black background color, white text, and a red bar on the left-hand side of the currently selected menu item.

There are any number of approaches to this type of feedback for the user (as we discussed in Chapter 4), but if you have access to the menu on all pages a simple way is to define a rule that can be applied to the corresponding menu element. Because much of the styling in this rule will only apply to the menu bar, the selector will be very specific.

Spry Menu Bar: MenuBar1

Home
Artists ▸
Exhibitions
Contact
About Us

FIGURE 6.21 With the selected rule applied, due to the box model, the border is pushing the text too far to the right.

1. Create a new rule in the mainStyles.css style sheet and specify its name to be `ul.MenuBarVertical a.selected`.

    You probably know what this means by now. We want the selected class to affect a link (anchor) that occurs in the unordered list designated as MenuBarVertical.

    To help the item stand out, we'll thicken the text in the link using the font-weight property and make it white on a black background.

2. Add the following properties and values to the rule:

    ```
    font-weight: bold;
    color: #FFF;
    background-color: #000;
    ```

3. Create the red bar on the left-hand side of the selected item using the border-left property as follows:

    ```
    border-left: 12px solid #AD2027;
    ```

4. Place the cursor in the Home link of the menu bar (you can turn off Live View and Live Code, if they are still enabled), and apply the rule named **selected** from the Style drop-down list in the Property inspector.

You should now see the black background, white text, and red left-hand border. But the text entry is too far to the right. Since the box model includes border and padding, the text is 12px further over due to the left border. The `<a>` element is inheriting padding from a previous rule and adding the border's 12px to it. To figure out where that padding is coming from, use the Summary for selection pane at the top of the CSS panel. Hover over the padding property and Dreamweaver will show you a tool tip that says the 30px of left padding is coming from the `ul.MenuBarVertical a` rule. (padding: 0.5em 0em 0.5em 30px;)

We need to create the proper amount of space by subtracting the 12px of left border from the 30px of left padding. That gives us 18px of left padding necessary for this selector.

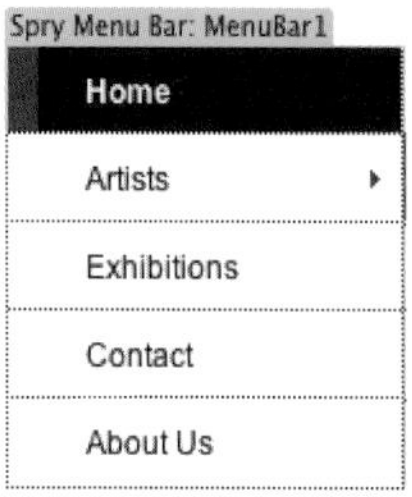

5. Add `padding-left: 18px` to the rule:

```
ul.MenuBarVertical a.selected {
    font-weight: bold;
    color: #FFF;
    background: #000;
    border-left: 12px solid #AD2027;
    padding-left: 18px; }
```

6. Save your work.

FIGURE 6.22 The properly aligned Spry Menu Bar.

As we add the Spry menu to subsequent pages within the site, we'll change the menu element to which the **selected** class applies to reflect this feedback for the visitor.

And with that, the index page of the site is complete.

A Word about Accessibility, JavaScript and Progressive Enhancement

You probably noticed that the fly-out portion of the menu is relying upon JavaScript to function. That's no surprise—the "J" in Ajax stands for JavaScript! But what about visitors who, for whatever reason, do not have JavaScript capabilities—whether by choice, such as those who turn it off, or by necessity, such as users who rely upon screen readers with limited or no JavaScript support?

In the first versions of the Spry framework, Adobe didn't have an answer: if JavaScript was turned off in the browser, the experience was over—any content that relied upon JavaScript was not delivered to the page. But as we'll see, version 1.6 of the Spry framework addresses these concerns with some, in our opinion, pretty incredible enhancements.

The Spry Menu Bar that we've just implemented continues to function even with no JavaScript present, because only the fly-out portion is controlled via JavaScript. The Artists entry in the menu is linked to artists.html, so visitors without JavaScript can click the link and be directed to the Artists page, bypassing the fly-out menu. The Artist's page would simply need to make it possible to move on to either the painters or sculptors pages by providing links to them. (Most visitors will choose from the flyout menu and never click on the Artist's page link at all, so the fact that it simply contains links to the submenu pages is a good accessibility feature to add.)

This approach is called **progressive enhancement**. We start with a basic, functioning page for all visitors. From there, we build (enhance) the page with additional functionality or interactivity for those users whose browser agent is able to support it.

The bottom line and our mantra must always be "no one gets left behind"!

Combining Two CSS Layouts for Use in a Single Site

The majority of the remaining pages within the site will rely upon the basic two-column layout already established for the index page. However, our designer wants a three-column layout for the artist detail pages that highlight an individual artist's work.

Of course it's always nice when we don't have to start completely from scratch as we start to work on a new page layout of our site. We've already done a lot of work. Since Dreamweaver CS4's CSS layouts were designed to be easily combined, we'll really only need to worry about elements specific to this single page!

1. Create a new (X)HTML page, selecting the 3 column hybrid, header and footer CSS layout as an XHTML 1.0 Transitional doctype.

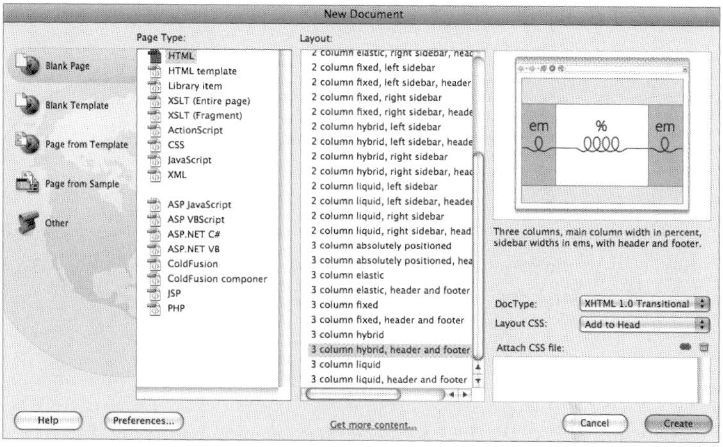

FIGURE 6.23 The basis for this page in the site will be a three-column hybrid layout with a header and footer.

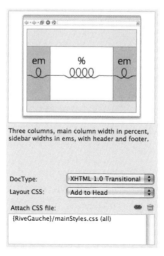

Notice that there's an option in the bottom-right corner of the dialog to attach the new document to an existing CSS file. Wouldn't you think that we could attach the mainStyles.css file that we've already created and have a good starting point to continue modifying the page? Unfortunately, this would give us some... uh... unexpected results. (Go ahead—try it. Told you!)

When you specify "Link to existing file" in the drop-down list, you are telling Dreamweaver that you don't need any of the CSS that would normally be associated with the file. That's a little more than we wanted to do!

FIGURE 6.24 We can attach an external style sheet to the page while placing the default CSS for the layout in the head of the document.

In order to combine (our terminology for using the CSS from two distinct CSS layouts) two layouts, we'll need a different strategy.

2. Leave the Layout CSS drop-down list in the New Document dialog set to Add to Head.

3. Click the Attach Style Sheet icon in the lower-right corner of the dialog and navigate to your mainStyles.css file.

4. Click OK to create the file and go ahead and save it in your site structure as artist_detail.html.

We're going to simplify our styles. It's not as scary as it sounds. You should remember that all the CSS layouts have the same div naming conventions and contain the same basic components. We'll walk you through the process of determining which ones to keep and which can be deleted.

You might have just noticed a change to your page—the body text changed when we deleted the embedded body rule, because it has now taken on the values defined for the body element in the external style sheet. An embedded style always overrides an external rule with equal specificity!

5. Switch to the All view in the CSS panel. Expand the individual style sheet groupings by clicking the toggle.

Notice that we now have a link to both the mainStyles.css and the `<style>` block in the head of the document containing the default CSS styles that belong to the three-column layout.

Scroll through the list of CSS rules. Notice anything? Each layout contains basically the same rules. They're simply modified through the specific body class indicating the given layout type. Remember, by default each `<body>` element has a class attached to it that declares what type of page it is.

Let's take a closer look. We have a rule for the container element in both the external mainStyles.css file and the internal CSS styles in the header. But the two rules could differ because each is specific to a defined class: `.twoColHybLtHdr #container` and `.thrColHybHdr #container`.

While we could easily append all of our internal styles to the external style sheet (and many people do), it's not a best practice. It results in redundancy, more rules to manage than needed, more complicated upkeep, and a larger physical file size for user agents.

Let's start by deleting a number of duplicate rules that don't have the extra specificity.

1. In the All mode of the CSS panel, right-click on the following rules in the `<style>` section (the embedded rules) and choose Delete: `body`, `.fltrt`, `.fltlft`, and `.clearfloat`.

This leaves us with nine embedded rules. But again, we've got some redundancy. We have a specific rule defined for the two-column layout's container element giving the values we decided on for the home page. Since the container for both pages should be the same—we want both pages to fill the browser window, have the same background color, etc.—we'll remove the page-specific prefix so that it will apply to all our pages.

2. In the All mode, click the name for the `.twoColHybLtHdr #container` rule in mainStyles.css so that it is editable. Rename the rule `#container`, and delete the `.thrColHybHdr #container` rule from the embedded (`<style>`) styles.

FIGURE 6.25 There are still a number of redundant embedded rules that we need to remove.

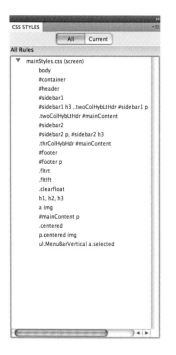

N *Notice there are two grouped selectors for the sidebars here—one for each layout. You may want to switch to the CSS file to edit this by hand instead of using the CSS panel as Dreamweaver can get a little quirky with the code it can't display in the panel—or simply drag your CSS panel very wide to see the full name of the grouped selector.*

FIGURE 6.26 Our consolidated styles—notice that only a few are specific to a two-column or three-column layout.

The header, `sidebar1`, and footer elements will also be the same for all of our pages.

3. Repeat the process above for all rules in mainStyles.css that relate to the header, footer, and `sidebar1` since they'll be the same on all our pages. Delete the same rules from the `<style>` block in the three-column page.

   If you look closely at the embedded styles left on the page, you'll notice a grouped selector that includes both `sidebar1` and `sidebar2` rules.

4. Remove the `#sidebar1` rules altogether since they're already defined in the linked CSS file. If you like, you can even remove the prefix for the `#sidebar2` rules that are left since the two-column pages won't include a `sidebar2`. This simply leaves:

   `#sidebar2 p, #sidebar2 h3`

   Check the index.html page to make sure that everything still looks the same. If it's still looking good, we know that our modifications to the specificity of our rules haven't had any effect on our original page.

   You should, however, already be noticing several differences to our new artist_detail.html page. There are some spacing differences as well as red borders below the header and above the footer.

5. Finally let's move the remaining three embedded rules into mainStyles.css by Shift-selecting the three rules in the All mode of the CSS panel and dragging them up to the mainStyles.css area.

6. Click to select the `<style>` element in the All mode of the CSS panel and delete it.

We're now left with an optimized style sheet that works for both a two-column and three-column hybrid layout.

Common Page Elements in a Flash!

Our next step is perhaps the fastest (and maybe most enjoyable) step in the process—we'll use good old copy/paste to grab the common elements from the index page for the artist_detail page.

1. Switch back to (or open) index.html and select the header element by placing the cursor in the header and clicking `<div#header>` in the tag selector.

2. Choose Edit > Copy and then switch back to artist_detail.html and select its header element using the tag selector.

3. Choose Edit > Paste to replace its contents with the contents copied from index.html.

4. Repeat the process for the `<div#sidebar1>` and `<div#footer>`.

   Now that was easy!

5. Save your work, and as you do, you'll notice that Dreamweaver is once again prompting you to copy Spry-related files. This is simply because Dreamweaver doesn't know whether we are using a horizontal or vertical menu since we didn't use the Spry MenuBar widget to insert the menu into this page. Because we know that we're only going to need the vertical menu, you can delete the link to the SpryMenuBarHorizontal. css file in the head of the page (and if you are certain you won't need it, from your file structure as well).

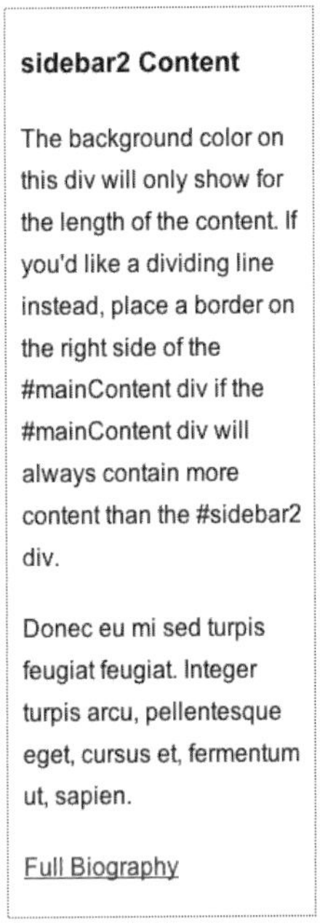

Styling Sidebar2

Before we move into the more complicated (but fun) part of the page, let's get the `sidebar2` area properly styled. This area provides details about the particular artist, their bio, and so on.

By default, the `sidebar2` div has a width of 11em. Since this is too narrow, we'll widen it, remembering this will require tweaks to the `mainContent` area as well since it has margins on both the left and right sides.

1. Click to place the cursor into `sidebar2` and switch to the Current mode of the CSS panel. Select `#sidebar2` in the Rules section of the CSS panel and change the width property to `13em`.

2. Remove the background property and modify the padding to have a value of 0.

   The `h3` is still not as far up as we'd like, so we'll create a rule to override the default margin of the `h3`.

sidebar2 Content

The background color on this div will only show for the length of the content. If you'd like a dividing line instead, place a border on the right side of the #mainContent div if the #mainContent div will always contain more content than the #sidebar2 div.

Donec eu mi sed turpis feugiat feugiat. Integer turpis arcu, pellentesque eget, cursus et, fermentum ut, sapien.

Full Biography

FIGURE 6.27 The sidebar needs some work to match our comp.

N *Be very careful when creating a rule when you have more than one style sheet attached to a page. Dreamweaver usually suggests the last style sheet that you've worked with, but not always—especially if you've just linked a new style sheet. Check and double check where the rule is being placed to be sure it's being added to the right style sheet. We'll continue to add ours to the mainStyles.css.*

N *Visitors expect links to have underlines, so we'll leave the underline style on the links on our page.*

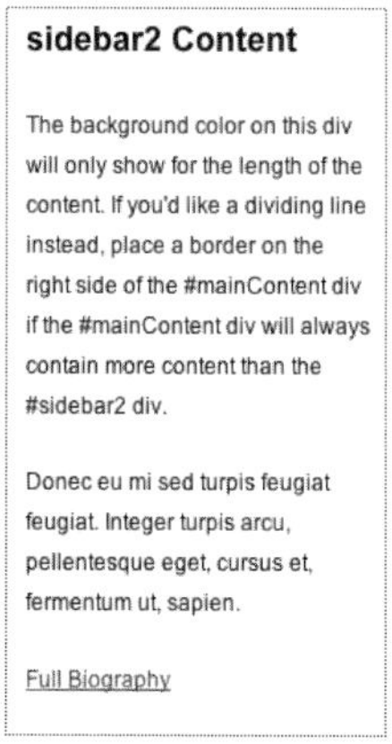

---

sidebar2 Content

The background color on this div will only show for the length of the content. If you'd like a dividing line instead, place a border on the right side of the #mainContent div if the #mainContent div will always contain more content than the #sidebar2 div.

Donec eu mi sed turpis feugiat feugiat. Integer turpis arcu, pellentesque eget, cursus et, fermentum ut, sapien.

Full Biography

FIGURE 6.28 The finished sidebar2 element.

3. Place the cursor in the **h3** and click the New CSS Rule button in the CSS panel. Create a rule for **#sidebar2 h3** with a margin-top of 0.

We also need to decrease the font-size of the text in **sidebar2**.

4. Create a rule for **#sidebar2 p** and set the **font-size** to **0.8em** to match the rest of the text on our page.

Each short description of the artist is designed to end with a link to his or her full biography.

5. Place the cursor at the end of the text in **sidebar2** and then press Enter to create a new paragraph. Type the words "Full Biography", select the text and add a # link in the link field of the HTML area of the Property inspector.

We've used a hash mark to cause the text to render as a link since we won't actually be creating a page for this link in this exercise. Our new link is the traditional blue, underlined text. But the color doesn't really fit in with our design.

6. Create a new rule **a**.

We want all text links in the site to take on this style, so the rule has no specificity.

7. Set the color for the rule to **#AD2027** to match the red we've been using throughout the site.

Finally, since we modified the width of the sidebar, we also need to adjust the margins of the **mainContent** div.

8. Place the cursor in the **mainContent** area and use the CSS panel to adjust the margins for the **#mainContent** rule to **0 13em 30px 13em**.

We've matched the 13em left margin that we also used in the index page's **mainContent** area.

And with that, we're ready to concentrate on the picture gallery content for the artist_detail.html page!

Building the Gallery—Part One

The layout of this page needs to be flexible enough to accommodate artists with both large and small portfolios. Our approach will use a welcome new feature within Spry 1.6 that draws upon the page's content and "repurposes" it with additional functionality.

This method takes advantage of our "no one gets left behind" mantra. We'll start by finishing the page design as older browsers and non-JavaScript-enabled browsers will experience it.

1. Delete the content of the `mainContent` div.

2. Switch to the Common section of the Insert panel and click the Insert Div Tag tool to insert a `<div>`.

3. Type gallery into the ID field and click OK.

   This div will hold an individual image and its corresponding title, artist name and price, but we don't need to establish any properties for the div as it will, by default, fill the width of the `mainContent` element.

   Within the image folder in this site, you'll find a number of images entitled IMAGENAME_thumb.jpg. Each of these images has been optimized to a maximum width or height of 138 pixels, making it easier for us to create an appropriately sized container.

4. Delete the placeholder text "Content for id 'gallery' Goes Here" and then click the Insert Div Tag again to add a nested div.

5. Click the New CSS Rule button to create the rule for the nested div. Give the rule a name of `.galleryItem`, once again adding it to mainStyles.css.

6. Within the CSS Rule Definition dialog, specify the following properties and values for the rule:

```
.galleryItem {
  width: 16em;
  float: left;
  padding: 6px;
  border: solid 1px #AD2027; }
```

7. Click OK to create the rule and click OK again to create the div. Select all inside the div and delete the placeholder text.

8. Click the Image tool in the Insert panel or use the menu Insert > Image command. Choose one of the _thumb images—your choice. Add an appropriate alternative text for the image.

9. With the image selected on the page, add a link to the high-resolution version of the image also located in the images folder of the site.

10. Leaving the image still selected, press the right arrow key to position the cursor immediately after the image and then press the Enter key to add a **<p>** element.

11. In separate paragraph elements, add a title for the image, the artist's name, the price, and the filename of the high-resolution version of the picture (the name without the _thumb attached).

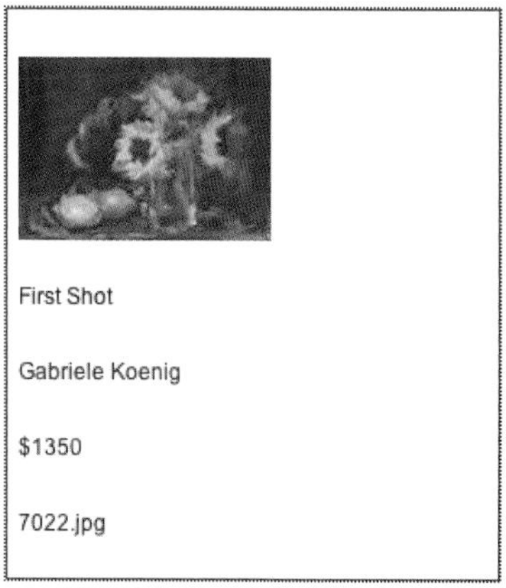

FIGURE 6.29
The **<div.galleryItem>** will be our basic building block for this section of the page.

First Shot

Gabriele Koenig

$1350

7022.jpg

The completed HTML code for the div looks like this:

```
<div class="galleryItem">
  <p><a href="images/7022.jpg"><img src="images/7022_
thumb.jpg" width="138" height="97" /></a></p>
  <p>First Shot</p>
  <p>Gabriele Koenig</p>
  <p>$1350</p>
  <p>7022.jpg</p> </div>
```

Our basic (X)HTML is here, but obviously we need to add a bit of styling to the contents of the **<div.galleryItem>**.

12. Create a new class `.thumbnail` and add it to mainStyles.css with the following attributes:

```
.thumbnail {
  width: 144px;
  float: left;
  height: 140px;
  margin: 0;
  text-align: center; }
```

This class will float the `<p>` element containing the image to the left of the text. Notice that we've specified `text-align: center` to cause the images to center themselves within the defined 144px width.

13. Click to select the image in the `<div.galleryItem>` and use the tag selector to select the `<p>` element surrounding it. Apply the `.thumbnail` class to the `<p>` element.

For the text about each image, we'll use three classes: `.pictureTitle`, `.pictureArtist`, and `.picturePrice`.

14. Create three rules with the following properties, adding them to mainStyles.css:

```
.pictureTitle {
  font-size: .9em;
  font-weight: bold;
  padding-bottom: 0.8em;
  margin: 0;
  line-height: 1.2em; }
.pictureArtist {
  font-style: italic;
  padding: 0;
  margin: 0; }
.picturePrice {
  padding: 0;
  margin: 0; }
```

15. Apply the rules to their corresponding `<p>` elements—leaving only the last `<p>` unstyled.

The final `<p>` element contains the filename of the high-resolution version of the image. We'll be using this as we begin to progressively enhance the page, but for now it serves no purpose on the page so we should prevent it from being seen by the browser.

FIGURE 6.30
The `<div.galleryItem>` element—almost finished.

We can either use `display:none` or position the element off screen as we did with the fly-out menu. Since there's no reason for assistive technologies to see the name of the files, we'll prevent it from rendering entirely, using `display:none`.

16. Create a rule, `.pictureHirez`:

```
.pictureHirez {
    display: none; }
```

17. Apply the `.pictureHirez` class to the paragraph.

You should see the paragraph and its contents disappear from the page.

FIGURE 6.31 Let the cloning begin—we'll simply duplicate the `<div.galleryItem>` for each picture in the portfolio.

N *Using a dynamic language like ColdFusion or PHP to pull the information into your page works perfectly as well. You simply place the code for the repeating regions into the classes you've built and the HTML data set will be created dynamically. If Dreamweaver prompts you about the JavaScript files that need to be copied into the site structure, click OK.*

We've now established the basic building block that we'll duplicate to accommodate as many images as are present in the artist's portfolio. Go ahead and make a few copies, giving them whatever names and prices you like—or, if you'd prefer, you can open up artist_detail2.html from the builds folder.

FIGURE 6.32 We've chosen to use six images—and so far, things look okay.

All set? Notice that the bottoms of the last frames are sitting directly on top of the footer even though we specified that the `mainContent` element should have a 30px bottom border. Hmm…

Take a look at the code for the `.galleryItem` rule again. One line should jump out at you:

```
.galleryItem {
  width: 16em;
  float: left;
  padding: 6px;
  border: solid 1px #AD2027;
  }
```

Pop quiz time—what happens to a container when all of its contents are floated? Since the `<div.galleryItem>` elements are all floated, the `mainContent` element has no way to know when to grow vertically and in turn, when to apply the 30px of bottom margin to push the footer away from its contents.

We need to clear the element in order to push the footer away.

1. Add a `<br>` immediately preceding the `</div>` tag for the `<div.gallery>` element and assign the `.clearfloat` class to the `<br>`.

   The final few lines of the code look like this:

   ```html
   <div class="galleryItem">
    <p class="thumbnail"><a href="images/7087.jpg">
   <img src="images/7087_thumb.jpg" width="109" height="138"
   /></a></p>
     <p class="pictureTitle">Tournesols</p>
     <p class="pictureArtist">Gabriele Koenig</p>
     <p class="picturePrice">$1850</p>
     <p class="pictureHirez">7087.jpg</p>
     </div>
     </div>
     <br class="clearfloat" />
     </div>
   <!-- This clearing element should immediately follow the
   #mainContent div in order to force the #container div to
   contain all child floats -->
   <br class="clearfloat" />
   <div id="footer">
   ```

2. Save the mainStyles.css and the artist_detail.html page.

FIGURE 6.33 If we make the browser too narrow, our page doesn't look as good.

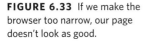

Preview the artist_detail.html page in a standards-compliant browser. You should be able to resize the browser viewport and have your `galleryItem` elements reflow according to the available space on the page.

But we don't want the page to become too unsightly. Let's limit this functionality to keep the page from being collapsed to a point where we only have one `galleryItem` on a row.

1. Place the cursor in the `mainContent` element and select the `#container` rule from the Rules section of the CSS panel.

   You'll notice it already contains the `min-width` rule from our home page.

2. Create a new selector called `.thrColHybHdr #container` and give it a minimum width property: `min-width: 64em`.

   The single `#container` rule will apply to all pages and the descendant selector we just created will override only the `min-width` property on the three-column pages.

3. Save the mainStyles.css file and preview the artist_detail.html again in a standards-compliant browser. Notice that you can no longer make the page too narrow to accommodate the images.

FIGURE 6.34 With a min-width in place, we are assured of having a nice layout even with a narrow browser window.

Progressive Enhancement— Making the Gallery "Cool"

We now have a nice-looking page, regardless of the capabilities of the visitor's browser. Of course, our example only uses six images. Imagine if an artist had a bigger portfolio—say, 12 or 20 pictures or even more. The more images, the more a visitor would need to scroll.

The solution: a progressive enhancement to our page, thanks to the Spry framework. To reiterate, a progressive enhancement builds upon the core functionality of a page, adding features that will be available to advanced browsers, while ensuring that the stage still functions for less capable browsers. Now that we have the core functionality in place, we'll add a different method of displaying the gallery of images.

FIGURE 6.35 Our page (as seen in Firefox) with a Spry Sliding Panels widget to reveal the gallery images.

The Spry Sliding Panels widget lets us display an unlimited number of images in a limited space. Instead of a link that opens a larger version of an image (as is the case now), even the detail image gets displayed in the page—and without a single page refresh!

In Spry 1.6, we can use an HTML Data Set to instruct the browser to read (X)HTML as its data source. This provides us with an incredible amount of flexibility because, after all, we're already designing with (X)HTML.

Our particular page is already laid out as standards-compliant (X)HTML and CSS. We'll leverage that page structure by using it as our data source for our progressive enhancement.

Creating an HTML Data Set

The enhancement that we've already made to the page using the Spry Menu Bar has made some additions to our code. Let's take a quick look at that.

1. Switch to Code view and scroll to the top of the document.

2. Locate the code just above the closing `</head>` tag:

    ```
    <script src="SpryAssets/SpryMenuBar.js"
    type="text/javascript"></script>
    <link href="SpryAssets/SpryMenuBarVertical.css"
    rel="stylesheet" type="text/css" />
    ```

    When we saved our page(s) earlier, Dreamweaver informed us that it would need to copy some files into our site structure. These files were the JavaScript file for our menu, providing its functionality, as well as the CSS that defined the look of the menu.

    Dreamweaver also added a `<script>` tag to link to the JavaScript file and a `<link>` tag attaching the CSS for the menu to our document.

    For our soon-to-be-created Spry Sliding Panels widget, we need to tell the browser what to display in the sliding panel: this information composes our data set. We'll also tell the browser to load a JavaScript file provided as a part of the Spry framework, in order for it to read and understand the data set.

3. Locate the Spry framework folder that you downloaded from labs.adobe.com and unzip it.

4. Inside this unzipped folder, you will find a folder named includes. Open it.

   The includes folder contains all of the JavaScript files for the Spry framework. Keep this folder handy as we'll need several of these files.

5. Open the widgets folder and locate the slidingpanels folder.

6. In the slidingpanels folder, locate the file SprySlidingPanels.js and copy it to the SpryAssets folder within your local site.

   We now need to tell the browser to use this file.

7. Add the following line of code to the <head> of the document immediately preceding the </head> tag:

   ```
   <script src="SpryAssets/SprySlidingPanels.js"
   type="text/javascript"></script>
   ```

   This will instruct the user agent to load SprySlidingPanels.js, providing the sliding panels functionality we're about to implement.

   We'll now tell the browser to build a data set using a particular item or items on the page as our source data.

8. Switch to the Spry section of the Insert panel and click the Spry Data Set icon.

   The Spry Data Set wizard will step us through the process of accessing our data and preparing it for use in our page.

9. From the Data Type drop-down menu, select HTML.

10. Select Divs from the Detect drop-down menu.

    The wizard will automatically examine the structure of the HTML page and locate the element(s) that we specify here.

11. Click the Browse button and select the artist_detail.html page that we are currently working in.

FIGURE 6.36 The Spry Data Set wizard provides a visual representation of the page to help identify possible data sources.

You'll immediately notice a couple of things. First of all, we can actually see a preview of the page that we've selected, and second, yellow markers identify individual divs as possible data sources.

The Spry Data Set wizard can intelligently analyze an HTML table and determine the rows and columns, but when using divs, lists, or custom elements, you'll need to manually identify the Row Selector and Column Selector.

12. Click to select the `mainContent` div that contains all of our pictures.

The Data Preview in the lower half of the window shows us the actual HTML that has been selected. And unfortunately, Dreamweaver is having a bit of trouble determining what should be a row of data and what should be a column.

13. Click to select the Advanced data selection check box, and in the Row Selectors field enter:

`div.galleryItem`

You should immediately see the Data Preview update because each of the `div.galleryItem`s has now been identified as containing data—much like the row of a table.

FIGURE 6.37 Each gallery item is now identified as a row of data.

14. Enter p in the Column Selectors field and then tap the Tab key.

Again the Data Preview has updated, and we can see that Dreamweaver now understands that each <p> element should be treated like a column in a virtual table.

FIGURE 6.38 Hey, we turned a collection of divs into a table!

You'll notice that Dreamweaver has arbitrarily assigned column names to our data. We could use these names, but column0, column1 and column2 don't strike us as an easy way to remember what data is in the column. Let's take care of that as well.

15. Click the Next button, then change the name for column0 to Thumbnail in the Column Name field.

16. Click on column1 in the Data Preview to select it, then change its name to PictureTitle.

17. Repeat the process for the other three columns, naming them Artist, Price, and HiRez, respectively.

In the bottom half of the window, you also have the option of defining other parameters, such as sorting and filtering duplicates. For our purposes, we'll leave everything set to its default.

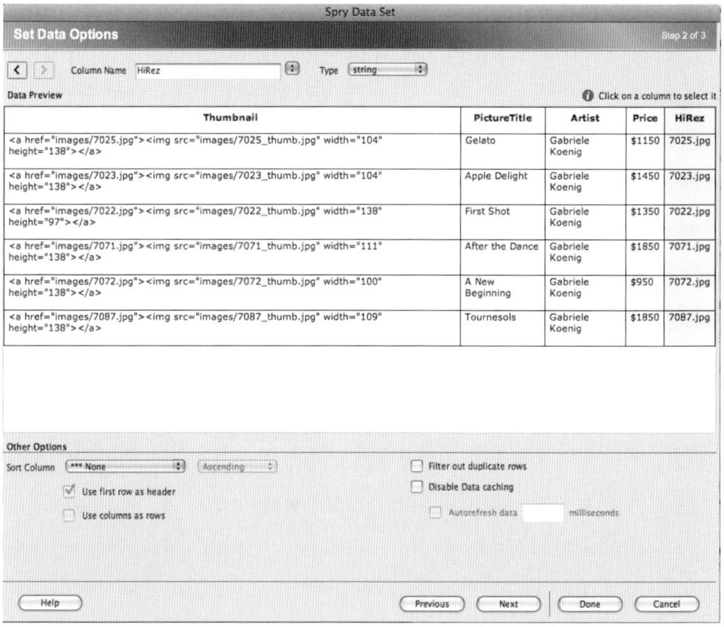

FIGURE 6.39 Our columns now make a little more sense.

18. Click Next. Now we're presented with our output options.

The wizard is capable of building three different types of layouts for our data. The first, a data table, doesn't make a whole lot of sense, since we already have a nice div structure in place. The second option is to build a master/detail relationship made up of two columns, where one column shows a list of data entries and the other column displays the details about the entry. This is sort of what we'll be doing in a moment, but we're going to build our own layout. The third option is a stack of elements—which is basically what we've already built. Each one of the prebuilt layouts is nothing more than CSS and HTML, and can therefore be completely customized to meet your own needs.

19. Since we only need to add the data set, select "Do not insert HTML", then Done.

20. Save your work, at which point you'll be notified that Dreamweaver will be adding two additional JavaScript files to the SpryAssets folder: SpryData.js and SpryHTMLDataSet.js. These files control the retrieval and manipulation of the data that we defined in the wizard.

FIGURE 6.40 Two more JavaScript files for our collection.

Fixing a Dreamweaver Limitation, er, Bug

Just when things were going so smoothly, we're about to encounter a limitation of the way in which the wizard works—but don't panic, we'll fix it.

To understand the issue, let's first look at the source code to see exactly what the wizard wrote.

```
<script type="text/javascript"> <!-- var ds1 =
new Spry.Data.HTMLDataSet(null, "mainContent",
{columnNames: ['Thumbnail', 'PictureTitle', 'Artist',
'Price', 'HiRez'], rowSelector: "div.galleryItem",
dataSelector: "p"}); //--> </script>
```

As you can no doubt tell, we're writing JavaScript. The first part of the script `var ds1` is telling the browser to create a variable named `ds1`. We're then telling the browser that this variable will be a HTML data set that will be processed by the Spry framework.

A Spry HTML data set is built using several parameters, which are listed in the parentheses. The first parameter, `null`, defines the HTML page to be used as the source of the rest of the parameters. In our case, `null` says "use the page that we are currently on." The second parameter, `mainContent`, defines the HTML element that will contain the data. We're telling the browser to find the element with an ID of `mainContent`.

And therein lies the problem. You see, whatever element is defined as the data source will be automatically hidden by the JavaScript when the page is enhanced (which we're about to do). You'll recall that we put all of the gallery items into a div with an ID of gallery. It's actually this div that we'd like to use as the data source (and automatically hide), instead of `mainContent`, which is the central content area of the page.

So, why didn't we just select `<div#gallery>` in the wizard? Well, that is the limitation that we were referring to. The Data Set wizard can only see elements that have a height of 20 pixels or more. We, of course, didn't put a height on the gallery element, and because all of its contents are floated, there's nothing holding it open, making it appear to have a height of 0.

To fix the problem, simply change `"mainContent"` to `"gallery"` in the source code.

```
<script type="text/javascript"> <!-- var ds1 =
new Spry.Data.HTMLDataSet(null, "gallery", {columnNames:
['Thumbnail', 'PictureTitle', 'Artist', 'Price', 'HiRez'],
rowSelector: "div.galleryItem", dataSelector: "p"}); //-->
</script>
```

A Quick Sanity Check

Before moving on, let's make sure that our page works. We won't actually use the following bit of code in our final page, but it's sure nice to know that we've gotten the groundwork done properly.

1. In the Design area, click anywhere in gallery of images, then use the tag selector to select `<div#gallery>`.

For more information about using HTML as a source for dynamic data—or even using XML as a data source—spend some time reading the Spry framework documentation and looking at the examples, all included in the zip file you downloaded earlier.

There are two other ways to fix the problem and cause the wizard to see the gallery div. We could create a rule for #gallery and assign overflow:auto to it and assign overflow:auto to it causing the parent container to contain its floats. Or we could add a clearing element after the final .galleryItem element, such as `<br class="clearfloat" />`. But these methods add unnecessary markup to the page or CSS, so we chose to simply make the change in code.

2. Add a `<p>` element immediately before the opening `<div#gallery>` element by tapping the arrow left key and then hitting Enter. If you have your source code visible, you can glance over to ensure that your cursor and the resulting `<p>` element are in front of the opening `<div id="gallery">` tag.

3. Open the Bindings panel from the Window menu.

FIGURE 6.41 The Bindings panel displaying our data.

The Bindings panel is what we'll use to "bind" the individual elements from our data set to their respective places on the page.

4. Click and drag the PictureTitle item from the Bindings panel onto the page in the `<p>` element that we just added.

In order for the browser to understand that the placeholder `{ds1::PictureTitle}` needs to be processed by the Spry framework, we need to add an attribute of **spry:region** to the parent container of the placeholder. We can do this quickly using the Spry Region tool in the Insert panel.

5. With the placeholder `{ds1::PictureTitle}` still selected in the Design area, click the Spry Region tool, and choose span as the Container. Leave the other options set to their defaults. You'll also notice that the data set has been automatically chosen. Click OK.

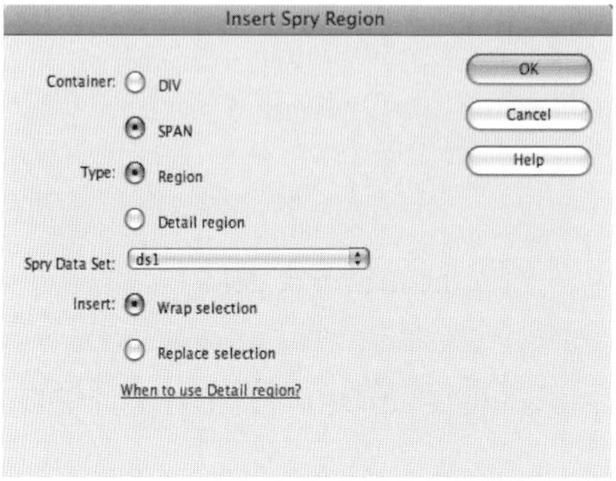

FIGURE 6.42 A spry:region is the trigger for the browser that causes it to replace a dynamic placeholder.

In the source code, the paragraph now looks like this:

```
<p><span spry:region="ds1">{PictureTitle}</span></p>
```

6. Turn on Live View—and hold your breath!

You might have been shocked when you saw your page—providing everything worked for you. If you didn't get a result like that shown in Figure 6.43, check to make sure that you have, in fact, copied the JavaScript files into the SpryAssets folder.

FIGURE 6.43 The Spry framework has successfully enhanced the page, so we know everything is working properly.

What happened to the page content that we had before? We're only seeing a piece of text where we previously had our nice gallery of images. This is the essence of a progressive enhancement to the page. The Spry framework has removed the element on the page identified as our HTML data set and rendered only the result of the processing—in our case a single `<p>` element with the name of the first data item.

The Spry Sliding Panels Widget

Now that we know that everything is working, we can add the Spry Sliding Panels widget to the page.

The Spry Sliding Panels widget is simply a div that contains panels (actually nested div elements) that slide either vertically or horizontally to reveal themselves within the confines of the declared width and height of the parent div.

All Spry widgets have a defined structure that must be adhered to. Check the Spry documentation for a description of the structure of each widget. For the Spry Sliding Panels widget the structure is as follows:

```
<div id="slidingGallery" class="SlidingPanels">
  <div id="galleryContentGroup" class="SlidingPanelsContent
Group">
    <div id="panelContents" class="SlidingPanelsContent">
    [contents of the panel]
    </div>
  </div> </div>
```

In other words, the widget is made up of three nested `<div>` elements. The first `<div>` identifies the bounding box of the visible overall panel area on the page. The second `<div>` identifies the bounding box of the contents within the panel that will be sliding. If this `<div>` element's width matches the width of the first `<div>`, the elements within it will slide vertically. If its width is wider than the first `<div>`, contents will slide horizontally until they reach the edge of their bounding box and then begin to slide vertically. Don't worry if this doesn't seem clear right now; we'll experiment with these values in a minute.

The third `<div>` is the actual contents of an individual pane or piece of content. We'll repeat this `<div>` for the number of items that we wish to scroll through the panel.

All of this will become clear as we work our way through the next few steps—so let's build it! (If you need it, you can start with artist_detail3.html in the builds folder.)

Creating the Structure for the Spry Sliding Panels

1. Delete the `<p>` element that we added to the page for testing, and in its place, just before the `<div#gallery>`, add the following code:

```
<div id="slidingGallery" class="SlidingPanels">
   <div id="galleryContentGroup" class="SlidingPanelsContent
Group">
      <div id="panelContents" class="SlidingPanelsContent">
      </div>
   </div> </div>
```

We've already discussed the significance of this code, so we now need to define what the content of each of the panels will be.

2. Add the following code to be used as the contents of each panel:

```
<div id="slidingGallery" class="SlidingPanels">
  <div id="galleryContentGroup" class="SlidingPanelsContent
Group">
    <div id="panelContents" class="SlidingPanelsContent">
      <div class="galleryItem">
      <p class="thumbnail">{Thumbnail}</p>
      <p class="pictureTitle">{PictureTitle}</p>
      <p class="pictureArtist">{Artist}</p>
      <p class="picturePrice">{Price}</p>
      </div>
    </div>
    </div> </div>
```

We've defined a container that will hold each of the individual images and their related data. Notice that we used the same classes that we've already created—this saves time since we won't have to create any new rules for the panel's actual content.

FIGURE 6.44 The placeholder for our sliding panels in Design view.

If you were to check the page in the browser, you'd notice that it doesn't seem to be working—the new `<div>` element is simply sitting on the page along with all of the other content and no dynamic data is appearing. (It's okay—we know you want to do it, so go ahead, save the page and turn on Live View!)

Our placeholders aren't being replaced because the browser doesn't understand that it needs to pass this area of the page to the Spry framework for processing. We need to add a `spry:region` attribute to the element to clue the browser in.

3. In the source code, add a `spry:region` attribute to the `<div#slidingGallery>` element—as you do so, notice that Dreamweaver offers full code hinting and completion for the Spry framework:

```
<div id="slidingGallery" class="SlidingPanels"
spry:region="ds1">
```

And we know you're wondering why we didn't just use the Spry Region tool like we did before. Well, we don't really like using that tool because it won't simply tag the `spry:region` on to a selected element, but instead insists on wrapping the element in either a div or a span. This is unnecessary markup that we prefer to avoid—and besides, we like writing code by hand!

4. Turn on Live View to check your work.

FIGURE 6.45 Once again, the Spry framework is doing its job, replacing our page content dynamically!

Okay, so things are working, but where's the rest of our content? Well, so far we have only told the Spry framework that we're interested in one item from the data set, not all of the items. We need to instruct it to loop over the data set and duplicate the `<div#panelContents>` element for each entry in the data set. We do this using another Spry attribute known as `repeat`, telling it which data set it should loop through.

5. Add the following code to the `<div#panelContents>` element:

```
<div id="panelContents" class="SlidingPanelsContent"
spry:repeat="ds1">
```

If you're working in Split view, you don't even need to turn off Live View as you do this—just hit F5 to refresh the view after you finish adding the code.

6. If you turned Live View off, turn it back on.

Amazing! We're back to where we started—or so it seems... In reality, we're not looking at the same page. The data on the page has actually been generated dynamically via the Spry framework. But since we've not yet constrained the sliding panel area, the browser is simply repeating the individual items from the data set down the page.

In order to constrain the items so that we can "slide" through them, we'll create some simple CSS classes.

7. Create a new rule in mainStyles.css for the `<div>` with an ID of `#slidingGallery`:

```
#slidingGallery {
    float: left;
    height: 160px;
    border: solid 1px #AD2027; }
```

This rule constrains the height of the sliding panel to 160px and places a red line around the area to give the visitor some visual feedback that this is a distinct page element.

8. Create a new rule for the `<div>` with the ID `#galleryContentGroup`:

```
#slidingGallery #galleryContentGroup {
    width: 1000em; }
```

This `<div>` defines how the content is sliding. We've set the width to 1000em to accommodate all of our panel items in a single line. Without this width defined, the items within the panel area would simply exhibit the standard wrapping effect that occurs when multiple left floated elements reach the side of their parent container—they would continue on the next horizontal band.

9. Create a descendant selector for the `<div>` within the `#slidingGallery` with a class of `.SlidingPanelsContent`:

```
#slidingGallery .SlidingPanelsContent {
    float: left;
    width: 260px;
    height: 160px; }
```

This rule establishes the width and height of the individual sliding items within the panel.

We need to override some of the styling that we initially established for the `galleryItem` elements. We'll use a descendant selector.

10. Create a rule for the `.galleryItem` elements contained within the `slidingGallery`:

```
#slidingGallery .galleryItem {
    border: none;
    width: 247px;
    height: 142px;
    padding-top: 12px;
    border-right: solid 1px #AD2021; }
```

Because we've already established a red border around the entire sliding panel area, we've removed the old border and are simply placing a right border to give a visual separation between the items. We're also overriding the width (previously 16em) and giving it a fixed pixel width. We've also assigned a fixed height to the items.

Finally, we need two classes defined with a relative position in order to make the widget work a bit better.

11. Create a grouped selector as follows:

```
.SlidingPanels, .SlidingPanelsContentGroup {
    position: relative; }
```

You'll recognize the names of these classes as they were defined as part of the overall sliding panel structure. The SpySlidingPanels.js file looks for these classes in order to perform the sliding animation.

12. If you didn't look at Live View, do so now.

N *If you appreciate the accessibility of em units and want to be sure your sliding gallery remains easy to view at larger text sizes, setting element sizes in em units will let the entire gallery scale along with the text. Remember the formula is X(px) ÷ 16 = Y(em). So as an example, 260px ÷ 16 = 16.25em. Do the math and you'll have a great gallery for low-vision users. (In this interface, you'd need to change the following selectors: .thumbnail, #slidingGallery, #slidingGallery, .SlidingPanelsContent, and #slidingGallery .galleryItem.)*

FIGURE 6.46 Umm... something's not quite right here.

Egad! What's going on with the page now?! Well, most of our CSS seems to have kicked in—our items are arranged in a single line and they've taken on the other defined properties, but they're running out of the page!

Before you throw the book out the window, calm down. The browser, in this case Dreamweaver, is simply doing its job. You see, while our CSS is working, we're missing one final element. We need to tell the Spry framework that it should hide any of the elements that do not fit within the defined panel area.

This is a built-in function of the Spry Sliding Panels widget—and we've also not yet told the browser that one of these elements is on the page. You'll recall that we created a link to the SprySlidingPanels.js file. We'll now instruct the browser to use this file to create the sliding functionality.

13. Back in the source code, scroll to the very bottom of the page.

You'll notice that "someone" has already added a JavaScript to the bottom of the page:

```
<script type="text/javascript"> <!--
var MenuBar1 = new Spry.Widget.MenuBar("MenuBar1",
{imgRight:"SpryAssets/SpryMenuBarRightHover.gif"});
//--> </script>
```

This script was added to our page when we added the Spry Menu Bar. In fact, if you open up the index.html page, you'll find the same code at the bottom of that page.

The JavaScript is executed after the page completely loads in the browser—hence its position as the last element before the closing **\<body\>** tag. When placed within a page, the JavaScripts that create a Spry widget must be the last element processed by the browser.

14. Add the following line to the script:

```
<script type="text/javascript"> <!--
var MenuBar1 = new Spry.Widget.MenuBar("MenuBar1",
{imgRight:"SpryAssets/SpryMenuBarRightHover.gif"});
var sp = new Spry.Widget.SlidingPanels("slidingGallery");
//--> </script>
```

Once again, we're declaring a variable, this time named **sp**. This will be a new instance of a **Spry.Widget.SlidingPanels**. We then tell the Spry framework which unique (ID) element on the page will become a sliding panel.

15. Finally, constrain the width of the overall sliding panel by adding:

```
#slidingGallery {
    float: left;
    height: 160px;
    border: solid 1px #AD2027;
    overflow: hidden;
    width: 99%; }
```

The width property is obvious—however, if there is too much content, it can still leak out and cause the effect that we've been seeing. Therefore, we use the **overflow:hidden** declaration to tell the browser to hide anything that leaks out.

16. Go ahead and refresh Live View—and if you're satisfied, save your work.

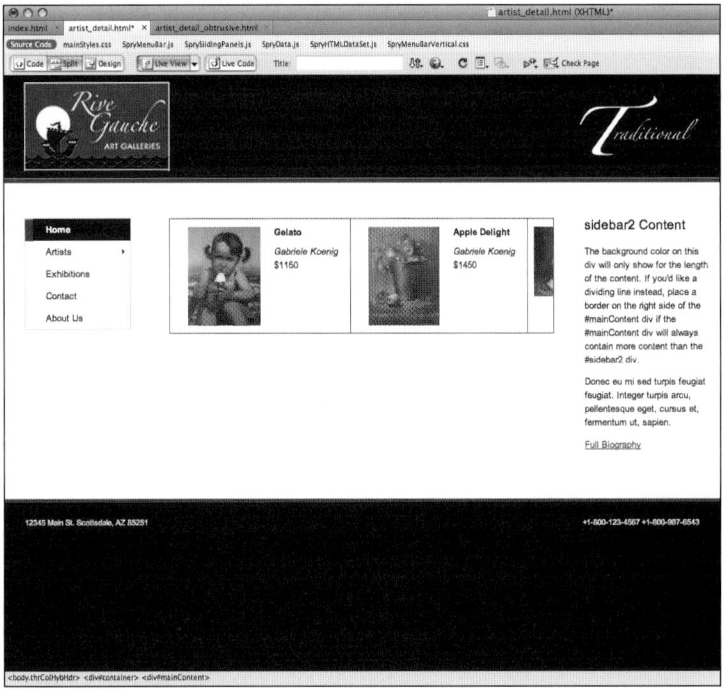

FIGURE 6.47 Much nicer—now if we could figure out how to make the panels actually slide, we'd be really excited!

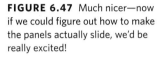

Now that looks a lot better, but you may have already asked yourself, "Um, self, how do the panels slide?" Well, you're not crazy... they don't slide. Or at least they don't slide yet. We need to establish some navigation to tell them how to slide.

Navigating Through a Sliding Panel

Head back over to the page in Dreamweaver's Code area (or open artist_detail4.html from the builds folder) and locate the opening `<div#gallery>` tag.

1. Insert the following code between the closing `<div>` tag for the `#slidingGallery` element and the opening `<div>` tag of the `#gallery` element:

```
<p id="panelNav" class="fltlft">
  <a href="#" id="firstPanel">First</a> |
  <a href="#" id="previousPanel">Previous</a> |
  <a href="#" id="nextPanel">Next</a> |
  <a href="#" id="lastPanel">Last</a> </p>
```

We're going to use simple anchors (links) to control the scrolling of the sliding panels. While the Spry Sliding Panels widget allows us to move in steps, i.e. three or four items at a time, we've chosen to use a simple "first/previous/next/last" navigation scheme. The next and previous links will move the panels forward or backward, one item at a time. The first and last links will slide the items back to the starting position or to the end of the items, respectively.

In order to make the Spry framework react to the clicking of the links, we'll need a bit more JavaScript—this time attached to each link itself.

2. Add the following `onclick` handlers to the links:

```
<p id="panelNav" class="fltlft">
  <a href="#" id="firstPanel" onclick="sp.
showFirstPanel(); return false;">First</a> |
  <a href="#" id="previousPanel" onclick="sp.
showPreviousPanel(); return false;">Previous</a> |
  <a href="#" id="nextPanel" onclick="sp.showNextPanel();
return false;">Next</a> |
  <a href="#" id="lastPanel" onclick="sp.showLastPanel();
return false;">Last</a> </p>
```

An `onclick` handler is simply an inline JavaScript that tells the browser to do something when the link is clicked. In our case, we are calling out to the Spry Sliding Panels widget **sp** that we created in the script at the bottom of the page. We're telling it to execute one of those built-in functions for each click of the link(s).

3. Refresh Live View.

FIGURE 6.48 The functioning Spry sliding panel—a very cool enhancement to the page!

You have to admit, that's pretty cool!

Adding a Detail Image

In our original, non-JavaScript version of the page, each thumbnail has a link to the high-resolution version of the image. But we're still missing the ability to click the thumbnail and see the hi-rez version of the image in this enhanced version of the page.

This relationship between the thumbnails and the hi-rez images is known as a master/detail relationship. We want the elements within the sliding panel to function as the master and when one of them is clicked, we want a detail area to react accordingly— in our case, to show us the image.

Do you remember the `<p>` element that simply contained the name of the high-resolution version of the image? We hid this element from view using the `display:none` property, but it's time to use that element.

1. Create a `<div>` element above the `.slidinggallery`, but still inside the `mainContent` element, and assign it an ID of "detailArea":

   ```
   <div id="detailArea"> </div>
   ```

2. Create a `<div>` within this element to contain the detail image—assign it a class of "detailImg":

   ```
   <div id="detailArea">
    <div class="detailImg"></div> </div>
   ```

N *When working with images it's usually best to define the container for the content with a fixed height. The reason for this is that the rest of the content on the page might have to shift due to the taller or shorter content. This can cause a "page flicker" very similar to a page refresh, which sort of defeats the purpose of our Ajax (i.e., no page refresh) approach. To see this for yourself, remove the height from the #mainContent #detailArea rule.*

3. Add an image element to the `<div.detailImg>` element along with a `<br>` element to clear the float:

   ```
   <div id="detailArea">
    <div class="detailImg"><img src="images/{HiRez}"
   alt="{PictureTitle}"  width="330" /><br class="clearfloat"
   /></div> </div>
   ```

   Notice that instead of identifying a specific image file, we've defined a Spry variable `{HiRez}`, which will tell the Spry framework to look at the data set and figure out which element to display. Additionally, the alt attribute, using the `{PictureTitle}` variable, will dynamically generate an image name for accessiblity.

   We've also added a `clearfloat` class to the `<br>` element to push the content down the page based on the height of the contents of the `<div.detailImg>`.

   We need to create a couple of rules to style these new elements.

4. Create a new rule for the `detailArea` in mainStyles.css as follows:

   ```
   #mainContent #detailArea {
       width: 40em;
       margin-right: auto;
       margin-left: auto;
       padding: 0px 0px 20px 0px;
       height: 460px;
       text-align: center; }
   ```

   Let's "pretty-up" the detail image with a border.

5. Create a rule for the detail image itself:

```
#detailArea img {
    padding: 4px;
    margin: 0px 10px;
    border: solid 1px #AD2021; }
```

All that's left to do is to identify the elements that we've just created for the Spry framework, indicating that the image itself should change when a thumbnail is clicked.

We'll do this by adding two more Spry attributes to the page.

6. Add the `spry:detailregion` attribute to the `detailArea`:

```
<div id="detailArea" spry:detailregion="ds1">
```

The `spry:detailregion` attribute tells the Spry framework to look at the current data set to determine what needs to be displayed on the page. This attribute works in conjunction with `spry:setrow` to find the "row" of data in which we are interested.

7. Add the `spry:setrow` attribute to the `panelContents` element:

```
<div id="panelContents" class="SlidingPanelsContent"
spry:repeat="ds1" spry:setrow="ds1">
```

8. Refresh Live View.

FIGURE 6.49 The detail image is placed above the sliding panel.

Raise your hand if it worked flawlessly… Hmm… nobody? Well, truth is, ours didn't work either. We have a detail image when we come to the page, but when we click on another image in the sliding panel area, we're taken to the high-resolution image itself. That's not right! But if we look at our code, it's logical.

```
<p class="thumbnail"><a href="images/7025.jpg"><img
src="images/7025_thumb.jpg" width="104" height="138"
/></a></p>
```

As we created our data set, we told the Spry framework to look at every `<p>` element within an individual `<div.galleryItem>`. The `<p>` element above contains our thumbnail image—but notice what is surrounding the image. It's an anchor (link). So, when we click on the image, the browser is doing what it thinks is natural and taking us to the image file.

If we could just get the browser to ignore the anchor when we're looking at the Spry version of the page…

Bet you saw this coming. Yes, Spry can provide this functionality too!

Go back to the folder you downloaded earlier and locate SpryDOMUtils.js in the Includes folder. This collection of JavaScript methods allows us to manipulate the DOM (Document Object Model). In other words, we can add attributes, change attributes or remove attributes, change styles, and much more. (See the Spry documentation for a complete list of its capabilities.)

We'll use a method called `removeAttribute` to remove the `href` attribute from the anchor when the page is viewed with JavaScript turned on.

1. Copy SpryDOMUtils.js into your SpryAssets folder, then return to the page in Dreamweaver, and scroll to the bottom of the page. Add the following line to the script:

    ```
    <script type="text/javascript"> <!--
    var MenuBar1 = new Spry.Widget.MenuBar("MenuBar1",
    {imgRight:"SpryAssets/SpryMenuBarRightHover.gif"});
    var sp = new Spry.Widget.SlidingPanels("slidingGallery");
    Spry.$$(".thumbnail a").removeAttribute("href"); //-->
    </script>
    ```

After the page is loaded into the browser, but before it actually renders, our script tells the browser to let the Spry framework find a selector on the page. In our case, it specifically says to find all of the `<a>` elements within an element with a class of `thumbnail`. Then the script instructs the browser to remove the specified attribute—in our case, the `href` attribute.

2. Scroll up to the top of the source code and add a reference to the SpryDOMUtils.js file:

```
<script src="SpryAssets/SpryDOMUtils.js" type="text/
javascript"></script>
```

3. Finally, refresh Live View. Feel free to save your work—or open artist_detail5.html.

Hopefully you're really excited now! But we're not quite finished…

Getting the Validation Gold Star

One of the primary criticisms from the web standards' community upon the initial release of the Spry framework for Ajax was the method in which Spry interactions happen within the page (including the methods we've implemented up to this point). Custom attributes and inline scripts, such as we've used, cause the page to fail when run through a validator. They make it easy to look at the page and understand what's happening, but the standards' approach is to separate presentation and content. In other words, JavaScript belongs in an external file, not embedded within the page. Additionally, the page markup should be semantic, and only contain tags and attributes that have been ratified by the W3C—and by adding things such as "spry:region", the framework is breaking the rules.

Fortunately, the Spry team at Adobe implemented a method of development within Spry 1.6 known as unobtrusive JavaScript. In a nutshell, this approach puts all of the Spry functionality into an external JavaScript file, leaving our page in its purest form. The result allows the page to validate just like any other well-structured (X)HTML and CSS document with all of our progressive enhancements occurring via this externally linked file.

So, to finish off our project, let's externalize our enhancements.

Creating an Unobtrusive JavaScript

Using CS3, moving all the Spry code and JavaScript out of the page was a tedious and very manual process. Thankfully, Dreamweaver CS4 makes it as simple as a click.

1. Make sure that Live View is turned off, then choose Commands > Externalize JavaScript.

FIGURE 6.50 You can choose a little or a lot.

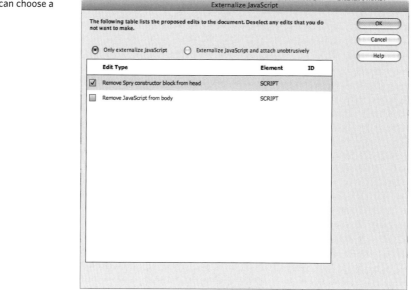

The Externalize JavaScript dialog allows you to simply move your inline and local JavaScripts to an external file by select- ing "Only externalize JavaScript" and choosing which scripts to move.

2. Select "Externalize JavaScript and attach unobtrusively."

When we choose this option, all of the visual help, such as the blue tabs identifying the presence of the Spry Menu Bar, and all other design-time functionality within Dreamweaver for these objects, will be lost. The page will still work, but we'll have to make any subsequent changes by hand, without much help from Dreamweaver. For this reason, it's always good to make a backup before proceeding.

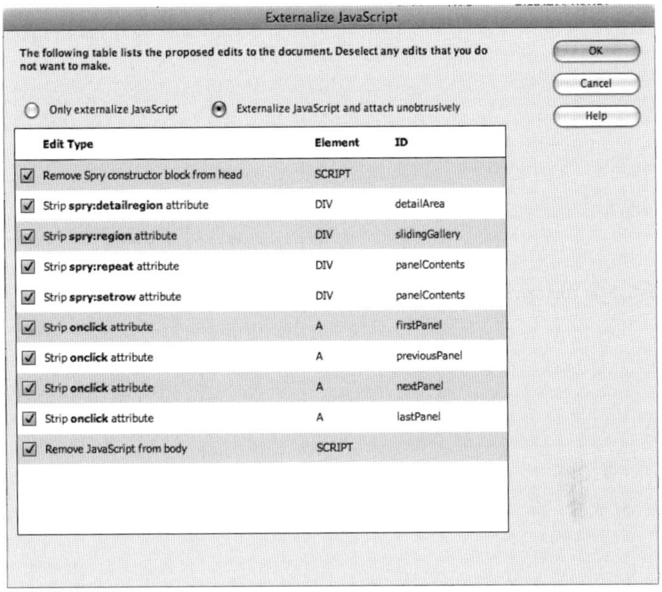

FIGURE 6.51 Let's move everything out of the page.

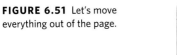

You can see a complete list of the things Dreamweaver will externalize, including all of the Spry attributes, inline JavaScript functions as well as local functions, and constructors from the head.

3. Leave everything selected and click OK.

FIGURE 6.52 Success!

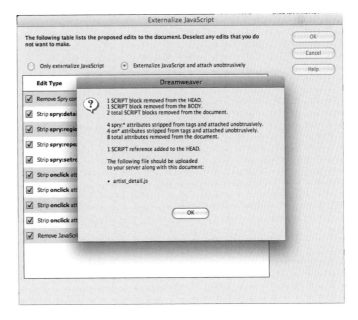

It only takes a second and everything is gone, leaving a perfectly clean HTML page, with a link established to the external JavaScript file, artist_detail.js.

4. Look at the source code of the artist_detail.html page.

   As you should be able to see, every piece of JavaScript and Spry-specific markup is gone.

5. Turn Live View back on and experiment with the page.

   Everything works exactly the same as it did before. The main difference is that the HTML markup is perfectly clean because all of the functionality now exists via the external JavaScript file. Or does it?

   You might notice that the first time you attempt to click on any of the navigation links for the sliding panel it doesn't react. Subsequent clicks work fine, however.

   The reason for this is simple, but fixing it will take a bit of manual work. First, let's understand what went wrong.

   In the external JavaScript, artist_detail.js, the construction script for the sliding panel has been added to a Spry utility function known as a LoadListener.

```
Spry.Utils.addLoadListener(function() {
...
var sp = new Spry.Widget.SlidingPanels("slidingGallery");
...
});
```

That's the problem. You see, the script is creating the sliding panel along with, and at the same time as, all of the other elements on the page. However, at that point, the page has not truly been completely processed, and as a result, the Sliding Panels widget is not yet aware of how much content it has. In fact, it's not until we click that first time that it becomes aware of its content.

To correct the problem, we need to delay the construction of the widget until after the page has completed its loading process and the manipulation of the data set is complete. We can do this using another JavaScript method of the framework known as an observer.

N   *The* Spry.Data.Region. addObserver *instructs the framework to pay attention to the data being loaded into the identified element, in this case* slidingGallery, *listening for it to finish and report back when everything is processed and in place. Upon receiving the word that everything is ready (the* Update *event), the* onPostUpdate *event then fires, instructing the Spry framework to go ahead and attach the sliding panels' behaviors to the* slidingGallery *element, turning it into a sliding panel ready to be navigated.*

If you want, you can go back to the index.html page and remove the Spry Menu Bar script from the bottom of the page. Then link the page to externalJavaScript.js as we've done in this section. That will ensure that index.html also will pass your validation tests.

6. In artist_detail.js, add the following code above the Spry.Utils. addLoadListener block:

```
Spry.Data.Region.addObserver("slidingGallery", {
onPostUpdate:
function()
{
sp = new Spry.Widget.SlidingPanels("slidingGallery");
}});
```

7. Remove sp = new Spry.Widget.SlidingPanels ("slidingGallery"); from the addLoadListener function.

Crossing the "T's" and Dotting the "I's"

At this point, you may think that we're finished—but before we reach for the champagne and party hats, what happens if we visit the page with JavaScript disabled in the browser, or with an older browser such as Internet Explorer 5.5, which we know can't interpret our more advanced JavaScript?

Let's find out…

N *If you are using Firefox, Chris Pederick has developed a widely used extension known as the Web Developer's toolbar. This is an incredibly useful tool for any web designer/developer. It can be found at http://chrispederick. com/work/web-developer/. Using the toolbar, we can easily turn JavaScript off to see the effects on the page. A similar, and equally good extension, is Firebug by Joe Hewitt which can be found at https://addons.mozilla.org/ en-US/firefox/addon/1843/.*

FIGURE 6.53 Our page doesn't look as good with JavaScript turned off!

FIGURE 6.54 The results in Internet Explorer 5.5 are equally disappointing.

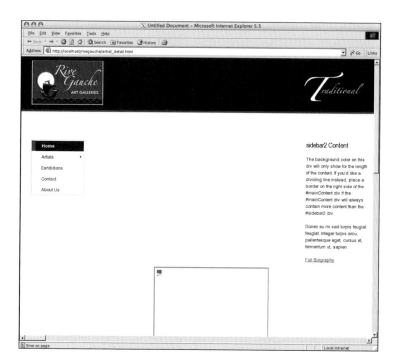

Oh no! This is definitely not acceptable. Didn't we do all this work in order to deliver a satisfactory experience to visitors to the site that have no JavaScript capabilities? The problem is that when the JavaScript isn't processed, the placeholders for our dynamically generated content are still visible on the page.

A couple of quick modifications can fix this.

1. Return to artist_detail.html in Dreamweaver and click in the Design area, where you might notice that the page is definitely looking a bit strange.

   Dreamweaver has no way of processing the JavaScript, so it's showing us pretty much what we saw with JavaScript turned off. Therefore, we'll use the Design area to help us get the page looking better for those non-JavaScript enabled browsers.

   The simplest fix to our problem is to hide the dynamic areas when JavaScript is not enabled. And we can do that using CSS!

2. Click to select the detail image placeholder on the page and in the CSS panel's Rules section, select the `#mainContent #detailArea` selector.

3. Click the Add Property link in the Properties section and add `display:none` to its rule.

4. Do the same for the `#slidingGallery` selector.

   This just leaves the `<p>` element that contains the panel's navigation. When we created the element, we assigned it an ID of `panelNav`.

5. Create a new rule in mainStyles.css for `panelNav` and assign its display property to `none`.

   ```
   #panelNav {
       display: none; }
   ```

6. Save mainStyles.css and preview artist_detail.html in Live View.

7. While in Live View, turn off JavaScript from the Live View drop-down menu.

FIGURE 6.55 Things look better in Dreamweaver—even without Live View turned on.

That's a much better result! The CSS has hidden the areas of the page that we aren't interested in seeing since they are only processed when JavaScript is enabled. And we're able to actually understand what we're looking at even without Live View turned on.

FIGURE 6.56 An equally satisfying result in Internet Explorer 5.5!

As we begin to exhale and contemplate a "Tom Cruise on Oprah" moment, a final check of the page in Firefox, now with JavaScript enabled again, has us completely panicked!

FIGURE 6.57 The page is a bit too clean now! Where are the pictures?

Because our CSS has hidden the Spry areas of the page, the browser has no way to know that we actually want to see them! Stupid browser!

For the non-programmers among you, a function is nothing more than a block of code, or instructions, that get executed together.

1. Return to Dreamweaver and switch to the artist_detail.js file.

2. Add the following lines of code to the function above the `Spry.Data.initRegions();` line:

    ```
    Spry.$$("#slidingGallery").setStyle("display:block");
    Spry.$$("#detailArea").setStyle("display:block");
    Spry.$$("#panelNav").setStyle("display:block");
    ```

    We're telling the Spry utilities that we used earlier to remove the **href** attribute to change the display property for our three selectors from **none** to **block**—allowing them to return to the page.

3. Save the JavaScript file and preview artist_detail.html in a standards-compliant browser with JavaScript enabled, or simply refresh in Live View with JavaScript back on.

FIGURE 6.58 With the display property switched, we're back in business.

4. Our last step should really be to constrain the width of the page for Internet Explorer in order to avoid any weird float drop issues. Add the following lines of code to the IECC:

```
.thrColHybHdr #container {
  width: expression(Math.max((document.documentElement
? document.documentElement.clientWidth : document.body.
clientWidth)/16, 1024/16)+'em'); }
#slidingGallery {width:99%;}
#mainContent #detailArea {width: 24em}
```

This constrains the page to the same width (64em) as we see in standards-compliant browsers. The rule for the **#sliding-Gallery** of 99% is to accommodate the 2px of border placed on the element. (You might remember that IE has a problem with a width set to 100% when there is a border present—it adds the width *to* the 100%.) Finally, we've created a rule to narrow the **detailArea** to fit into the allotted space when the page becomes narrow.

A Final Bit of Polish

As often happens—and you might have even noticed this already, while we were creating our menu—we forgot to double-check its look against the look of the comp. Close inspection shows that we need a thin dotted line between the entries of the menu bar. Thankfully, this is an easy and quick fix.

1. Place your cursor in any of the entries in the menu and in the CSS panel, select the last `ul.MenuBarVertical` entry in the CSS cascade.

2. Change the border property to `border-top: 1px dotted #CCC`.

3. Add a bottom border to all of the entries in the list by adding `border-bottom: 1px dotted #CCC` to the `ul.MenuBarVertical li` rule.

4. Repeat the process for the flyout menu: `ul.MenuBarVertical ul` and `ul.MenuBarVertical ul li`.

5. We'll change the page indicator button by moving the ID `#selected` from the home button to the artist button.

FIGURE 6.59 Our designer will be happy—the dotted lines are back.

One final suggestion—don't keep your Internet Explorer Conditional Comments (IECC) in the head of your document. Externalize them. This makes it much faster and easier to update them if you need to add some later. It's a simple process for our site since our IECC rules are set to be seen by all current versions of Internet Explorer.

We've zeroed the first element in both our side columns, so as discussed in Chapter 1, we no longer need the top padding for either of the side columns in our IECCs.

1. In both your artist_detail.html and index.html pages, remove the rules with the padding-top that are included by default with the CSS layouts from the IECC.

    Be sure to keep the `zoom: 1` for the #mainContent rule.

2. Create a new CSS document called ie_fixes.css.

3. In the head of the artist_detail.html page, cut out the rules within the IECC and paste them into the new CSS documents. Remove the `<style>` block within the IECC.

4. In the head of the index.html page, do the same.

    You'll notice the `zoom: 1` rule is duplicated in both pages, but with each page's unique prefix. We only need one and it can apply to both pages.

Remember that the Spry engineers have no way to add an IECC to your page, so the IE fixes are left in the bottom of the style sheet. Whenever you can, remove them and place them in your IECC so your page will validate.

5. Remove the prefix from either one of the **#mainContent** rules, and completely remove the other rule. You should be left with this: **#mainContent { zoom: 1; }**

6. The menu needs a tweak for Internet Explorer as well. First, as we saw in earlier chapters, `hasLayout` needs to be triggered to get rid of some extra vertical space. Add **ul.MenuBarVertical a** to your **zoom:1** rule.

7. We also find IE's rendering of dotted borders unsightly. We decided to feed it a solid line instead. To your IECC, add:

```
ul.MenuBarVertical li {
    border-bottom: solid 1px #666;
}
ul.MenuBarVertical {
    border-top: solid 1px #666;
}
```

8. Open the SpryMenuBarVertical.CSS and, at the very bottom, remove the section that begins with "BROWSER HACKS". Paste that into your ie_fixes.css document.

N   *With IE8 looming some-where on the horizon, we think it's a good idea to target IE7 and below for selectors that are currently needed to straighten out IE's rendering. Previously, IE was simply the old engine updated for a new version. IE8 will be using a new engine completely. For that reason, we may no longer need the same fixes. What if they got rid of the* hasLayout *trigger? What if divs no longer expand to contain all their content? We think it's better to leave your page in working order for current IE browsers and recheck your pages when IE8 is released.*

9. Finally, add the link to the CSS file you just created within each page's IECC and make the IECC target IE browsers less than or equal to IE7:

```
<!--[if lte IE 7]>
<link href="ie_fixes.css" rel="stylesheet"
type="text/css" />
<![endif]-->
```

10. Save the page and preview it in as many browsers as you want—you've created a beautiful layout that is progressively enhanced according to a browser's capabilities and that validates perfectly.

Now feel free to have that "Tom Cruise" moment! And thanks for spending what we're sure has been a lot of time with us—we hope you've learned a lot and had a fun time doing it!

Index

Safari
Books Online

Get free online access to this book!

And sign up for a free trial to Safari Books Online to get access to thousands more!

With the purchase of this book you have instant online, searchable access to it on Safari Books Online! And while you're there, be sure to check out the Safari on-demand digital library and its Free Trial Offer (a separate sign-up process)—where you can access thousands of technical and inspirational books, instructional videos, and articles from the world's leading creative professionals with a Safari Books Online subscription.

Simply visit www.peachpit.com/safarienabled and enter code OKKBAAA to try it today.